on the dot

on the dot

the speck that changed the world

Alexander Humez • Nicholas Humez

OXFORD
UNIVERSITY PRESS

2008

OXFORD
UNIVERSITY PRESS

Oxford University Press, Inc., publishes works that further
Oxford University's objective of excellence
in research, scholarship, and education.

Oxford New York
Auckland Cape Town Dar es Salaam Hong Kong Karachi
Kuala Lumpur Madrid Melbourne Mexico City Nairobi
New Delhi Shanghai Taipei Toronto

With offices in
Argentina Austria Brazil Chile Czech Republic France Greece
Guatemala Hungary Italy Japan Poland Portugal Singapore
South Korea Switzerland Thailand Turkey Ukraine Vietnam

Copyright © 2008 by Oxford University Press, Inc.

Published by Oxford University Press, Inc.
198 Madison Avenue, New York, New York 10016

www.oup.com

Oxford is a registered trademark of Oxford University Press

Library of Congress Cataloging-in-Publication Data
Humez, Alexander.
On the dot : the speck that changed the world /
Alexander Humez, Nicholas Humez.
p. cm.
Includes bibliographical references and index.
ISBN 978-0-19-532499-0
1. Dot—History.   I. Humez, Nicholas D.   II. Title.
P301.5.P86H86 2008
411—dc22   2008003320

3 5 7 9 8 6 4 2

Printed in the United States of America
on acid-free paper

To our mother,
Elisabeth Gleason Humez

contents

preface

On the Dot, as the title promises, is a book about dots—mostly, though not exclusively, the sort we use in print. It is subtitled *The Speck that Changed the World,* for despite the humble origins of its name (Anglo-Saxon for 'the speck at the head of a boil'), and its diminutive size (it is the smallest meaningful symbol that one can make with ink from a pen or a press, a stylus on wax or clay, or a hammer and chisel on stone), the dot has been one of the most versatile players in the history of human communication to the point that it has become virtually indispensable.

If this assertion seems just a tad grandiose, imagine for a moment what the world would be like if it awoke one morning to discover that during the night the dot had completely disappeared as though it had never been: The morning newspaper would be a single monster sentence, broken only by the occasional comma; accounts receivable would no longer distinguish between dollars and cents (at least in the United States); Internet addresses and much of the programming that supports the dot-coms that they identify would be unintelligible; the sheet music for your favorite jig would be quite out of kilter with the tune.... You get the idea.

The Romans called the dot a *punctus* (whence English *point*), and in the script they bequeathed to the West it is a constituent of the colon, the semicolon, the question mark, the exclamation mark, the dieresis, and the ellipsis…as well, of course, as a mark of punctuation in its own right—the period—signifying the end of a sentence. (We also put a dot at the end of an abbreviation to let the reader know that it is one: Mass is the Eucharist; Mass. is the Bay State.)

In the language of mathematics and money, the dot is the decimal point (at least in the United States), a sign for the operation of multiplication, and a marker in the representation of a repeating decimal (like 1/3). In the computer world, the dot has a number of specialized uses; the "dot" of "dot-com" is only the latest of these.

In Western musical notation, the dot signifies that you should prolong, by half as much time again, the note or a rest that precedes it; a dotted quarter rest equals a quarter rest tied to an eighth rest. In braille, raised dots represent numerals and the letters of the alphabet—and its eponymous inventor threw in a system of musical notation for good measure.

The dot can also function as a variant of the checkmark, in its most robust form (the bullet) arousing a heightened attention to items on a list. A row of three or four of them tells us that something is being left out of the text; a row under crossed-out text tells us not to delete it after all. *On the Dot* explores all of these uses of the dot, and more.

On the Dot is a study in the natural history of this most minimal of punctuation marks as carrier of meaning in its various sociolinguistic contexts: All languages are firmly embedded in the society of their speakers, and even the tiniest punctuation mark, as we shall see, imparts its meaning only insofar as it is embedded in a specific cultural context. Thus Aristophanes of Byzantium, the librarian at the Museum at Alexandria who is generally credited for the earliest punctuation in the West, created a system of three dots (low, middle, and high) to address a problem of vital interest to the readers of his day:

how to tell where (and for how long) to pause and take a breath while reading out loud. We may sympathize to a degree with the passion behind his purpose but would do so a great deal more were we dealing as he did with manuscripts altogether lacking in capital letters, and usually with no spaces between words.

Like Aristophanes, we may use a dot to signify the end of a sentence, but our mind-set is not—cannot be—that of a Greek working in a Hellenized Egyptian city within a few years of the Romans' definitive victory in their struggle with their Carthaginian rivals for control of the entire Mediterranean. We moderns bring our own cultural baggage to the dot instead, according to the several communities of thought and practice in which it has made itself at home: mathematicians and cryptographers, banks, pressrooms, telegraph offices, and clock factories. In the following pages we shall show how thoroughly the dot is embedded in our everyday traffic in words and ideas, to the point that it is so inconspicuous as to be nearly invisible—and in the process, has managed to acquire a semiotic power inversely proportional to its diminutive size.

Four points before we get on with the story: First, don't miss our endnotes; they contain plenty of cheerful facts not readily shoehorned into the body of the chapters themselves, in addition to the usual source citations for quoted material. (The reader may safely assume that unless an endnote says otherwise, all translations are our own.) Second, all fictitious characters whom we introduce by way of example are intended to bear only a generic relation to persons living or dead; any apparent resemblance beyond this is either (a) a figment of the reader's vivid imagination or (b) the merest coincidence—possibly both.

Third, today's world is a wired one: To burlesque a novelty song hit of our youth, "The information highway runs through the middle of the house." We will mention a number of helpful websites in the pages that follow. We must caution the reader, however, that URLs and their contents are subject to change without notice; the timeliness that is arguably the Internet's greatest virtue is the obverse of its weakest feature: its penchant for being unexpectedly ephemeral. We'll warrant that what we report from or about any given site was true at the time we were writing this book (spring 2006 through autumn 2007), but we simply cannot guarantee that these sites will remain as factual and germane as they were at the time we examined and cited them. *Caveat lector.*

And fourth (a corollary of number three), any non-dead language is by definition undergoing constant change and thus cannot admit of what Thomas Nagel nicely calls a "View from Nowhere." The story we propose to tell in this book is positioned knowledge, situated in our particular time and place, just as Aristophanes of Byzantium was firmly planted in his. Reality is always grander than words can capture, and when it comes to dynamic features of a living language, there is never an end in sight.

on the dot

time and chance
punctuality and the coin toss

"The train arrived at 6:34 on the dot." In other words, the train arrived punctually, at a precisely predicted point in time—the *appointed* time. Time viewed as a continuum is the analogue of the geometer's one-dimensional line, an infinite and straight succession of points. (Strictly speaking, a point has no dimensions at all; but mathematicians carefully distinguish between a half-line, i.e., a point plus all points on the line to one side of it, and a ray, which is the same thing as a half-line except without an initial endpoint.) Yet we have been conditioned to think of time elapsing in a succession of discrete ticks; to speak of a point in time in this latter sense would have been unthinkable prior to the invention of accurate enough clocks to tell not just the hour but the minute as well. It is presumably to the dot at which the minute hand stops on the face of a clock or watch that *on the dot* refers.

Accurate timekeeping was shown to be a matter of life and death when it came to knowing *when* as a function of *where*: For want of an accurate method of determining longitude, British admiral Sir

Clowdisley Shovell made an egregious navigational error that cost the lives of no fewer than 2,000 sailors in the spectacular wreck of his fleet off the Isles of Scilly in 1707. The key to longitude was the development of a clock that would run true to within a few minutes even when tossed around on a sailing ship for a month or two; if it could accurately tell you that it was noon in London, you could determine local noon from shipboard by the height of the sun, and therefore how far east or west of London you were.

To the development of accurate timekeeping was added coordinated time and time zones, necessitated by the development of railroads. David Landes writes that "wherever there were railroads, there soon developed standard times and time services...with the institution of time zones, which led in turn to international agreements for similar partition of the entire earth. So in October 1884 the International Meridian Conference voted to mark the prime meridian at Greenwich," England's official naval astronomical observatory. Prior to this reform, localities had marked time according to conspicuous public clocks; thus Samuel Hopkins Adams recalls his grandfather telling him about arriving in Troy, New York, on the newly inaugurated Rensselaer and Saratoga Railroad one late fall day in 1835 "at exactly eight o'clock, Baptist time.... Grandfather explained that some years earlier the Peculiar Baptists had set up a clock in their steeple. Thereafter, Troy had taken its time from that." But it soon became clear to the railroads that a system operating on uncoordinated time was an accident waiting to happen; this was particularly a risk on single-track lines such as the ill-starred Central Massachusetts, on which, even with everyone's watch synchronized, "trains came crashing together with monotonous regularity."

An additional boost to the popularization of knowing the precise time of day was the American Civil War, which made the fortunes of the Waltham Watch Company, in Waltham, Massachusetts (still a going concern at the end of the 20th century, albeit in a fraction of its original factory on the Charles River at Crescent Street, under the modernized name Waltham Precision Instruments), thanks to the Union army's need for cheap but accurate soldiers' watches. Waltham was known for many years as "the Watch City," a soubriquet capitalized upon by its local public transport company, the Middlesex and Boston Street Railway, whose fare tokens bore a watch face in their centers.

You might think that the French expression for arriving on the dot would *be arriver à point* or the like, *point* being the word for the dot over an *i*, and *points de suspension* being an ellipsis (dot dot dot). But no: *à point* (as the Allrecipes.com Cook's Encyclopedia defines it) is 'the French term used for food cooked just to the perfect point of doneness' (which, in the case of meat, an American would consider rare). Similarly, *arriver à l'heure pointe*, another seemingly likely candidate, actually means to arrive at the peak hour (the high point) of traffic. In fact, the French expression for arriving on the dot is *arriver pile—pile* being the term for the reverse side of a coin. (Compare *s'arrêter pile—* 'to stop short, stop on the spot'—to the American English expression "to stop on a dime." Tempting as it might be to relate this in turn to "on the money," the latter, according to *Picturesque Expressions: A Thematic Dictionary*, "appears to refer to money placed as a bet against a certain, previously stated outcome (p. 262). "On the button," on the other hand, alludes to striking the point of the chin with a fist; a precise blow of this sort will stun a boxing opponent through transmission of the shock up either side of the jaw to the brain-case just below the ears.)

The French word for the obverse of a coin is *face*; thus English "to flip for heads or tails" equals French *jouer à pile ou face* (literally, 'to play at tail or head'). *Face* for "heads" is straightforward enough, since the whole point of showing a head on a coin is that the face, whether that of divinity, sovereign, or famous citizen, should be recognizable. According to Leo Braudy's *The Frenzy of Renown*, a history of fame in the Western world, the coins issued by Ptolemy I of Egypt in about 320 B.C.E., showing the head of his deceased boss Alexander the Great, were "among the first coins to depict realistically an actual human being." But coins of the Persian empire under Darius Hystapis, two centuries earlier, had shown at least an idealized image of the Great King on their obverse. Called *darics* after him, they were to the Persian realms what the high-grade drachmas of Aegina were to the Greeks: renowned for their fineness, passing current for the settlement of financial obligations both public and private. Darius's conquest of Croesus and his gold-rich kingdom of Lydia in Asia Minor undoubtedly helped supply the necessary bullion for extensive minting of darics, which were still in wide circulation when the upstart prince Cyrus used them to pay Xenophon and 10,000 other Greek mercenaries at the beginning of the 4th century B.C.E. in an unsuccessful attempt to overthrow another king of Persia: Cyrus's older brother, Artaxerxes Mnemon.

6   Well, but what of French *pile*? In its sense of 'reverse side of a coin,' *pile* comes from Latin *pīla* ('pillar, column') and subsequently came by extension to mean the particular sort of pillar on which was fixed the die incised with the pattern for the back of a coin, against which the precious-metal blank was laid and struck from above with a second die (called in French the *trousseau*—trussell or tursall in English) bearing the face design. English "coin" itself comes from Old French *coin*, 'die for stamping coins,' from Latin *cuneus*, 'wedge.'

Another meaning of Latin *pīla* is 'mortar,' also surviving into French as *pile* but with the meaning "stamping trough in which a slurry of fibers is pressed into paper." It is not clear whether the two Latin *pīla* words have anything to do with each other etymologically, but, for what it's worth, the French word for 'pestle' is *pilon*, derived from *pīla* in its 'pillar' sense; *pestle* itself comes from Latin *pistillum*, whose root means 'pound, beat'—whence Latin *pistor*, which first meant 'miller' and later 'baker.'

The "heads" side of the coin has not always borne a face: In medieval and Renaissance Europe, it often bore a cross instead; thus the older term for "heads or tails" in French, dating from the 1600s, is *croix ou pile*. The monetary unit in Portuguese-speaking Brazil was formerly the *cruzeiro*, likewise derived from Latin *crux*, 'cross.' For "heads or tails" the Dutch still say *kruis of munt* ('cross or mint') even though the face side now bears the head of the reigning monarch; *munt* is related to Latin *moneta* (source of English *mint* and *money*) and indicated that the denomination of the coin is stamped on the back (compare German *Kopf oder Zahl*—'head or number' or Turkish *yazi mi tura mi*—'writing or face'). Other nations' coins had a cross on the reverse, which gave Spanish its *cara o cruz* ("face or cross") and Italian its *testa o croce* ('head or cross'). Other designs for the reverse of coins included a castle (Argentine Spanish says *cara y castillo*, though their word for "reverse side of a coin" is *sello*, 'seal'; compare Colombia's *cara y sello* for "heads and tails") or a shield (Cuba's *cara o escudo*); the *escudo* remains the currency unit in Portugal and Cape Verde. (When casting about for a name for what ultimately became the Euro, the community missed a golden opportunity for a fiduciary pun in overlooking *ecu*—old French both for "shield" and for the now-obsolete gold coin bearing one, but also a handy acronym for "European currency unit.")

7

Coin-flipping is probably as old as coins itself, and is attested in writers of antiquity; thus the *Saturnalia* of Macrobius, written about 400 C.E., mentions Roman children playing at *capita aut navia* ("heads or ships"), so called because the reverse of the *as*, the lowest-denomination copper coin of the Romans, commonly showed a ship. (The obverse bore the head of two-faced Janus, god of beginnings; according to Ovid's calendar-poem *Fasti*, written four centuries earlier. Such coins were often given out by way of good-luck wishes on the first day of January.)

The Romans were strong on divination, as were their Etruscan neighbors to the north. Two types of diviners whose specialty in reading portents was encoded in Rome's civic religion were the *augur*, who interpreted the flight of birds relative to a line of sight toward the Alban Hills from a viewing station on the Capitoline Hill, and the *haruspex*, who "read" the entrails of the sacrificial victim, especially the liver. Both types of divination had been previously practiced in Etruria, whose tombs have yielded brass models of the liver with its various lobes delineated and labeled—unfortunately in Etruscan, a language almost entirely lost despite modern attempts, ranging from the ingenious to the merely crackpot, to make sense of it.

Flipping a coin is, of course, only one of a number of ways of choosing by chance (or as the ancients might have put it, divining the will of the gods). There is also drawing straws: Only the one holding them knows which is the short one, and (at least when the draw is done fairly) has no control as to who draws it. (It is possible that such straws were originally counting sticks; see the Coyote story below.) Again, there are the "paper-scissors-rock" hand/finger signs, to be shown simultaneously upon an agreed signal (e.g., "One-two-three-shoot!")—flat palm for paper, two fingers for scissors, fist for rock (rock blunts scissors, scissors cut paper, paper wraps stone)—a variant of which is popular in China. Yet another, of course, is the throwing of dice. The standard European die nowadays is a cube, with between one and six dots to a face (sometimes called pips), and (unless loaded) have an equal probability of turning up any given number on a throw.

Roman dice (*astragali*) were made of knucklebones, usually thrown in sets of three; the emperor Claudius, according to the historian Suetonius, was said to be particularly addicted to dice games (and was expressly satirized for it in Seneca's "The Pumpkinification of the Divine Claudius"). Other types of animal bones have been used for dice elsewhere: The Klamath Indians of the American West Coast tell how Coyote tricked Old Man Thunder into giving human beings fire in a dice game using woodchuck and beaver teeth ("female" and "male" dice, respectively), the tally being kept with piles of counting sticks. Coyote won by cheating, distracting Old Man Thunder and turning the dice already thrown to alter the score, or stealing a few sticks from Old Man Thunder's pile. Although he knew Coyote had cheated him, Old Man Thunder was at a loss to see how. So he reluctantly relinquished fire, but not before attempting (unsuccessfully) to kill the trickster.

A variant on the die is the four-sided top called the dreydl, used in a game of put and take; the four Hebrew letters on the faces are the initials of words meaning "great miracle happened here," which refers to the one-day supply of oil that miraculously lasted over a week when the Maccabees were rededicating the temple after winning the revolt in Judea against its Greco-Roman defilers. The event is commemorated in the Jewish feast of Hanukkah ("purification"), and the game is played by children for matchsticks (and sometimes by adults for cash) during that winter festival.

In the 20th century, game designers and manufacturers have come up with alternatives to the six-faced cubic die: The game Dungeons and Dragons employs dice made from other regular polyhedra as well as the cube. Another game, called Pass the Pigs, uses two miniature hogs which, when thrown like dice, can land on their sides facing in the same ("Sider") or opposite directions ("Pig Out"), on four feet ("Trotter"), on their backs ("Razorback"), on their nose and front feet ("Snouter"), or on nose, one foot, and an ear ("Leaning Jowler"). The higher-scoring throw is a "Double Leaning Jowler," good for 60 points.

The gaming die is a persistent symbol of chance and the element of luck all the way back to the Romans; Julius Caesar is quoted as saying *Iacta est alea* ("the die is cast") to express the risk he was undertaking by crossing the stream called the Rubicon (the border between Italy proper and Cisalpine Gaul): By entering Italy under arms without the express consent of the senate, he was in effect making a declaration of civil war, as he well knew.

Since the 1950s a popular good-luck talisman for American automobiles, at least among youth whose driving may indeed still have left more to fortune than to skill, has been a pair of fuzzy dice suspended from the rearview mirror. This talisman has been immortalized by at least one rock band: In a song called "Dog Breath" (on side 1 of the double album *Uncle Meat*, released on the Bizarre Records label in 1968), a paean to the automotive cruising rituals of California teen low-rider freeway culture, Frank Zappa and his Mothers of Invention sang of "Fuzzy Dice / Bongos in the back / My ship of love / Is ready to attack," while elsewhere in the album the "Uncle Meat Theme" reprise (on side 2) elaborates: "…fuzzy dice / I got them at the Pep Boys," along with a "Brodie knob and spinners, chromium plated." (The "Brodie knob" was attached to one's steering wheel in imitation of the knobs on the much larger steering wheel on trucks and buses; also called a "suicide handle" because of being notoriously useless for control of the wheel in an emergency, it was named for Steve Brodie, who had claimed in 1886 to have leapt from the Brooklyn Bridge and survived, but had no witnesses to corroborate the event. Hence, in popular 20th-century American parlance, "to do a Brodie" came to mean both an extravagant failure and a suicide attempt.)

Since fuzzy dice are usually several inches on a side, they tend to block the driver's view, thus increasing the chances of an accident—which is why hanging them or any other good-luck charms (baby shoes, the garter caught at the wedding reception, multiple graduation mortarboard tassels, etc.) in the front windshield is often explicitly discouraged in auto safety pronouncements by such state agencies as the Massachusetts Registry of Motor Vehicles or the Pennsylvania Department of Transportation (usually abbreviated in vernacular speech as "PennDOT"). While prudently eschewing rearview mirror items, many motorists have miniature statues of patron saints mounted on the dashboard by suction cups instead. One of the commonest is St. Christopher, and so strong and widespread is popular belief in his efficacy as the patron of travelers that he continues to be acknowledged in car statuettes and neckchain medals down to the present day, notwithstanding his official decanonization by the Roman Catholic Church under Pope John XXIII in the early 1960s.

This is hardly a novel phenomenon: Religious iconography stimulated the medieval imagination to a fault, such that the Church had to "warn incessantly against want of discrimination," according to Jan Huizinga, between the veneration of saints and the worship of God; for "when faith is too directly connected with a pictured representation of doctrine, it runs the risk of no longer making qualitative distinctions between the nature and the degree of sanctity of the different elements of religion." Roman pagan culture had already had a tradition of domestic worship of one's own family's deities of house and field, the *lares* and *penates* respectively, a pattern of behavior strikingly similar to the modern Catholic's special relationship with individual saints, whether the believer's confirmation-namesake, patron of parish/town/profession, or specialist ameliorator of maladies and problems—whence the children's jingle seeking the intercession of St. Anthony of Padua in helping to turn up lost objects: "Tony, Tony, turn around: Find the (…) that can't be found."

Imperial Rome well understood the value of coins as a vehicle for disseminating the icons of civic religion. Even before the first emperor, Augustus, minted coins with his face on the obverse and such images as his triumphal chariot on the reverse, contenders in the Civil Wars had struck their own coinage to pay their soldiers, from the *denarius* issued by Brutus and his fellow tyrannicides depicting his famous ancestor who expelled the Tarquin kings (the reverse bore a pair of daggers flanking a freedman's cap and the single word *libertas*) to Marc Antony's war-galley *denarii*, issued to his legions just prior to the fateful sea-battle at Actium in the wake of which he and Cleopatra committed suicide. A coin identifying Antoninus Pius as *divus* (i.e., deified) bears a tolerable representation of his funeral pyre on the back. Several types of Roman coins (e.g., the *congiaria* and *alimenta*), show scenes of imperial largesse toward children, who represented the bright future of Roman society. And it is to the reverse of a *denarius* of Nero that we owe the only surviving depiction of the surprisingly modest temple of Janus, its doors closed and wreathed to indicate that at least for the moment Rome was at peace. "More than just a piece of money," says collector Ronald D'Argenio, "coinage was a way for the Roman senate, and later the emperor, to convey a message to the folks who lived out in the colonies." Money, in short, talks.

Pile in its meaning of 'heap, stack' (as in "the Hunt brothers hoped to make a pile of money manipulating silver futures, but then Kodak stepped in") first turns up unequivocally in print in 1611, in which it is used in the specialized sense of a cone-shaped stack of graduated weights. *Pile* in this sense (in both English and French) is derived from Latin *pīla* in its meaning of 'column.' (The unrelated *pile* that refers to the surface of certain fabrics, such as a pile rug, has its origin in Latin *pĭlus*, 'hair,' whence also the *-pil-* of *depilatory*.) *Heap* is attested much earlier (as 'large quantity of immaterial things,' it appears in a quotation from around 1200, spelled *hæp*). Both *heap* and *stack* (cognate with Old Norse *stakk-r* and Russian *stog*, both meaning 'haystack') appear in a generous array of figurative and combinatorial expressions: the fallacy of the heap (a.k.a. the Sorites Paradox), to drive a heap (sc. jalopy), heap big Indian Bingo prize ("in the representation of the speech of North American Indians used adverbially and as quasi-adj.," delicately says the *Oxford English Dictionary*), to knock/strike all of a heap; to swear on a stack of Bibles, to have a one-day stack pass at Widener Library, a stack of wood/coal (usually four cubic yards, or in cordwood 20 cubic feet short of a full cord), the (smoke)stack of a furnace or locomotive, hence to blow one's stack (cf. *go ballistic*)—a manifestation of temporary insanity on the opposite end of the spectrum of fury from one who is just pleasantly and chronically dotty.

on the dot

dit dah

codes to sigh for

Illustrious people's famous last words (actual or apocryphal) can fill volumes; perhaps it is time someone did a compendium of first words as well, or at least those first messages sent along any new medium of communication. In the case of Alexander Graham Bell, the first telephone message was an urgent request to his colleague Watson to come to him, as Bell had just spilled some battery acid on himself. (The phone Watson answered was in a neighboring building, so this was not as silly a request as it might have been had Watson been all the way across town.) Generally, however, the occasion is recognized as a momentous one, for which a suitably unforgettable inaugural line is crafted with some care well in advance. Neil Armstrong's "That's one small step for a man, one giant leap for mankind," his first words on alighting from the lunar lander onto the surface of the moon on July 20, 1969, were certainly not a spontaneous utterance, any more than was Samuel Finley Breese Morse's first telegraph message sent to his partner Albert Vail on May 24, 1844, on an experimental telegraph line from Washington to Baltimore: "What Hath God Wrought."

We are nowadays somewhat jaded at the pace at which one revolutionary technological advance succeeds another, so it may be hard to imagine how different the climate of opinion was in the first flush of the Industrial Revolution. This cut both ways: For every inventor there were plenty of skeptics, and despite having successfully tested a prototype along three miles of wire at Vail's Speedwell Iron Works in New Jersey in 1839 (the test message: "A patient waiter is no loser"), it took Morse another five years to persuade Congress to allocate $30,000 to fund the stringing of a Washington–Baltimore line that resulted in the textbook demonstration above.

After that, however, telegraphy caught on and rapidly spread out across the country. Western Union was founded in 1856 and its first transcontinental telegraph line in 1861 spelled the beginning of the end of the Pony Express; the first transatlantic cable was operational by 1866, and the first telegraphic stock ticker in 1867. (It gave stock quotes in Morse code; two years later Thomas Edison would invent an alphanumeric version similar to the ones in use until the 1960s.) Nor was the strategic value of telegraphic communications lost on the U.S. War Department, although its most dramatic effect on any single battle during the Civil War came from its hardware, not its informational content: On November 29, 1863, telegraph wire strung along tree stumps near Knoxville, Tennessee, literally tripped up Confederate general James Longstreet's attack on the forces of Union general Ambrose Burnside (whose eponymous side-whiskers were much admired and imitated; the name was later metathesized to *sideburns*, but they were also known as *dundrearies* from the name of the character who sported them in the comedy *Our American Cousin*, the last play Abraham Lincoln saw).

That fateful first message Morse actually sent was something like this: *Dit dah dah, dit dit dit dit, dit dah, dah* (pause), *dit dit dit dit, dit*

dah, dah, dit dit dit dit (pause), *dah dah dit, dah dah dah, dah dit dit*
(pause), *dit dah dah, dit dah dit, dah dah dah, dit dit dah, dah dah dit,*
dit dit dit dit, dah (· – – ·· · · – – [pause] ·· · · – – ···· [pause]
– – · – – – ·· [pause] · – – · – · – – – ·· – – – · ···· –). This string
displays in a nutshell most of what is good and bad about Morse code:
The good part is that it consists of just two elements, long and short
(as in classical prosody: D, for example, is the metrical equivalent of
a dactyl [*dah dit dit*], while A is an iamb [*dit dah*], N a trochee [*dah
dit*], U an anapaest [*dit dit dah*], M a spondee [*dah dah*], and R an
amphibrach [*dit dah dit*].) As such, Morse code was tailor-made for an
electronic age then still very far in the future. The bad part is that relative to speech (let alone to reading the printed page) it's awfully slow
going, even under the touch of an experienced telegrapher: 40 words
per minute is doing very well, and the best anyone has ever done (Ted
R. Elroy, at a July 1939 contest in Asheville, North Carolina) is a little
over 75 WPM. By contrast, a radio announcer reading into the mike
from index cards or typescript can usually count on about 125 WPM,
and most people can read silently at speeds approaching or even sur-
passing twice that.

    A further problem is that the variable length of the characters has
proven to be an impediment to adapting Morse code to automated-
communication media. The last Western Union telegram from one
member of the public to another was sent on January 26, 2006, 150
years after the founding of the company—which, however, continues to do a brisk and expanding business in money-by-wire transfers:
In 2007 Western Union, in partnership with the retail and financial
services company Grupo Elektra, acquired a consumer wire-transfer
franchise in 587 locations of Farmacias Benavides, a Mexican drugstore chain. (The company's website boasts "over 280,000 agents
worldwide.")

    There are several reasons that Morse code is likely to complete its
second century, however. For one thing, amateur radio license holders

15

("hams") can broadcast long distances at low power, yet their Morse code exchanges will still remain mutually intelligible, even with a fair amount of white noise and static in the background. For another, Morse code is adaptable to a variety of low-tech media: pulses keyed in and sent on a telegraph wire activating a magnet on the other end, bips and bleeps on a radio frequency, the on-off of a flashing light (Aldis lamp or heliograph), or even surreptitious gestures by a prisoner of war; in 1966, Jeremiah Denton, captured by the North Vietnamese, seized the opportunity to eye-blink the word "torture" in Morse code when he was out before a television camera in the company of his guards.

This is an instance of Morse code as "code" in its most familiar sense (at least until computer software and poststructuralist literary/social critics came along): a language not intended to be decipherable by just anybody, i.e., a cipher. The word *cipher* comes from the Arabic *sifr*, meaning both 'empty' and 'zero,' a meaning it retains in British English, in which an unremarkable and unprepossessing person may still be referred to as a cipher (compare American *Joe Zilch*); up until the early 20th century, at least among rural Americans, it also meant "to do arithmetic," as the hillbilly said to the schoolma'am: "The boy's all right at cipherin', but I reckon he needs more of that there trigger-nometry, for he's the worst shot in the family!"

A cipher begins with a plain text and encodes it such that the sender hopes it will be rendered incomprehensible to anyone who might intercept it on its way to the intended recipient—as opposed to simply concealing the message in the expectation that it won't be intercepted (such as shaving the head of one's slave, tattooing the message on his scalp, waiting for his hair to grow back, and sending him off right under the noses of the unsuspecting spies of the Great King on an ostensible errand to one's kinsman in Ionia). Such a method is more properly an instance of *steganography*, the science of concealing a message in plain sight embedded in something else.

For example, there are trellis ciphers, in which an opaque sheet with windows, identical to a template in the possession of the recipient, is laid over a printed or handwritten message, exposing only words here and there. Its success rests on the sender's talent for creative writing seamlessly embedding the message in a plausibly innocuous-seeming superficial text, e.g., a letter ostensibly from someone on vacation in the borderlands, concealing a terse report on the gaps in an unfriendly neighbor's frontier that might be suitable crossing points for refugees or spies planted behind the lines.

Then there are *microdots*, developed by Germany during World War II: By taking a photograph of a document and reducing it to a very tiny circular phototransparency, an agent can convey a large amount of information in a miniature form that can be hidden as the dot over an i in a typewritten document. All the recipient needs is to know where to look for it, peel it off, and put it under a powerful enough overhead projector or photographic enlarger, with the enemy unaware that anything other than the full-sized cover message has changed hands.

Still another steganographic technique, unthinkable before the desktop computer age, is to conceal strings of electronic text in graphic files several orders of magnitude larger. Of course, just because a technology exists does not mean that it is being used: In February 2001, two *USA Today* stories by Jack Kelley claimed that Islamic terrorists were already sending steganographic messages embedded in the code of pornographic image files. This started an urban legend that got a dramatic boost seven months later with the World Trade Center and Pentagon attacks, notwithstanding the fact that a team with networked computers and sophisticated software at the University of Michigan's Center for Information Technology had already been scrutinizing promising Internet images for what Andrew Glass called "the tell-tale 'signature' of steganography" concealing terrorist plans. The results? The researchers reported that despite scanning two million

17

digital graphic files they had "not been able to find a single hidden message." (*Steganos*, by the way, is Greek for 'roofed over,' and *stegē* means 'roof,' which is why the familiar Jurassic dinosaur with those plates on its back got named *stegosaurus*.)

By contrast, *cryptography* is all about enciphering the actual text of a message itself. The *crypt-* part means 'hidden,' as in *cryptofascist* or just plain *crypt*; it's the same root as the *cryph-* in *apocrypha* and the *krypt-* of *kryptonite*, the one thing in the universe that can put Superman at a serious disadvantage against the forces of evil (apart from a growing scarcity of phone booths to change clothes in). One of the simplest ciphers is an alphabetical substitution algorithm such as Augustus Caesar used, writing b̲ for a̲, c̲ for b̲, and so on down to x̲, the last letter of the Romans' alphabet, for which the emperor substituted a̲a̲. (Thus *pax romana* would be written *qbaa spnbob*, which at least would have given the opposition something to scratch their heads over.)

A much later "Father of His Country," George Washington, preferred to use a cipher that substituted three-digit numbers for words; the recipients of his messages would have an identical codebook and decipher his message with that. A subtler variant is to use numbers to stand for syllables, the method of the father-and-son team Antoine and Bonaventure Rossignol in devising the so-called Grand Chiffre ('Great Cipher') for Louis XIV. (*Chiffre* is French for both 'cipher' and 'number on a clock or watch face.') The Grand Chiffre's codebooks do not seem to have long survived the three men themselves and it was not until the 1890s that Étienne Bazeries, a French army officer and cryptographer, was able to make headway in cracking the code, starting from the lucky guess that a frequent combination in the surviving encoded texts should be decoded as *les ennemis* ("the enemies"). In 1893 Bazeries caused considerable excitement by claiming to have decoded a letter positively identifying the "Man in the Iron Mask," the mysterious high-ranking prisoner whose hidden identity

on the dot

was the subject of much speculation in the two centuries following his death in 1703, not to say fair game for the pen of Alexandre Dumas. The letter named Vivien Labbé, Seigneur de Bulonde, a general who had led a botched assault on the fortifications of Coni (Cuneo) in the Piedmont; that he was the fellow with the mask, however, is an assertion that has drawn only mixed support, since while the letter certainly is about Bulonde and provides for his being able to take his exercise on the prison rampart as did the mystery prisoner, the final phrase about the mask rests on Bazeries' reading of two Grand Chiffre numbers for whose interpretation there is no other evidence.

Nevertheless, frequency of letters often furnishes a very sound starting point for cracking alphabetic codes. In both English and French, the most common letter is e̲ (around 13% in English and 15% in French, not including é, è, or ê, which would raise the latter to over 16%). In English the first twelve letters in order of frequency were determined to be e̲, t̲, a̲, o̲, i, n̲, s̲, h̲, r̲, d̲, l̲, and u̲ at the time the linotype machine was put on the market, which is why, during the many years that newspapers were set by linotype operators, readers would sometimes stumble on a string of one or more "etaoin shrdlu"s embedded in the middle of a column (or as temporary boilerplate on the end) where the typesetter's hand had swiped the top line of the keyboard and the proofreader missed it. In France the distribution is somewhat different, notably because English uses h̲ about five times as often as French does (less than 1%). Note that different samplings will produce different frequencies, though one might suppose that the larger the sample the closer it will be to a reasonably accurate prediction of future writings as well—and if a major part of one's only sample were the entire Georges Perec novel *La Disparition*, a tour de force of lipography without a single e̲ in it, all bets would be off, or at least awfully dicey.

It is pure coincidence that the six pips drilled into the highest-numbered face of a die should resemble the two-by-three array of raised dots in the alphabetic code developed by Louis Braille. Blinded in one eye as a three-year-old and having lost the sight of the other to ophthalmia by the age of four, Braille was enrolled as a child of 10 in the National Institute for Blind Children in Paris in 1819; there he became acquainted with the raised-dot "night writing" invented by Charles Barbier for military use as a way for soldiers to communicate silently in the dark or during the smoke and noise of artillery exchanges. Barbier's 12-dot matrix had proved too difficult for the ordinary recruit to master (though Braille had no difficulty in doing so) and had the further drawback that none of its characters (each of which stood for a different sound rather than a letter) could be read in its entirety without moving one's fingertip. Braille came up with a more compact and tactile-friendly six-dot alphabet starting in 1824, publishing it in 1829 in his *Method of Writing Words, Music, and Plain Songs by Means of Dots*; thanks to the school's strong music program, which had turned him into an accomplished cellist and church organist, he also invented a method of raised-dot music notation, adding it to his system in 1828. (His best friend, Gabriel Gauthier, who later would be his colleague on the school's faculty, was also an organist and composed some of the earliest music to be printed in braille.)

While there are typewriters and printing presses to produce braille text, the ordinary person uses a braille slate, a six-hole template with a second plate in back with shallow pits in it in the same grid, as a backstop for the stylus with which the individual dots are to be made. The braille text is consequently written in mirror image, right to left; since punching the paper on the front raises dots on the back, the sheet must be flipped over in order to read the text correctly, left to right. Braille is code, not cipher; and encrypted only to the extent that one is ignorant of the alphabet, as were the besiegers, during the 1857 war in India, of a British commander whose message to summon reinforcements was written in plain English disguised in Greek characters (σομεθινγ λικε θις).

on the dot

Indeed, the students at Braille's school became such quick studies at his system that they put their teachers to shame; they successfully resisted attempts to suppress its use on the part of administrators with considerably less facility in it than their charges, another instance in which something that is a mere code to some people can function as a de facto cipher to others. (This is also, of course, the utility value of second languages that parents use in front of children for conversations whose contents they do not wish their little-pitchers-with-big-ears to understand. This has the added benefit of furnishing a powerful incentive for their offspring to learn that language for themselves, a win-win situation if the parents really would like them to grow up fluent in it anyway.) An antique dealer may do something of this sort when tagging stock with letter codes indicating the cost of acquisition, in order to be better able to haggle with the client while never losing sight of the bottom line: A substitution for the numbers one through ten can be made from any ten-letter word or phrase that does not repeat a letter, such as *dumbwaiter*, by which a dollar amount such as "135" can be encoded as DMW. (Other possibilities: *stenograph, anteloping, quicksandy, polytheism, psychotica, Mary Joseph*, and *zydeco fans*.)

Most ham radio operators use Q code, which collapses a great number of standard character strings into more compact form: QST is "general call to all stations" (compare CQ), QTH is "location" (as in "My QTH is Quimper, Kansas"), QSB is "fading signal," QRN is "natural interference," QTA is "disregard last message," and QRRR, "distress." The Q codes originated in Britain, promulgated by the British government for naval use but eventually propagating into aviation as well; a list of 45 of them was adopted at the Third International Radiotelegraph Convention in 1912.

The Second International Radiotelegraph Convention in 1906 had adopted the German distress call SOS, effective July 1, 1908. For a while this was used interchangeably with CQD, which the Marconi

International Marine Communications Company had promulgated for all its stations at the beginning of 1904; the sinking *Titanic*'s radio operator sent out both. SOS is a "prosign" (procedural signal), properly written with a bar over it because there is no space between the three letters (unlike, for example, the first three letters of the names of the Polish city Sosnowiec or the early Christian Sosthenes). Normally a *dah* is equal in length to three *dits*, and each *dah* or *dit* making up a letter is separated from its neighbor by a silence equal in duration to one *dit*. Each letter or character is set off from the next by a three-*dit* silence, and adjacent words are separated by a seven-*dit* one. Such backronyms as "Save our Ship" or "Sink or Swim" are mnemonics only: The SOS string actually was just an alteration of SOE (three dots, three dashes, and one more dot), the German "calling-all-stations" code used to summon the attention of any receiving operator.

Citizens' Band users and truck-song afficionados will be familiar with 10-code, the prefixed 10 (like Q or the European Z) being a sign that what follows is code rather than plain text. Probably the most familiar of these is "10-4," i.e.,"Acknowledging your message." Unlike Q code, police 10-codes can vary from one jurisdiction to another: a "10-45" in Portland, Maine, is a domestic disturbance; in Shippensburg, Pennsylvania, it's an automobile collision—and elsewhere in the Keystone State it can mean "large dead animal on road."

Encodings also take place in the language of rhetoric: Every allegory is an encoding, and one the allegorist wants us to decode. So we may say that Arthur Miller's *The Crucible*, ostensibly a play about the Salem witch trials, encodes a narrative of the '50s red-baiting hearings staged by the House Un-American Activities Committee and Senator Joseph McCarthy, or that jazz as portrayed in such postwar films as *DOA* is code for sexual and racial transgression. Political advertising is notorious for this, of course, particularly those attack ads that try to sell the idea that certain types of people with whom the opposing candidate has been shaking hands are emblematic of everything that

on the dot

is nasty, dangerous, and unpatriotic. (Close-up of long-haired bearded man blessing leper pulls back to pan as he goes into home of tax collector followed by seedy-looking extras. Voice-over: " 'Reb' Yeshua says that 'clean' versus 'unclean' doesn't matter. Publicans, robbers, riffraff from Samaria—HE doesn't care; he'll tuck in and chow down with just anyone. Is THIS the sort of faith healer you want laying hands on your daughter?" Zoom in on leper's hand grabbing at hem of the young rabbi's garment, then fade.) Of course, as our dramatization of Matthew 9:11 shows, this sort of thing has been going on for millennia; but it's gotten a lot slicker in our technologically sophisticated age.

A form of encoding that employs an everyday variety of low-level steganography is the acrostic, in which the first letter of the first word in each line can be read vertically. Lewis Carroll famously did this in his poem "A boat beneath a sunny sky," with which he concludes the second of the Wonderland books, *Through the Looking Glass*. The initial letters of its 21 lines spell "Alice Pleasance Liddell." The original Christian acrostic was the Greek word *ichthys* ('fish'), which was an acrostic for *Iesous Christos Theou Huios Sōtēr* ('Jesus [the] Annointed, God's Son, [the] Savior'), so in the early days of the Roman empire a graffito of a fish (that is, two curving horizontal lines meeting each other at one end and crossing each other to form a tail at the other) was a code sign indicating Christians in the vicinity, much as tramps leave signs for one another chalked on the sides of houses down to this day.

During the Nazi occupation of France and the Low Countries, the resistance in Belgium would write "R.A.F." (as in Royal Air Force) on walls as a taunt to the Germans. A Belgian lawyer named Victor De Lavelaye came up with "V" instead on January 14, 1941. It had the advantages of being short for victory (*victoire* in French), as well as for Dutch/Flemish *vrijheid* ('freedom'), and took only two swipes of a crayon or chalk (RAF requires nine, omitting the dots). "The B.B.C. mounted a highly successful propaganda campaign employing

23

dit dah

the Morse code symbol for V (dot-dot-dot-dash) and the opening bars of Beethoven's Fifth Symphony," write Desmond Morris and his colleagues. "Churchill took up the sign and used it publicly at every opportunity." It was revived in America by the antiwar movement in the 1960s and rapidly became a fashionable greeting sign among hippies, many of whom referred to it as the "peace sign" (as opposed to the "peace symbol," the nuclear disarmament semaphore icon mentioned below) with only dim awareness, if any, of its role in the gestural rhetoric of an earlier military conflict.

The great cryptographic triumph of the Second World War was the Allied discovery of how to decipher messages sent by the Germans with their Enigma encryption devices, which used a set of cylinders to change the algorithm for encoding of letters with every letter. According to Hans-Peter Bischof, "As the plain text letter passed through the first rotor, the first rotor would rotate one position. The other two rotors would remain stationary until the first rotor had rotated 26 times. Then the second rotor would rotate one position. After the second rotor had rotated 26 times, [t]hen the third rotor would rotate one position." Hence, deciphering the encrypted text meant one had to "know the initial settings of the rotors, and then put the cipher text through the machine to find the plain text.... [A]ll of the recipients would set their rotors to predetermined settings according to the date. Each clerk had a book" specifying the day's settings.

The Allies, however, managed to figure out how the German encoding machines worked, thanks to getting their hands on one smuggled out of Germany by a British cryptographer. By 1939 they had cracked the code and were routinely intercepting and decoding Axis top-secret communications without the Germans knowing it. The price of this was high: A year later, decoded messages revealed that a huge air raid on Coventry was about to take place. The British high command made the agonized decision not to warn the inhabitants, for to do so would have put Hitler's own cryptographers on notice that the Enigma apparatus had been at least compromised, if not rendered useless in its existing form. In the massive Luftwaffe assault on November 15, 1940, the city's cathedral and 50,000 houses were destroyed, with the loss of 1,000 lives.

In contrast to times of openly declared war, encryption nowadays is by no means the monopoly of the war departments of belligerent nations or of cold warriors. The technological explosion has put computers on the ordinary person's desktop or lap that have proved to be quite hackable, and even private citizens have taken an interest in the security of their e-mail and the threat of rogue access to their files. Commercial data users have an even stronger incentive than just a dislike of snoops: When financial transactions and other proprietary information are computerized, the opportunities for unauthorized users to get at them are legion, but if the information is reasonably well encrypted, the only people who will be able to unlock and read such files are those with the right key.

A burgeoning ancillary industry strives to meet this need for encryption, and in America the Bureau of Standards has gotten in on the act as well, approving and promulgating an algorithm called the Data Encryption Standard (DES for short) that applies to symmetric encryption, i.e., encryption in which the key for encoding and decoding a message is the same. Asymmetric encryption, on the other hand, uses two keys, one for encryption and one for deciphering the encrypted message, which obviates the necessity of transferring the key as well as the message. Encryption keys chosen at random are virtually uncrackable if they are long enough; it would take four trillion years—a thousand times the age of the earth—at 10,000 guesses a second to examine all the possible permutations of characters in a ten-character key selected from the first 256 ASCII characters. This is a long way from Augustus's letter-substitution cipher!

People's names play a role as substitutes for letters in a wide variety of alphabets; here the process is the opposite of decoding in that it seeks to make plain and unambiguous the names of letters that would be clearly audible but for static and the limitations of certain electrical transmission devices in carrying the high formants of phonemes. Telephones, for example, typically chop the sound spectrum off at both the lower and higher frequencies, thus making it virtually impossible to distinguish between the nasals [m] and [n], for example, or the fricatives [f], [θ], [s], and [š]. (The authors can speak from personal experience, having spent much of their lives spelling out "H, U, M-as-in-Mary, E, Z-as-in-zebra" to people on the other end of phone lines—and this was before cell phones.) The military alphabet during World War II began "Able, Baker, Charlie, Dog…" whereas the U. S. armed forces now use "Alpha, Bravo, Charlie, Delta…."

No discussion of encryption would be complete without a nod to Alice and Bob, a couple constantly popping up in exemplary narratives from cryptography to physics. They are personifications of A and B (joined by Carol, Dave, and Eve et al.—that is, C, D, E, and so forth—as the encryption/decryption story gets more complex). For example, Alice sends a message to Bob and wants to make sure that the message remains private (i.e., secret/encrypted), and that it is indeed Bob whom she is contacting (and not, say, Eve, who is the perennial eavesdropper). So she sends Bob a random number and asks him to encrypt it using a key number she knows Bob knows. If he passes the test, she knows it's really Bob. Usually Bob wants to send a reply (also secret/encrypted)…and so on. A French website shows how Alice and Bob can play at heads-or-tails (French *pile ou face*) via e-mail, using encryption keys to keep each other honest. (Then again, they *could* just get a life.)

Literary and musical references to codes and ciphers abound; ever since someone figured out that you could turn a piece of tape around and splice it so that it played backward (one of the earliest was the instrumental bridge in the Beatles song "I'm Only Sleeping," released on their *Yesterday, Today and Tomorrow* album in 1966), rock fans and do-gooders alike have looked for subversive hidden messages in popular music's backward breaks. And for those whose turntables wouldn't spin backward, there was the song "Oh Dear, Miss Morse," on Pearls Before Swine's eponymous first album, with its refrain "*Dit dit dah dit, dit dit dah, dah dit dah dit, dah dit dah*"—probably a dead heat in the in-your-face disguised-naughty-song category with the thin encryption in the Aerosmith number "Devil's Got a New Disguise," whose chorus begins with the line "If you see Kay, tell her I love her." As well one might: If scarcely a code of honor, at least words to live by.

dit dah

with a bullet
checklists and dingbats

"Funny you should mention it," sang Frank Zappa: "Our new single hit the charts last week—with a *bullet*!" Amidst proliferating Power-Point presentations and burgeoning books of lists, the bullet seems as ubiquitous as blazing six-guns in a spaghetti Western. Like bar codes, they're everywhere, even where one can't tell exactly why (e.g., the one next to the sub-headline on a feature story about tree houses in our local paper). The use of *bullet points*, as a synonym for *list items*, has become so commonplace as to have worn out its novelty. We live in a bulleted age.

Bulleted lists are lists of things that (at least in theory) you can do in any order you like (and perhaps skip the ones you don't feel like doing). In the context of a list, a bullet is simply a raised dot:

- Do this (maybe).
- And/or this (maybe).
- And/or that (maybe).

The raised dot as bullet item marker does not have a monopoly on that typographical niche: Alternative representations, such as the asterisk and the checkmark, also serve to mark items in an unordered list (the latter being why we sometimes refer to such an inventory as a *checklist*). This convention is at least three thousand years old: Butehamun, chief scribe of the corps of tomb workers near the Valley of the Kings in the days of Ramesses XI, left faint little red dots, as if checking them off, next to each of the short prayers from the Book of the Dead written on the inside of the gesso mummy-cover that was to go inside his own innermost coffin (he would finally come to rest in it around 1056 B.C.E.):

- My mouth is opened by Ptah....
- Thoth...has come and loosened my bindings....
- Anubis has freed my hands....

Note that in a bulleted list one needn't do or eliminate things in order of appearance on the list, nor is it implicitly necessary to do/eliminate every one of them—in marked contrast to numbered lists, which say you have to do the first item before getting on to the second, the second before the third...and the $(n\text{-}1)^{\text{th}}$ before the nth—in short, any given thing before you can go on to the next thing. Some ordered lists—the best-dressed movie stars of the year, the worst movies of the year (or of all time so far)—are a variant of the first-this-then-that school of thought, usually in descending order, the best/most agreeable being number one.

Numbered lists are sometimes bulleted lists in mufti: The take-out menu from your favorite ethnic restaurant often will number its items (sometimes in categories, but almost always serially: Items 1–10 are appetizers, items 11–20 are the pork dishes, and so on). Of course, one advantage to numbering menu items is to spare everybody involved the heartbreak of trying to pronounce the names of the dishes or, on the restaurant's end of the phone, understand such attempts ("I'd like an order of number 23" being shorthand for "I'd like an order of that exotic-looking combo with the squid, eggplant, and lotus-flower sauce, whose name I can't pronounce but it's number 23 on the menu"), allowing one to order by the numbers in any order, and pick up (or have delivered) everything in a few minutes.

Another variant on menus as ordered/unordered lists: The restaurant offers a prix fixe dinner: appetizer, main course, dessert. The ravenous diner gets a choice of each of these—escargots, pâté; canard à l'orange, langues des grenouilles Saint-Nytouche; crème brûlée, gâteaux. The appetizer, the main course, and dessert typically come in order; one picks an option for each. It is presumed that one can skip anything (e.g., dessert), though not usually the main course.

Grocery shopping lists are typically unordered—get milk, bread, and a bunch of other stuff. This may be incorporated into an ordered list of errands:

1. Pick up prescription at the pharmacy.
2. Get stuff at the grocery store:
   - Milk
   - Bread
   - Etc.
3. Buy stamps at post office.
4. Go home.

Or, more elaborately,

1. Run errands:
   - Pick up prescriptions at the pharmacy.
   - Get stuff at the grocery store:

- [✓] Bread
- [✓] Milk
- [✓] Etc.
- Get stamps at post office.
2. Go home.

The idea is that you run errands and then go home in that order. Your errands are to go to the pharmacy and grocery store and post office in whichever order you like (though the presumption is that you will do all three) and that while at the grocery store you'll get the stuff on the shopping list. Putting bullets within bullets is generally discouraged by the editorial police, and probably rightly so, but sometimes logic needs to trump literary convention.

While a grocery list is unordered, if you skip anything or make substitutions, you may or may not get away with it (as many a spouse or domestic partner can ruefully attest). But if it's an ordered list (e.g., get the car key, go to the car, open the door, get in, put on your seat belt, start the car...), that's a different story: You can't do any of those operations in random order or omit any of them (except the seat belt one if you like to live dangerously or, at least in certain states, don't mind risking a fine if the highway patrol pulls you over for something else). This has become increasingly true in an era of "smart" devices, from appliances to automobiles: In order to open the windows of the 2000 Kia Sephia, for example, one must not merely get inside the car as in the old crank-window days but also have inserted one's key in the ignition *and* have turned it past "accessories" to the "on" position—whereupon a bell starts bonging because one has not fastened one's seat belt! (One might think manual override options would come with all such electronic-nanny modules, given our culture's widespread belief in free will, but no.)

Even though the Ten Commandments look like an ordered list and are always supposed to be read in the same sequence, at least in public, with the exception of the first (monotheism being of the essence), the order in which one does or refrains from doing the items on the list would not appear to matter a great deal. To be sure, none are optional, but not coveting your neighbor's donkey is probably lower on the order of importance than, say, not murdering. Order of importance is another system for list-making, sort of a hybrid of the ordered and unordered list: it's more important to do A, B, and C than to do D if you don't have time to do everything. You don't necessarily have to do A, B, and C in any order as long as you do them. Elections offer another hybrid: Vote for one person for mayor from those on the ballot (or write in someone, but it's still a vote for one person, or for nobody), vote for (up to) five aldermen, etc. The order in which one fills out the ballot doesn't matter.

Here might be mentioned also the empty bullet list, i.e., the multiple-choice test printed to be read by an optical scanner (familiar from our standardized-tested childhoods: the Iowa Test of Educational Development, the CEEB Achievement Tests, the National Merit Scholarship exam, etc.). By making one's mark (#2 pencil, black only, good and dark, and within the lines; if you make a false mark, erase it) on one and only one of the empty bullets, one turned it into a proper bullet and the scanner would record it as such. A more sophisticated algorithm, of course, can allow for programmable options if the empty-bullet form to be scanned is an electoral ballot instead.

The *American Heritage Dictionary* (4th ed.) defines *laundry list* as "[a]n item-by-item enumeration"—something of a misnomer, since the usual way of thinking of a laundry is that one needn't do it in any particular order, *and* one can skip some (though hope springs eternal that it will all come to pass, in the fullness of time at least). Wash and iron the shirts, but you don't have to do the pants if you don't get around to it; iron the shirts but, if you don't have time, skip the washing part (?)—compare *wish list*: Ideally, I'd like all the stuff on this list (possibly prioritized), but I won't be surprised if I don't get everything. (Senator Sludge's press secretary: "I'm happy to report

33

that the senator did manage to obtain funding for both the Hogtown Bypass and the Dry Gulch bridge improvement projects, but the withdrawal of all our state's National Guard units from Armageddistan by Thanksgiving—well, it just wasn't in the cards.")

A variant of this is the *hit list*, until recently the province of mobsters but now coming into favor as an expressive art form among disgruntled secondary-school students. A recent *New York Times* article noted that some of these lists distinguish among people the writer wants to kill, people merely to hurt, and people to knock out cold. Since kids who have the leisure time (and compulsiveness) to write a hit list nowadays generally are computer-literate and have access to word-processing software—several of the examples in the article are culled from Internet chat rooms—presumably such a list would have looked something like this:

- Billy
- Bobby
- ✓ Brad
- ✓ Bink
- ➤ Barowski

Key:

- Kill
- ✓ Harm
- ➤ KO

Whether a potential perpetrator would also order the lists within the list—get Billy first because he's the guy you really don't like, or get Billy first because he comes alphabetically before Bobby, do the killing first and then do the hurting—was not discussed in the article. Nor is

on the dot

there a clearly implicit order in which one would kill, harm, or knock out cold. (A variant from a town in Massachusetts, reported in the same article: A youth who compiled both a hit list and a "protect" list, fortunately found by school officials before either could be implemented.)

●

Of course, *real* bullets (that is, projectiles discharged by firearms) nowadays do have points *on* them—the technical term is *cylindroconoidal*—but this is the result of an evolution in weapons technology from muzzle-loaders charged with powder and ball (the French term for bullet remains *balle* to this day) and even further back to the little balls hurled by auxiliary soldiers with slings, working from the fringes of the regular Roman sword-and-spear-bearing infantry.

Tempting though it is to see a connection between the *ball* of a musket (or cannon) and *ballistic*, such an etymology is a wash: The latter comes from the Greek verb *ballein*, 'to throw,' ultimately derived from the Proto-Indo-European root *g^wel-* ('to throw, reach, pierce'), the former from an Old Germanic word *balluz*, also the probable source for Italian *palla* ('ball')—whose diminutive, *pallotta*, means 'little ball, bullet' (as does French *balle*)—and ultimately from a different PIE root, *bhel-*, meaning "to blow, swell," whose other derivatives include *bale, balloon, ballot, bawd, boil, bold, boulder, bowl* (but not *bowel*, which derives via Old French *boel* from Latin *botulus*, 'sausage'—as does *botulism*), *bulk, bull* (of the sort that comes from the pope), and *bullet* itself.

Latin *bulla* means 'bubble,' a meaning close to the underlying 'blow, swell' above; by extension it means both an envelope and, since the Middle Ages, the blob of sealing-wax with an official imprint that is used to seal it, hence by synechdoche 'sealed official document,' especially Vatican encyclicals down to the present day.

Bulla is also the term used by archaeologists to describe the curious closed vessels unearthed in Mesopotamia and found to contain clay tokens, depicting miniature animals and other commodities, which had apparently been pressed into the still-soft surface of the container before it was sealed up. These seem to have been bills of lading to guarantee that as many donkeys (pigs, sheep,...) got to the recipient as were intended by the sender, the bulla serving to ensure that the inventory hadn't been fiddled with, and the surface impressions to show what was inside so as to obviate the need of breaking it at any point in transit. ("Say, Upshilummi, was that *nine* donkeys we were supposed to bring with us, or only eight?") From there it was a short if crucial conceptual leap to dispensing with the token transfer entirely and instead simply sending with the livestock a fired slab with the same donkey token pressed into it so many times; from the usual donkey token to a standard character meaning "donkey" would be only a matter of time.

Bulletin also comes from *bulla* in its sense of 'seal (pressed into a blob of wax).' English got it from French, which had it from Italian *bulletino*, a double diminutive of *bulla* that means 'safe-conduct, pass' (appropriately enough for a specific kind of sealed official document much smaller than a papal epistle-general). The "sealed" (i.e., official, trustworthy) part of the sense has largely been lost, though not altogether (radio announcer: "This is an all-points bulletin...."), while the "short" part is still with us: A bulletin board typically houses relatively small pieces of paper.

●

"Roll a-bowl a ball, a penny a pitch!" sings the barker at the coconut-shy stand in Fred Heatherton's 1944 song "I've Got a Lovely Bunch o' Coconuts," picked up by Danny Kaye during a phenomenally successful tour of the British Isles. Recorded in his best Cockney accent, the song earned him his only spot on U.S. pop-music charts in 1950, and he sang it as well in the film *I Could Go On Singing* (also starring Judy Garland; it would be her last film). The game is a variant of the carnie shooting-gallery booths familiar in America: Buy a certain number of balls, shy (throw) them at several coconuts sitting on posts at the back of the booth, and whatever coconuts you knock off, you get to keep (or earn some other prize, depending on the rules. If you're doing it to impress your sweetie, she'd probably prefer that stuffed fuzzy pink woodchuck over there).

The *bowl* in the chorus has the sense of 'set a ball in motion toward a target,' more familiar to us as the gerund in *bowling alley* or *bowling green* (and as a plural noun, *bowls*, the name of the game played on the latter, also called *lawn bowling*). It's a straightforward borrowing from *bulla* via French *boule*, fastidiously glossed by the *Nouveau Petit Larousse Illustré* as *corps sphérique* ('spherical body'); in one of his songs, the French *chansonnier* Charles Trenêt reduced cosmology to asserting that *La terre est une grosse boule / Qui tourne autour de l'univers* ("The earth is a great big ball / That circles the universe") and vice versa, underscoring the fact that spherical entities often prove to be hollow (a point also made by former physical education major Bill Cosby in his monologue "Why Is There Air?" from the album of the same name). From *boule* comes *boulet*, which means both 'cannonball' and '(convict's) ball and chain' (and by extension, 'tiresome person from whom one cannot escape'); by contrast, a *boulette* is a pellet or grain of shot.

Then there's *bowl* as 'hemispherical vessel' (salad bowl, toilet bowl), artificial or natural amphitheaters resembling it (the Hollywood Bowl, the Devil's Punch Bowl—site of an infamous murder in Sussex, England), or eponymous end-of-season football games played in them (the Rose Bowl, the Orange Bowl). This *bowl* is derived from **bhel-* too, but by a different route: It comes from Middle English *bolla* ("pot, bowl") and is one of a cluster of Germanic words from this stem having to do with roundness, including *boll* (as in *boll weevil*) from Middle Dutch *bolle* ('ball'), *bulk* from Norse *bulki* ('[rolled up] cargo'), the garlic-like plant called *rocambole* (borrowed into French from German *Rockenbolle*, from Middle High German *rocke*, 'distaff,' plus *bolle*, 'bulb'), and the *bil-* of South Africa's *biltong* ('dried meat,' *bille* being Dutch for 'buttock'). The Greeks used various types of bowls for wine-drinking, from large deep ones in which to mix the wine with water to the smaller shallow two-handled cups for the serious drinking itself. (The term for a drinking-party was *symposion*—Latinized to *symposium* and borrowed into English to indicate a gathering where ideas rather than wine would flow; the *-pos-* part is Greek for 'drink,' and is the same root as the *pot-* of *hippopotamus* and *potation*.) Through the rhetorical logic of container-for-the-thing-contained, *the bowl* came to mean liquor of any sort, implicitly consumed to the point of general merriment and perhaps beyond, whence the rousing old temperance song beginning "Old Alcohol is king of tears, /Away, away the bowl!"

Students of classical antiquity will occasionally come on a reference to the *boulē*, the Athenian Council of 500, and be tempted to see some connection with French *boule*. No go: The former comes from the Greek verb *bouleuein*, 'to take counsel/consider/deliberate.' (The block of theater seats reserved for the councilors at Athens down front by the orchestra was accordingly known as the *bouleutikon*.) The 1972 edition of Harrap's *Modern College French and English Dictionary* gives *Boule de feu, boule de fer* ("ball of fire, ball of iron") as a gloss for "Cross my heart and hope to die"—though this item seems quietly to have disappeared from the 1998 edition, and our efforts to find a single native speaker of French who would corroborate it met with no success. However, *Croix de bois, croix de fer* (*et si je mens, je vais en enfer*)—literally, 'wood cross, iron cross (and if I'm lying, I'm going to Hell)' is well attested, as is the pithier *juré craché* ('sworn spat') which

on the dot

is current in Canada but documented elsewhere in the francophone world as well; one of our informants (born and brought up in France) tells us that the *craché* part involves spitting on the ground when you swear you're telling the truth. To this a Canadian informant adds that when she was growing up, she and her peers would say, "Cross my heart and hope to die, and if I die I'll spit in your eye." She points out that this doesn't make logical sense, but, then, who thinks about the actual meaning of the words that constitute received sayings, especially when one is a kid? Compare crossing one's fingers when telling a lie.

●

Among the Celts of Gaul and Britain, the Druids had considerable **39** power in settling disputes, up to and including coming between opposite sides of an impending battle and calling the hostilities off. Diodorus Siculus, a contemporary of the emperor Augustus, approvingly writes that "they and the singing bards are likewise obeyed, and this by enemies as well as their own side." As indeed they might be, for it was well known that a well-composed satire could bring boils onto the object's face, among other afflictions; and in Ireland at least this general belief persisted well into the Middle Ages. (Under an increasingly repressive occupation, satire composed in Irish also became a gratifying means of subtle resistance to overlords ignorant of the language and remains a robust strain in Irish writing down to the present.) A boil—from Old English *byl*, related to Icelandic *beyla* ('hump')—is also called (in medical school at least) a *furuncle* (a diminutive of *fur* 'thief,' the original sense of *furunculus* having been "knob on a vine [that steals its sap]," hence a knob on your body). The boil to which one brings water, on the other hand, is an uncomplicated descendant of *bullire*, 'to boil, to make bubbles' (*bullae*).

An indispensible term in the discourse of Western medicine is *magic bullet* for any substance that will target a particular disease and do no damage to the rest of the body. The *Oxford English Dictionary* gives as its first citation for this phrase in an article published in 1907 by microbe hunter Paul Erlich, who said that the body's own antibacterial agents and antitoxins were "charmed bullets which strike only those objects for whose destruction they have been produced by the organism," and *magic bullet* has been a standard metaphor for antibodies since at least midcentury.

There are two possible sources for this image: The first is a Germanic legend about diabolically accurate bullets, recycled by Weber for his opera *Der Freischütz* (literally, "The Freeshooter," sometimes translated as "The Marksman"); the second is the belief that *silver bullets* are the only kind with which one can shoot and kill werewolves, a widespread but relatively late accretion onto those ubiquitous legends of lycanthropy throughout Europe that go back at least to Herodotus in the fifth century B.C.E. But the association of silver with the moon (like that of gold with the sun) is much older; and since werewolves are supposed to turn from human to wolf at the full moon, the homeopathic connection seems logical enough.

The connection is more tenuous for the silver bullets of the Lone Ranger, an enduring figure of popular American culture who was created by George W. Trendle and who first galloped onto the airwaves on Detroit radio station WXYZ on January 30, 1933. *His* silver bullets, supplied from the workings of a secret silver mine by his mentor, who had discovered it, were a reminder never to shoot anyone unfairly, the outward and visible sign of an inward commitment to distributive justice. Given that lead's molecular weight is 207.2 and silver's is just over half that (106.4), and presupposing a standard load of powder in his cartridges, it is left as an exercise for students of military science to determine how much closer to his target the Lone Ranger would

on the dot

have to be to inflict the same damage as a conventional gunman firing lead bullets; but this of course discounts the shock-and-awe factor produced by a fellow in a black mask on a white horse galloping off into a cloud of dust with his faithful companion, Tonto, to the strains of the overture to Rossini's *William Tell.*

And what of the bullet next to that hit single in the charts? According to chart manager Silvio Petroluongo, bulleted records on the website "R&R" (radioandrecords.com) are "[S]ongs showing an increase in plays over the previous week, regardless of chart movement. A song will also receive a bullet if its percentage loss in plays does not exceed the percentage of monitored station downtime for the format," but "[a] song that has been on the chart for more than 20 weeks will generally not receive a bullet, even if it registers an increase in plays."

Thus Ken Barnes's May 29, 2007, posting about Chris Daughtry on his "Idol Chatter" site (http://blogs.usatoday.com/idolchatter/ idol_airplay/index.html), which tracks *American Idol* performers, including Chris Daughtry:

> Daughtry['s] It's Not Over is hanging in there at 8 on the Hot 100 Airplay chart, the overall multi-format grab-bag. It was No. 8 last week and has no bullet, exactly the same story as on the similar national radio airplay audience chart USA TODAY uses. In other words, it is over, for all intents and purposes, but what a ride! It moves 3–3 (no bullet) on the Pop 100 Airplay chart (equivalent, more or less, to a national top 40 radio chart); 5–5 (no bullet) on the Mainstream Rock chart; 19–17 (bullet) on the Modern Rock chart; 27–21 on the Adult Contemporary chart, where it's just starting out; and is No. 1 with a bullet on the Adult Top 40 chart.

So motion—whether ballooning inflation or hurtling at a speed giving Superman a run for his money—seems to be what it's all about. With bullet points, though, you needn't be bound by time's inexorable forward flow: Though they are invariably ordered in the PowerPoint presentation that you're reading to your comatose audience, one page following another, one *can* always go back to a previous PowerPoint screen, in a way that you can't in some other ordered lists (undo handcuffs, go back to the scene of the crime, unshoot the guy behind the counter). Or in other words, the bullet that you bite needn't be your own.

. . . and a half

musical dots

In musical notation, the dot signifies that the note preceding it is to be increased in duration by half its length: A dotted half note is equal to a half note tied to a quarter note, a dotted quarter note equals a quarter tied to an eighth, and so on. (By the same token, a quarter-note rest with a dot after it means a rest equal to a quarter-note rest plus an eighth-note rest.) This has saved composers and their printers a great deal of ink over the years; without the dotted quarter, a jig (time signature 6/8), with an underlying two-beat rhythm of two dotted quarters to the measure, would be a thicket of tied quarters and eighths—and as for a concert polonaise jam-packed with dotted-eighths-plus-sixteenths, don't even go there.

In modern editions of Gregorian chant using the old square notation, which dates from about the 12th century, the dot *doubles* the value of the note it follows. (A horizontal line over a note—the equivalent of a macron in scansion or phonology—indicated that a note was to be prolonged slightly, but not by any measured quantity.)

However, the "Rules for Interpretation" at the beginning of the *Liber Usualis* (the 2,000-page compendium of Roman Catholic plainsong) concede that the demands of breathing at the ends of phrases will sometimes require that "the dotted note before the bar must necessarily be shortened slightly—almost to half its value."

Medieval composers wishing to represent rhythm, such as Perotinus at the cathedral of Notre Dame in Paris in the 13th century, adopted existing types of neumes (a neum(e) being a note or group of notes sung on a single syllable; the word comes either from Greek *pneuma*, 'breath, spirit' or *neuma*, 'nod, sign'—choral conductors would sometimes indicate pitch through gesture). By the 1300s, however, notes of different lengths were in use with distinct shapes for each: the long, breve, semibreve, and minim, in effect corresponding to our whole note, half note, quarter note, and eighth. The "dot of addition," adding half the value of the note before it, first appears around the same time: A treatise called "The Art of Mensurable Song" whose author is known today only as "Anonymous V" says that "a dot, when it perfects [makes complete] always adds to the note after which it is placed the neighboring part," that is, the next smallest note value. (But some of the French and Italian composers of the 14th century used a dot instead as the equivalent of a bar-line, to indicate the end of a group of notes corresponding to a given longer note. In such manuscripts a note prolonged by half its value might instead be indicated by a vertical stem plus a second stem, horizontal and to the left.)

Baroque musical notation was clear on the convention that a dot lengthened the previous note by half. However, as David Fuller points out, "[T]here is evidence that written dotted rhythms were often altered in performance.... The flexibility of dotted rhythms was...an aspect of good execution, along with many other kinds of rhythmic alteration or nuance." This is borne out in the fifth chapter of the classic treatise on flute-playing written by Johann Joachim Quantz (1697–1773), resident flute teacher to Frederick the Great: Quantz states that

on the dot

"a dot standing after a note has half the value of the preceding note" (§9) but later on qualifies this by saying that "the time of the short notes after the dots cannot actually be fixed with complete exactness" (§21)—the difference between theory and practice.

There were several innovations in dotted notation toward the middle of the 18th century as Baroque music turned into Rococo: Examples in Fuller's article include a harpsichord piece by Chambonnières with a vertical double dot (looking like a colon straddling the middle line of the staff) followed by a single dot, as a sign that the preceding note is to be prolonged by three-quarters of its value, where we would simply use a double horizontal dot today. And C. P. E. Bach proposed a vertical wedge over the second dot of a double-dotted note to signify an actual silence. In both of these cases the dots were not written immediately after the note but further along in the measure where the tied second note would have been had the long one been notated without a dot and tied to the next one instead. A vestige of this, persisting well into the 1800s, was carrying the dot over the bar line from the last note of a measure intended to be held over half its length into the new bar.

45

Other uses of the dot in musical notation today include writing a dot over a note to indicate that whatever its length, it is to be played staccato (in Broadway pit orchestra slang, a *stinger*); in string music, dotted notes under a slur are to be played in a single bow stroke but detached, with the bow actually bouncing off the string, variously called *portato*, *saltato*, or *ricochet* (this last is on a down-bow only). A vertical pair of dots to the right or left of a double bar indicates the beginning or end of a section to be repeated. In wind music, however, two or three dots may be printed over a single note with a tremolo crossbar on its staff to indicate double- or triple-tonguing, which is actually the player alternating unvoiced dental and palatal stops behind the breath going into the instrument: *t-k* for a duplet and *t-k-t* for a triplet. The dot is also a component of other musical signs including the fermata, which looks like an eyeball with a brow over it (whence musicians' slang "eyebrow") and whose effect is to prolong the duration of the note underneath it by an indeterminate amount (i.e., as long as the performer or conductor feels like it).

Perhaps it is no surprise that in our everyday speech and thought, doubling and halving are often in the foreground. For one thing, we are creatures of bilateral symmetry (at least on the surface); for another, we come in two sexes. As developing infants, moreover, we make the jump from mere animal awareness to human consciousness when we understand that there is a distinction between self and other, and begin to sort out where that boundary lies. (Indeed, one of the clinical signs that is apt to elicit the psychiatric label "schizophrenic" is when this boundary seems seriously compromised or incoherent, as when a patient doesn't bother to close the door to the therapist's conference room because he believes that everybody can listen in on his thoughts anyway.)

Feminist critics have taken dominant Western ideologies to task for what is seen as their common reductionism, a shared tendency to recast all sorts of complex realities into simplistic binaries (whose net effect, not surprisingly, is to reinforce existing power structures). Biologists might argue (as do Wells, Huxley, and Wells below) that we are creatures with a front and a back, and as such can empathize at least to a limited extent with creatures built along even vaguely similar lines, but when it comes to echinoderms such imaginings balk, for "with a few exceptions, they do not know front and back, right and left. They are not bilaterally symmetrical, as we are. They do not 'look before and after.' One cannot imagine oneself a starfish or a sea-urchin however hard one exerts one's mind." However, the protagonist in Naomi Mitchison's 1976 novel *Memoirs of a Spacewoman* sets out to achieve just that: "radial" thinking, undertaken in order to communicate with an alien species, the inhabitants of Lambda 771, who are descended from "a radial form, something like a five-armed starfish." Mitchison's parable deconstructs the either-or mind-set that is crucial to conventional scientific thinking, the rational empiricism that brought the 20th century such spectacular successes as aviation, penicillin, radar, television, nuclear reactors, catalytic converters, human space-suit footprints on the moon, DNA mapping, and cell phones.

Aside from all the technological goodies, it's not all that easy to transcend the ineluctable modality of the dual when it's built right into the language. Indeed, the older Indoeuropean languages (e.g., Sanskrit, Avestan, Classical Greek) attest a grammatical number that is neither singular nor undifferentiated plural, namely the dual, particularly handy for talking about things that come in pairs, such as hands, eyes, or oxen. (Modern Hebrew and Arabic also have a grammatical dual as distinct from singular and plural.) Latin shows vestiges of the Indoeuropean dual as well, notably the *-o* ending in the masculine and neuter nominative of the adjectives *duo*, 'two,' and *ambo*, 'both,' as well as the adjective *bini/-ae/-a*, meaning 'both (of a boxed set),' the *bin-* of *binoculars* and *binaural*.

47

A natural subject for the dual, of course, would be a pair of twins. The Greek word for 'twin' or 'double' is *didymos*, related to the adverb *dis*, 'doubly, twofold.' This reduplication of the first syllable as an intensifier recalls the *Si-* of *Sisyphus*, thought to be derived from *sophos*, 'wise,' and thus meaning 'wise-and-then-some, too smart for his own good'—an apt enough name for a man who tried to pull a fast one on the powers of the underworld and almost got away with it. While identical twins are always special and often considered preternatural by their very existence as doubles of one another, the Greeks had a great interest in dizygotic twins as well; mythic pairs of this sort, such as Castor and Polydeuces or Heracles and Iphicles, were explained as having been simultaneously fathered on the same woman by a mortal man and a god.

This is tidier than both twins being half mortal and half divine, a condition not unlike that of Strephon, offspring of the Lord Chancellor and a fairy named Iolanthe in her eponymous Gilbert and Sullivan operetta. Offered a Parliament seat by the Queen of the Fairies, who has a couple of pocket boroughs at her disposal, Strephon objects that he is a Tory from the waist up but his legs are Radicals and "sure to take me into the wrong lobby." The Queen replies, "Don't let that distress you; you shall be returned as a Liberal-Unionist, and your legs shall be our peculiar care." Strephon bows, observing that "I see your Majesty does not do things by halves."

Doing things by halves is one of those sayings that grammatically should allow of both a negative and positive, but in practice only the negative is actually used. (Compare *It isn't worth the powder to blow it to Hell, He hasn't the sense to come in out of the rain,* and *I wouldn't give a plugged nickel for it.*) Of course, in a sense we *do* do things by halves every time we *go halvesies* (or in some places *halfsies*), which is to say *even Steven,* probably rhyming slang and usually referring to a two-way division, as opposed to *share and share alike,* which can be any number. (Phrases with *even*—as in *even-handed, even-tempered, on an even keel,* and so on—seem generally to have a positive sense in the West, with the possible exception of *get even,* which doesn't have much of a feeling of warm and fuzzy for its intended object, though the implication of the maxim "Don't get mad, get even" would seem to be that the person who does so, at least, will feel good.) But in any case there are plenty of expressions about something having or being half of what it might, mostly pejorative: *half-wit, half-pint Hitler,* a *half-assed job,* a *half-baked scheme,* to *go off half-cocked,* to be *half in the bag, half-and-half* (in the sexual demi-monde, either a hermaphrodite or bisexual, but also a sexual act that starts out oral and concludes genital; in dairy discourse, it's half milk and half cream, while for bartenders it may signify a mixture of two ingredients in equal quantities, such as Guinness stout and Bass ale, a.k.a. a Black-and-Tan).

A half-note is the same as a *semibreve,* two of which equal a whole note or *breve,* also equal to four quarter notes (British *crotchet*), of which

on the dot

half is an eighth note (British *minim*), half of that a sixteenth (British *quaver*), half of that a 32d (*semiquaver*), half of that a 64th (*demisemiquaver*), and half of that a 128th (*hemidemisemiquaver*), with five flags on its stem (and as may be imagined, quite rarely needed). There are rests corresponding to the same notes, of the same duration, with an interesting exception: The whole-note rest is equal to a whole measure in 4/4 time, but it is also used to signify a whole measure rest in 3/4 time as well—rather than, say, a dotted half-note rest, or three quarter-note ones. (Another oddity: The first 256 characters of ASCII code—the ones that you pull up on your Character Map screen when you can't remember the keystroke combination for the final a̱ of *voilà* [it's alt-133]—include three fractions: ¼, ½, and ¾. The half is handy enough, and sometimes the quarter too, but ¾? Why not 1/5, which surely gets used more in our decimal world? Or, for that matter, 1/8, for stock-market quotes? Just one more anomaly for the Life's Little Mysteries file.)

As a prefix, *semi-* (the Latin cognate of Greek *hēmi-*, as in *-sphere*) leads to less confusion than *bi-*: Does a *bimonthly* publication appear every two months, or twice a month? We know where we can expect to be and for how long when we take a class that meets *triweekly*, but if we're told *biweekly* are we talking 12–1:15 on, say, Wednesdays and Fridays, or 9–12 and 12:45–3:45 with a break for lunch, every two weeks? No such problem with *semi-*: It is general knowledge that semiautomatic is less than fully automatic, that a semicircle doesn't go all the way around, and hence that publishers of a semimonthly had better produce an issue every 15 days or so, or subscribers will start ringing the phone off the hook in its circulation office.

Hemi- and *semi-* are both from an Indoeuropean root **sem-*, meaning 'one,' which also turns up as the *sim-* of *simple*, *similar*, and *simplex* (the *-plex* being from Latin *plecto*, 'I braid/weave/interfold.' *Multiplex* literally means "braided of many strands," though by extension the word has come to be applied to lots of things that can be separated into discrete entities, such as movie houses; an *organum* *triplex*, such as Perotinus repeatedly wrote, is a composition, for three voices, one of which sings a text as a *cantus firmus*, holding very long notes with the other two parts in motion above it); and if your house is a *duplex*, it has two floors. Ernout and Meillet say that Indoeuropean **sēmi-* has the sense of 'that which has just one side,' which seems reasonable enough, especially if it happens to be the very one you're concerned with (a possible comeback line when you're just starting to jack up your car and some passing Elihu offers the wiseacre consolation that your tire is "only flat on one side.")

Semi- in its sense of 'partly-' is also nicely manifest in the grammatical term *semi-deponent:* Deponent verbs have an active sense but their conjugation makes use entirely of passive-voice forms (e.g., *progredior*, 'I go forth,' whose past participle gives us the word *progress*), while a *semi-deponent* is only partly deponent, having active forms in the present tense but passive ones in the perfect. Thus in the Latin version of Genesis 1:3, *Dixitque Deus: Fiat lux* ('And God said: Let there [come to] be light') is followed by *et facta est lux* ('and there was light,' literally, 'and light came to be.' *Factus* is also, by no coincidence, the supine stem of the verb *facere*, 'to do/make.')

Demi-, on the other hand, is from the Latin adjective *medius* ('central'), prefixed by the *dis-* ('separate') that also turns up in *divide*, *dismiss*, *distinct*, *dissociate*, *disallow*, *diversity*, and a host of other words that entail splitting up of one sort or another. (*Dis-* is probably from the Indoeuropean root **dwo*, 'two,' whose adverbial form **dwi-* gives Greek *di-* as in *digamma* and Latin *bi-* as in *biped*, mentioned above.) No connection with *demi-* of *demiurge*, whose *e* is actually the long vowel eta (η) in Greek *dēmos* (δημος), 'people, tribe, deme,' a *dēmiourgos* originally being an official who ran a town or a ward in a city, and later by extension a divinity whose job it was to get the wheels of the universe going.

Demi- replaced *semi-* in almost all French compounds (though still alive and well in Spanish): A *demitasse* is a half-size cup (*tasse*), usually for coffee; the *demi-monde* is that part of the social world with all the interesting naughty bits, as opposed to the straight and narrow half; a half-note rest in French is a *demi-pause*, and a sports semi-final is a *demi-finale*. *Demi-deuil* means half-mourning, the clothes worn when one comes out of full mourning that signal that one is still not yet fully over it; the *Petit Larousse* describes it as *mi-partie noir et blanc, ou de toute couleur sombre* ('half-and-half white and black, or all of somber color'). The *mi-* of *mi-partie, minuit* ('midnight'), *midi* ('noon') and *mi-clos* ('half-closed') is from the part of *demi-* that isn't from **dwo*, which also gives English the *med-* of *medium, median, medieval, mediocre,* and (from Italian through French) the *mez-* of *mezzanine*. (The same Indoeuropean root, **medhyo-*, turns up in the Germanic languages as well; English has *middle* and the *mid-* of such compounds as *midshipman, midnight, midriff,* and *midwife*.)

The Latin prefix meaning 'one and a half, half as much again' is **51** *sesqui-*, as in "In 1959 the Department of the Treasury marked the sesquicentennial of Lincoln's birth by changing the obverse of Brenner's 'wheat straw' cent to bear an image of the Lincoln Memorial instead." The *sesquialtera* (*sesqui-* plus *alter,* 'other, more') is an organ stop, a mixture whose pipes sound a fifth higher than the keyboard note played. (Compare *hemiola*—Greek *hēmi-* plus *holos,* 'whole'—a musical figure in which two measures of three beats each are subdivided to form an overarching structure of three two-beat groups, often seen in baroque music in the two measures immediately preceding the last one in a strophe, e.g., in the hornpipe from Handel's *Water Music*.) *Sesquipedalian words* are words a foot and a half long; this is a direct translation of *sesquipedalia verba,* a jocular coinage going all the way back to the Roman poet Horace.

Sesqui- is formed by sticking *-que* ('and' as suffix, as in *Senatus Populusque Romanus,* "The Roman Senate and People," commonly abbreviated S.P.Q.R.) on the end of *semis,* a contraction of *semi-* plus *as,* the *as* being originally a unit of weight divided into twelve *uncia* (the Latin word for 'inch' and 'ounce,' and the ancestor of both), and later the name for the lowest-denomination Roman coin. *Sestertius*, the Roman coin equal to two and a half *asses*, is itself a contraction of *semis* and *tertius* ('third') meaning something like 'half for the third time.' Here the idea is that the 'half' is on the way to three, a logic shared with the German way of saying "half past" a given hour: *Halb drei* (literally, 'half three') means 'half past two,' not 'half past three.' (By contrast, French has *deux heures et demie*, 'two hours and a half.' English, French, and German use similar phrases, however, once it's past the half hour: "Quarter to three" is *trois heures moins le quart*— 'three hours less the quarter'—and *Viertel vor drei*–'a quarter before three.')

It probably goes without saying that "and a half" refers to an implied unit. Suppose you're trundling your offspring down the street in a stroller, and someone asks you, "How old is your kid?" Up to 18 months or so, the inclination may be to answer in months; but after that, unless you or your interlocutor happen to be a developmental psychologist, who's counting months anymore? So you would probably answer "X" or "X and a half" (e.g., "Two and a half") up to some point when you don't bother with the "and a half." (Nobody says "14 and a half" when asked how old Billy is; at some point, you start rounding off.) The point is that two and a half doesn't mean "two plus half two" (i.e., one) = 3; the "half" means half a year.

Other halves from everyday life: *My better half* (= "my spouse"), *'arf a mo'* ("half a moment"), the *half-time show* at a football game (compare baseball's *seventh-inning stretch*, usually at around six and a half), the *half-timer* whom the company doesn't have to pay benefits, see *how the other half lives*, your flag is at *half-mast*, he said he had *half a mind* to do something drastic, there's a *half-tone* mugshot of him on page 7, and he lives in a *halfway house*. In trying to sort out ethnicity while remaining firmly on top, a dominant class may speak of *half-bloods*, *half-breeds*, or *half-castes*; here the binary division has at least the justification that, pending some radical advances in reproductive technology, every child is the product of two biological parents. (The anonymous poets of the Gilgamesh epic surely knew this as well as we do, yet deliberately chose to depict the eponymous hero as one-third human and two-thirds divine. Guess they just wanted to mess with our heads a little.)

In any case, *well begun is half done*, and *half a loaf is better than none*. Then there's the old brain-teaser about if "a hen and a half lays an egg and a half, how long does it take ten hens to lay ten eggs?" (See below.) Hint: This is a little like the old shell game: There may be three compound fractions in motion here, but only one of them has the pebble under it.

Could there be such a thing as a pebble and a half? Isaac Asimov told a story about an argument he had once as an undergraduate with a friend's professor, who scoffed at imaginary numbers by challenging Asimov to show him "the square root of minus one pieces of chalk." Asimov replied that he would be happy to do so if his interlocutor could first show him half a piece of chalk. The professor smiled and broke a piece in half and handed it to him. Asimov, however, countered by saying that it was still a piece of chalk, not half of one. The professor, faced with the choice of conceding defeat in front of the amused onlookers or losing his cool and kicking Asimov out of the classroom, did the latter. Half a piece of chalk, half a pebble, half a beach, half a bay, half a hurricane, half omnipotent, half unique...: Evidently there are at least *some* things in this world that do not come by halves.

(Oh yes, and the answer: "A day and a half.")

for short

mr., sr., et al.

Q.: What do Mr. Natural, Dr. Doolittle, Mrs. Malaprop, Ms. Airy-chord, Capt. Dandelion, Sen. Dreckslinger, Sr. Dymphna-Joseph, Prof. Mamamouchi, Fr. Feeley, and the Rev. Byron Frimstone have in common? A: The fact that each has an abbreviated title, followed (at least in America) by a period. In this abbreviations differ from acronyms, which generally lose their dots as soon as people start pronouncing them as though they were words in their own right: The North American Treaty Organization, initially N.A.T.O., increasingly gets referred to as "nate-oh" until poof! the periods vanish, and NATO it is.

The distinction between abbreviations and acronyms is one that American English speakers, at least, appear to find increasingly confusing at least terminologically. The most recent edition of the University of Chicago Press *Manual of Style* calls everything an abbreviation, periods or no periods, whether you pronounce it as a word or say the letters (AWOL *vs.* A.W.O.L.). This is a difference with a decreasing orthographic distinction (at least as far as periods go), especially in the linguistic domains of Computerspeak: Compare SQL (Structured Query Language), which doesn't have periods and is sometimes pronounced *ess-cue-ell* and sometimes *sequel.*

Sometimes an acronym can inadvertently backfire, thanks to the myopia of the organizers: Concerning Exodus, an evangelical Christian group whose mission is to try to "convert" gay people to heterosexuality, Ohio State University professor Tanya Erzen wrote that the organization

> emerged in the early 1970s, when [Frank] Worthen became a born-again Christian at age 44 after living his entire adult life as a gay man. He soon began counseling people who were "homosexual strugglers" at his church. According to one of its early leaders, Exodus chose its name because "homosexuals finding freedom reminds me of the children of Israel leaving the bondage of Egypt and moving towards the Promised Land." (The original name, "Free All Gays" was eliminated after the organizers realized the potential contradictions of its acronym.)

A variant of the acronym is the syllabic abbreviation, pronounceable because the syllables include vowels: *Benelux* for **Bel**gium, the **Net**herlands, and **Lux**emburg, *Soweto* for **So**uth**we**st **To**wnships, the New York City districts *SoHo* for **So**uth of **Ho**uston and *Tribeca* for **Tri**angle **Be**low **Ca**nal, *Comintern* for **Com**munist **Intern**ational, *Proletcult* for **Pro**letarian **Cult**ural and Educational Association, *agitprop* for **agit**ation and **prop**aganda, *MiG* for aircraft designers **Mi**koyan and **G**urevich, *Gestapo* for **Ge**heime **Sta**atspolizei ("Secret State Police"), *Nazi* for **Na**tional So**zi**alismus, *Frelimo* for **Fre**nte de **Li**bertação de **Mo**çambique (the Mozambique Liberation Front), *Pornsec* for **Porn**ography **Sec**tion (Winston Smith's day job in Orwell's *Nineteen Eighty-Four*).

Abbreviations come in multiple flavors: truncated forms such as F.B.I., from which the ends of the words Federal Bureau of Investigation have been lopped off, and contractions, where one leaves out stuff between the beginning and end of the word, e.g., *Mr.* or *Ph.D.* (sometimes in jest pronounced *Fud*[*d*], as in Uncle or Elmer), short for *Philosophiae Doctor.* The third edition of the *American Heritage Dictionary* (1992) includes the dots, while the fourth edition (2000) eliminates them (as do the British). Acronyms come in similar flavors—just initial letters or syllables: MADD (Mothers Against Drunk Driving)—but are pronounceable as though they were words. (A borderline case is QWERTY, not an acronym per se but rather the first six keys on the top row of letters on a standard English typewriter keyboard, and therefore a useful term when discussing alternatives such as the Dvorak or linotype keyboards: Nobody asks "Having tried both, do you prefer the Dvorak or the *cue-double-you-ee-are-tee-wye* keyboard?"—it has come to be sounded as if spelled *querty* instead.)

Indeed, no small amount of effort and ingenuity may go into coming up with an acronym that is both pronounceable and represents in a favorable light something suggestive of the entity it stands for: CARE (Cooperative for American Relief Everywhere), h.o.m.e. (Homeworkers Organized for More Employment, an Emmaus-movement community in Orland, Maine, and a conspicuous exception to the rule that acronyms are upper case and have no periods), PEACE (Peace Education and Action CommitteE—slick recovery there, heh heh), SCORE (Service Corps of Retired Executives), ASSET (the U.S. Air Force's aerodynamic-elastic structural systems evironmental tests), and of course the egregious USA PATRIOT Act (Uniting and Strengthening America by Providing Appropriate Tools Required to Intercept and Obstruct Terrorism—rather a stretch any way one looks at it). Such inventions are known as *backronyms.*

Of course, satiric opportunities are legion. Cartoonist Al Capp featured the organization SWINE ("Students Wildly Indignant about

Nearly Everything") in the sad sunset years of his strip *Li'l Abner*. COBOL (Common Business-Oriented Language) was said to be short for "Compiles Only Because of Luck." During the Depression, the W.P.A's earthier critics asserted that it stood for "Whistle, Piss, and Argue." (It was actually short for Works Progress Administration.) The Italian automobile makers probably never anticipated the American quip that Fiat was an acronym for "Fix It Again, Tony." And it is impossible to earn a Bachelor of Science degree without encountering vulgar jokes, while if going on for an M.S., one may expect to hear at least the euphemism "More of the Same," with Ph.D. standing for "Piled Higher and Deeper."

Some abbreviations invariably include the dots, such as the Latin borrowings *etc.* (*et cetera*, 'and the rest'), *e.g.* (*exempli gratia*, 'by way of an example'), *i.e.* (*id est*, 'it is'), *et al.* (*et alii*, 'and others'), *sc.* (*scilicet*, a truncation of *scirelicet*, literally 'it is permitted to know,' more or less interchangeable with *i.e.*, but implying a degree of amplification; cf. *viz.*, short for *videlicet* [a truncation of *viderelicet*, 'it is permitted to see'], the final *z* being actually a shorthand squiggle denoting several conflated letters, like the tail on the proofreader's delete sign), *cf.* (for *confer*, 'bring together,' i.e., 'compare'), *ibid.* (a contraction of *ibi*, 'there' and *idem*, 'the same'), *op. cit.* (*opere citato*, 'in the work cited'), and *v. infra/supra* (the *v.* is short for *vide*, 'see' with *infra* meaning 'below' and *supra* 'above'). Virtually all of these abbreviations are nowadays printed in English without italics, as a sign that they are fully naturalized citizens of our native tongue. Style manuals, however, increasingly urge writers to eschew such Latinisms, if only because of the reality that many people don't know the difference between *e.g.*, and *i.e.*, and won't even recognize some of the others—holdovers from the days when every educated person was presumed to know at least *some* Latin.

Other abbreviations may or not include periods but are always pronounced as though they were there. An S(.)O(.)B(.) is always an *ess-oh-bee*, as opposed to a *sob*; R.I.P. is not a *rip* but is pronounced *are-eye-pee*, fortuitously standing for both the original Latin *requiescat in pace* and its English translation, *rest in peace*. Likewise FOB (whether standing for Freight on Board or Friend(s) of Bill): It's *eff-oh-bee*, not *fob*. Interestingly, if one types either *FOB* or *F.O.B.* into the search field of Google, identical return sets come up on the screen; evidently Google ignores periods in search strings (not the case with the Yahoo search engine or Answers.com). Likewise always pronounced as three letters was the multiple-entendre *F.T.A.*, originally a slogan of disaffected soldiers during the Vietnam War (it stood for 'Fun, Travel, and Adventure,' 'Free the Army,' or 'Fuck the Army,' depending on who asked), subsequently the title of both an antiwar touring show and the movie made about it. And nobody attempts to pronounce IOU as *yew*, since it is not strictly an abbreviation so much as a typographic rebus. (Compare the old wheeze about the four letters most feared by a night burglar: "OICU!")

Thanks to the ubiquity of personal computing, e-mail and its spin-offs instant messaging (IM for short) and cell-phone text-messaging have evolved a shorthand that now seems remarkably commonplace considering that it has been with us no more than two or three decades. Its abbreviations are dotless *initialisms* and are almost all unpronounceable as words: *BTW* ('By the way'), *FYI* ('For your information'—this one is pre-cybernetic, already in common use by the time James Blish published his apocalyptic sci-fi short story "FYI" in 1953), *LOL* ('laughing out loud'), often preceded by *ROTF* ('rolling on the floor') as in the superlative, *ROTFLMAO* ('rolling on the floor laughing my ass off'), and *CUL*, or sometimes *CUL8R* ('See you later'), the longer version less likely to evoke a raised eyebrow (?-:) from one's francophone friends.

French cybernauts have evolved their own set of e-mail/IM abbreviations, including *A+* and *@+* for *à plus* [*tard*] ('later'), one of the French names for the "at" sign being *a commercial*. Some are translations: English *IMHO* ('in my humble opinion') equals French

AMHA (*à mon humble avis*); *BJ* (for *bien joué*, 'well played') is pretty close to English *GJ* ('good job'), *JRB* (*je ris beaucoup*, 'I'm laughing a lot') somewhat tamely glosses *LOL*, and *GETA*, short for *Google est ton ami*, is the same as *GIYF*, 'Google is your friend,' i.e., 'look it up with your search engine (before you come asking me).' Some abbreviations, however, have no exact English Cybershorthand equivalents, such as *KOID9* for *quoi de neuf* ('what's new?'), *EXPLDR* for *explosé de rire* ('burst from laughing'), *A2M1* (pronounced as if it were spelled *ah-deux-m'un*) for *à demain* ('till tomorrow'), *TLM* for *tout le monde* ('everybody'), or *OQP* (pronounced *oküpay*), for *occupé* ('busy').

The fundamental rule of e-mail, IM, and text-messaging abbreviations is that they should express the writer's sentiments in as few characters as possible; the strategy is reminiscent of the goal of conveying the maximum amount of information in the fewest number of words in telegrams priced by the word. The result is a mix and match of phonetics and actual abbreviations: *IOU* for 'I owe you' is pure phonetics, *CUL* mix and match, and *LOL* pure abbreviation (though LAWL has turned up as a substitute, a phonetic approximation of the sounds of LOL if anyone *were* to speak it).

A related phenomenon is *Leet Speak* (or *Leetspeak*, or *L33t Speak*, or *L33tspeak*), a contraction from "(computer) elite." Leetspeak replaces alphabetic characters with numbers and/or combinations of other characters, and is thus a valuable tool for spammers trying to get a message past message filters that will automatically toss out any e-mail containing such words as *mortgage* or *Viagra*, or a phrase such as *prescription drugs:* "V14gr4" will elude spam filtering, as will "|-|0T C|-|1C|<5 \/\/4/|/T 2 ∧∧ [-[-T U 2|)4Y!" (For an excellent treatment of spam and how to thwart it, see the chapter on spam in David Wood's *Programming Internet Email*.)

In classified or personal ads (*adverts* in Britain) in the newspapers, dots are out, for the most part. Like telegrams, these are usually charged by the word, which is to say per string of characters with a

60

on the dot

space between them. (According to the *American Heritage Dictionary*, in addition to 'advertisement' *ad* can mean an advantage in tennis; *AD* as abbreviation can stand for 'active duty' and 'air-dried,' while A.D. with dots means *anno Domini*, 'in the year of the Lord,' now in deference to non-Christians rendered as C.E., "Common Era" and B.C. ['before Christ'] as B.C.E. C.E. is not to be confused with *Ce*, the symbol for the element cerium, nor with *CE*, the abbreviation for *chemical engineer* or *civil engineer*. *ADD* stands for—Oh look! a hummingbird, right outside the window!—*Attention Deficit Disorder*, while .*ad* [with leading dot] stands for Andorra in e-mail addresses, the dot here being the standard delimiter for, among other things, a country address in a URL, such as .*ca* for Canada.)

Here's a personal ad from the "Dating" page of the *Boston Phoenix*, which has a separate section for adult ads, the difference between the ads in the one and the other being somewhat hard to distinguish in some cases: "**Look Me Up** SBF, Virgo, never married, N/S, N/D, no kids, 5'8," 190 lbs, brown eyes, fair-complected, likes movies, concerts, museums, dining out/in, relaxing. ISO low-key, affectionate SBM, 38–50, 5'9'+, childless, for friendship/relationship." The *Phoenix* is kind enough to provide its readers with a key defining some but not all of the shorthand: M = Male, F = Female, W = White, Wi = Widowed, B = Black/African-American, Bi = Bisexual, D/D-free = Drug + Disease Free [*sic*], WLTM = Would Like To Meet, though the paper's list interestingly omits LTR (long-term relationship, usually preceded by "for possible") or ISO, which stands for "I'm Seeking Only" (that is, someone with whatever attributes I've specified, so, presumably, if you don't in fact enjoy long walks on the beach or you're not really an SBM, don't bother to respond to this ad). Use of the virgule (as in N/S—non-smoking) is standard; the authors have yet to see D/D–free, however, perhaps because "Drug and Disease Free" could be taken as an additional offering on the part of the person posting the ad: "If you date me, I'll throw in a drug and a disease for free."

As with telegrams, the object is to save words (and from the newspaper's angle, column-inches) yet maintain the high degree of specificity desired for a viable match, a critical consideration in the more exotic "adult" ads, where a bad match means an unarousing encounter or worse. The woman who writes "SSWF seeks DBM 35+" is making it clear that she has no intention of wasting her time with another submissive white female who's just turned 23! Abbreviations rule "adult" ads in that they allow expressions the newspaper might be reluctant to print in their full form. (This is true of demi-monde vocabulary in general; as anthropologist Michelle Buchanan writes, in a vanilla world "one has at least to mask oneself with the aura of plausible deniability," of which "[t]he terms D/S and B&D are perfect examples. D/S stands for dominance and submission, which sounds a tad less scary than SM [sadomasochism].")

62   And here's an example of a real estate ad: "Watertown, OH Sat. 12:30–2 (91 Spring St #13) 6rm 2/br 2.5 bath TH W/2c Garg. Grt loc! Only [*sic*] $399.9K!" Note the punctuation, or rather the lack thereof; *TH* stands for *townhouse* and *OH* is presumably *open house* (and not Ohio!), while *2c/Garg* is *two-car garage*, *Grt loc* is *great location*, and *K* is thousand. Spelled out, the ad would read "Watertown, open house Saturday 12:30 to 2 pm, at 91 Spring Street, unit 13: six-room, two-bedroom, two-and-a-half bathroom townhouse with two-car garage. Great location! Only three hundred ninety-nine thousand nine hundred dollars!"—201 characters to the actual ad's 82.

•

The canonical family of personal titles: *master* (abbreviated M. or M^r, depending on your source); *mister* as *Mr.* (the plural is *Messrs.*); *Mrs.* (plural *Mmes.*), sometimes, when used as a noun, spelled out *missus* for humorous effect, as in "the missus don't like us lettin' the

on the dot

pigs in the parlor"—and the unabbreviable *Miss* (plural *Misses*). *Ms.* is a latecomer of the 1960s, and both product and, as magazine title, standard-bearer of second-wave feminism, designed to level the playing field by rendering marital status of the bearer as irrelevant as it is with *Mr. Ms.* was greeted with sardonic amusement by at least some publishing workers, all too familiar with it in lower-case throughout as the standard abbreviation for *manuscript. Mss.*, according to the *American Heritage Dictionary*, is an acceptable plural of both words, though *Mses.* is listed as the preferred form for the title, whose singular is pronounced *miz* (which in some areas of the country, just to help the conflation along, is also the pronunciation of *Mrs.*).

Miss and *Mrs.* (and presumably *Ms.* as well) are from *mistress*, the feminine of *master* and still used as a combining form in job titles (U.S. *postmistress, headmistress, wardrobe mistress*, U.K. *games mistress*, i.e., female phys.-ed. teacher). It was formerly a title in its own right in Britain's stratified society: One addresses someone as "Lady Letitia" or "Lady Percy" if she is gentry (or "Lady Northumberland" if her husband, Peredur Lord Percy, is the present Earl of same), as "Mistress Percy" if she's of yeoman status, but as just "Percy" if she's the servant. But *mistress* has also come to mean a (usually married) man's female lover, generally receiving support from him (as in "Juliette Drouet, Victor Hugo's mistress, was installed in a house on one of the Channel Isles from which she could see his balcony during his years of exile there").

In America, mistresses tend to be frowned upon; the "strong presumption in favor of marriage" noted by one legal historian in his study of the marriage litigation in England's medieval court at York remains robust six or seven centuries later. Judith Martin ("Miss Manners") cites a French diplomat's assumption that "young ladies should be single and old ones should be married," and both widows and divorcees have the weight of conventional etiquette behind them in retaining the title "Mrs. *N.*" where *N.* is the surname of their former

for short

husband. However, it is still expected that Letitia Percy, née Brown, will remain Mrs. Perry Percy as a widow (let us assume that his Lordship, in a Senior Moment of born-again egalitarianism, abdicates his title in favor of his formerly happy-go-lucky younger brother Eustace and emigrates to Bar Harbor, in his retirement playing golf at Kebo Valley in yellow slacks and going by "Perry"—in preference to his old school nickname, "Boojums"—before catching a fatal case of pneumonia on the links one foggy evening), whereas she will call herself Mrs. Letitia Percy if the old bounder throws her off in favor of Mlle. Fifi Nytouche, the *au pair* from the chalet next door, so that nobody will be tempted to confuse her with "That Woman" when the latter begins styling herself Mrs. Perry Percy as well. An alternative increasingly favored by divorcing women is to resume their premarital—or "maiden"—names, so that the former Mrs. Percy goes back to being Miss or Ms. Letitia Brown. This is a petition the courts normally will grant without batting an eyelash unless there are minor children still at home, and even then will merely ask, like a Windows prompt, if the litigant really wants to do this.

Face-to-face, however, an older woman can expect to be addressed, by persons unacquainted with her, as *madam* or *ma'am* to her face while the generic *miss* will be used with young ones: Thus "Miss, could I have some more coffee, please?" but "No, ma'am, I'm sure the stain won't be permanent." (This does not apply to women in holy orders, of course. Nuns are addressed thus: "Yes, Sister, I cleaned the blackboard like you said," the title in practice sometimes shortened to 'Ster when one is answering quickly and under duress, as in "No-'Ster-I-swear-I-never-touched-him.")

Master as boy ("Master James will take his dinner in front of the TV tonight"), like *mister*, comes from French *maître* (as in *maître d'hôtel*, shortened in English to *maitre d'*, pronounced "mayter dee"—compare "Noter Daym"), and is ultimately from Latin *magister*, as in *Magister Artium* (*M.A.* for short), 'Master of Arts.' (Compare use of

Russian *gospodin*, literally 'Lord,' to mean 'Mister—,' as in "*Gospodin* Staum didn't do his homework.") A *magister* was originally a keeper of animals, a shepherd or other sort of herdsman, and only later a professional teacher, schoolmaster, or a slave put in charge of boys (equivalent to Greek *paidagogos*, "pedagogue"). 'Master' in the me-master-you-slave sense was *dominus*, the source of Spanish *don* (and its feminine, *doña* from *domina*, "mistress"); French *monsieur* is *mon* ('my') plus *sieur*, cognate with Italian *signor* and Spanish *señor*, all derived from Latin *senior*, 'older.' (Compare *priest*, from Greek *presbyteros*, '[church] elder.') Most *magistrates*, at least while robed and seated in court, are about as far from boyish as one can get; but a *magisterium* was a teacher's office, and by extension in the Roman Catholic Church the Magisterium denotes the authority to teach doctrine, however much the grumblers complain that it appears to be exercised by a sclerotic old-boy network.

65

•

The fundamental appeal of acronyms and abbreviations is that they are brief. *Brief, breve, brevet,* and *breviary* all ultimately come from Latin *brevis/breve*, 'short.' A brief in the legal sense is a summary of the case one is going to argue (whence the term *to brief someone:* Originally, a solicitor, who could not actually appear in court, briefed a barrister, who could. [Hence the Lord Chancellor in Gilbert and Sullivan's *Iolanthe* sings: "I'll never assume that a rogue or a thief / Is a gentleman worthy implicit belief / Because his attorney has sent me a brief, / Said I to myself, said I."])

Briefs in the plural are underpants, and are to this category of feminine intimate apparel what the breve is to the rest of the notes in modern music: the longest currently in everyday general use (as opposed to high-cuts, thigh-cuts, bikinis, and thongs). But it was not

for short

always so; at the time they were first introduced in the 1930s, they were a great deal shorter than the old-fashioned directoire drawers that went partway down the thigh, and even shorter than the "step-ins" (essentially what we now refer to as tap pants) then very much in fashion. Briefs were originally called *Hollywood panties* because they were much favored by extras who had to dance in them: You could do a high kick without either looking like Granny in her snuggies or exposing yourself, as the original cut of the garment allowed for a generous three to four inches across in the crotch.

Men's briefs, often called jockey shorts or BVDs (short for the gentlemen whose firm first offered them to the public—Bradley, Voorhees, and Day—but subsequently thought to be an abbreviation of Better Ventilated Drawers), were likewise briefer than the elastic-waist boxers still worn by some men and the button-down-front shorts still available from old-line haberdashery lines such as Brooks Brothers. In the British Isles and Australia they are often called Y-fronts, owing to their crisscross construction. The Scottish musician Dougie Pinock once remarked that nobody in Scotland took Batman or Superman seriously because they wore their underpants outside their trousers.

In addition to being the other name for the whole note, a *breve* is the sign for a short vowel, an upside-down rounded circumflex used in teaching scansion in poetry, or, in dictionaries, as a guide to pronunciation. A *brevet* is a commission that advances a military officer in rank but doesn't augment the paycheck to go with it; as a verb it means to promote someone in this fashion. Like the attorney's brief, it's from the Anglo-Norman diminutive of *bref*, 'letter' (compare German *Brief*). *Breviary* (a book of prayers, psalms, and hymns for the various canonical hours of worship in the Catholic Church) comes from *breviarium*, Medieval Latin for 'summary.' (This is the sense in which the word is used in the title of the *Breviary of Alaric*, also called the *Lex Romana Visigothorum* ['Roman Law of the Visigoths'], a codification and set of commentaries on Roman law promulgated by Alaric II in 506 for use with his subjects in southern France and Spain.)

Hamlet identified brevity as the soul of wit; we are reminded of a friend who, when asked during a job interview the standard "What is the one word you'd use to describe yourself?" replied "Terse." This in turn calls to mind the possibly apocryphal tale of the taciturn Calvin Coolidge, seated next to a woman at dinner who was at pains to try to engage him in conversation, but in vain. Finally she exclaimed, "Oh, Mr. Coolidge, some of my friends bet me I couldn't get you to say more than two words." Replied the president, "You lose."

for short

dot dot dot

ellipses, lacunae, and missing links

"Nine tailors make a man..." and three dots make an ellipsis. The urge to leave some of the story out is probably as old as storytelling itself. More recent is the feeling that we should at least leave evidence that something is missing. Suetonius relates that the emperor Claudius, when approached by a man in hopes of getting the black mark against his friend's name removed from the Censor's rolls, granted the request saying, "But I want the erasure to show."

The ellipsis discloses that there used to be text here but it's gone, whether because we don't know what it was (e.g., the damaged cuneiform tablet: "We shall bring about his..., we shall bind his wings/ ...we shall.../ His..., we shall stand upon him") or because we know but aren't telling (e.g., the unscrupulously edited dust-jacket blurb: "Morgenschwein's long-awaited book is a serious...contribution to the field of sociolinguistics" could very well be an abridgement from a withering review that *actually* said, "Morgenschwein's long-awaited book is a serious disappointment, the sort of brummagem contribution to the field of sociolinguistics that only gives this discipline a bad name").

The word *ellipsis* is from the Greek *leipein*, 'leave behind,' whose passive voice means 'I am wanting.' The same root also turns up, not surprisingly, in *ellipse*, which falls short of being a circle, and in *lipography*, the writing of a text without using one of the letters of the alphabet, such as French novelist Georges Perec's *La Disparition*, and its translation by Gilbert Adair, *A Void:* Both eschew the letter e̱, no mean feat in either French or English. (Notwithstanding something being made to disappear, however, the Greek root *lip-* in *liposuction, liposome, lipid,* and *lipolysis* comes not from *leipein* but from *lipos*, 'fat.')

Ellipsis can be a way of signaling a pause: "Our eyes met and she hoarsely whispered, 'Your place...or mine?'" The same three dots, of course, could equally well stand for a missing parenthetical: "Our eyes met and she hoarsely whispered, 'Your place (not the summer place in the Hamptons but the penthouse on the Upper West Side) or mine?'" But usually the reader should be able to tell from the context (if in a dimly lit nightclub after the second Scotch, the former; if in the back of a speeding taxi being shot at by a gang of ruffians leaning out all available windows of a pursuing glossy black Hummer, probably the latter).

Jacques Drillon's book on French punctuation gives an example of length of pause signified by how many dots the ellipsis contains: "Some writers consider [the dot] a unity that can be multiplied at will. Thus Bernanos, in *Nouvelle Histoire de Mouchette*, seeks to render the long notes in a song by doubling the sign: '"Have hope...And more hope! Three / days," Columbus tells them, "I'll give a wor..r..rld to you" / towards which his finger points, while his eye, to view/it, scans the hori..i.i.zon's dee..e.p, its deep i..mme..n-sity...'"—a typographic innovation we have yet to see duplicated, however, by an American press. (You saw it here first....)

In his homage to the typing keyboard, *Quirky Qwerty*, Torbjörn Lundmark notes that the ellipsis "can be seen as a companion to the asterisk," which can be "used to signify omission of something that can be found elsewhere (as in the footnote) or gathered intuitively (as in a f***-letter word)." This is of course a double-entendre; we are so used to the "f-word" that we really do fill in the expected blanks here. Just so with *f*—, whose dash leaves little doubt. (It's a bit murkier in *b*—*d*, but context-specificity again comes to the rescue: " 'I'll be b—d if they take me alive!' swore the pirate captain" versus " 'Pull over, you stupid b—d!' yelled the state trooper.") Cartoonists, because actual profanity in the funny papers is absolutely taboo, rely on strings of characters such as the ampersand, pound sign, and asterisk, together with jarns (little spirals) and quimps (little Saturn icons) to indicate swearing in the text of what is called a maledicta balloon: Funny animal hits thumb with hammer, shouts "#&@#*!"

The asterisk is what is sometimes called a wildcard character, in that it can be used to stand for anything and nothing in particular including multiples of itself. Thus "Tom Dick and Harry" would be one each of the possible referents of "T*m, Di*k and Har*." Some varieties of Computerese use the question mark instead to represent a single character (or no character), as in T?m, Di?k and Har?? but in either case the answers could just as well be "Tim, Dirk, and Harpo." In the publishing trades, a call-out for a page as yet unknown (because final pagination will not occur until page-proofs), will be given as "page 000" instead, although here, as with f—, the missing characters are knowable enough, and the expectation is that the typesetter will be told what the real numbers are when the uncorrected proofs are sent back with the editorial revisions added. By contrast, "Find all files of the form *.jpg" means "find every jaypeg file you've got," the filename (of however many characters) being wild-carded while the extension is not.

Another way in which the asterisk signifies something that isn't there is in its use by philologists as a marker meaning "this utterance is unattested" (thus: "I'm to preach next Sunday at the Church of the Dormition; last Sunday I *praught at St. Gwénolé-on-the-Shoals").

Most often, however, we encounter it as a footnote call-out when there aren't enough notes to warrant numbers and every note will be printed, or at least will begin, on the foot of the page from which it is called out. (Thus: "St. Gwénolé*-on-the-Shoals" steers the reader down to the footnote "*Spiritual advisor to King Gradlon, the last king of the sunken city of Ys.") As with any substantive footnote, this saves the text from getting bogged down in interesting but secondary facts while still permitting the writer to have them right there on the same page. If one has more notes there are the dagger (†), double dagger (‡), pound sign (#), and section sign (§). (When there are more than four footnotes on a page, they really should be numbered and be done with it.) The asterisk is also known as the *star* (universally so in phonespeak: "Press star 82, then redial," is how one is told to override caller-ID line blocking by rendering one's number visible to the recipient of the call on a one-shot basis) and, in journalism especially, the *splat*. To call attention to a passage that follows, printers will sometimes set a triangle of three asterisks called an *asterism* (⁎⁎⁎), while astronomers use the same term to refer to a coherent group of stars smaller than a constellation. Both *asterism* and *asterisk* come from Greek *astēr* ('star').

Another indispensable component of a maledicta balloon string is the "at-sign" (@). Formerly confined to commerce (in which it turned up in Italy as early as 1500), since 1972 it has come into worldwide use as the indicator separating individual user from domain in e-mail addresses. In France it is jocularly referred to as an *escargot* ('snail') from its appearance, but it is more formally called an *arobase*, *arobas*, *arrobace*, or *ar(r)obe*. The origins of the sign are obscure and have provoked what its webmaster calls "regular but calm" debate on a French language discussion site: One theory says it's a digraph for Latin *ad* ('at'); another would have it be shorthand for 'ea(ch),' which has certainly been its primary use in English-speaking countries until computers came along (one comment mentions the much earlier term 'commercial a̲').

on the dot

Perhaps the most intriguing derivation is the most fantastic: that the *arobase* is somehow connected with the spiral glyph called the *gidouille* on the front of the gown of Père Ubu, the Macbeth-like protagonist in Alfred Jarry's play *Ubu Roi*. One of Jarry's more lasting flights of fancy was what he described as a "science of imaginary solutions, symbolically harmonizing in their contours those physical properties described by objects in their virtuality," which he named 'Pataphysics, meaning "that which is close to that which comes after metaphysics" (in Greek, *epi ta meta ta physika—ta meta physika* being the stock Greek philosophical phrase that we translate today as 'metaphysics'). The "History" page of one 'pataphysical website advances the ingenious argument that the e-mail pioneer Ray Tomlinson "was a 'pataphysician and hence the symbol he chose was that which most closely resembled the gidouille." It's a tempting thought.

•

Print journalists have always enjoyed leeway in editing out white noise in direct quotes—pauses, "speech-pillow" words such as *ah* and *um*, and sometimes even whole buzzwords such as *like, you know, really*, and *basically*, though some editors discourage this more than others. The AP style manual says that quotations "should be corrected to avoid the errors of grammar and word usage that often occur unnoticed in speech, but are embarrassing in print." Editors are apt to strike out parentheticals, almost by reflex: "He said ~~(and I quote)~~, 'D—n the torpedoes!'" Both writers and editors, however, may also insert words to clarify the elliptical direct quote: "'The boys just love the [Rolling] Stones,' she told us." Such clarifications generally appear in parentheses in newspapers, but between square brackets in books.

There are other types of parenthetical insertions as well: "The novelist Elmore Leonard has been variously quoted as saying 'I (try to) leave out the parts that people skip.'" Here what's in parentheses might or might not be part of the original quote, depending on who you ask. (For an interesting discussion of whether Edwin Stanton, Lincoln's secretary of war, did or did not say "Now he belongs to the ages" just after the president breathed his last, see Adam Gopnik's "Angels and Ages" in the May 28, 2007, issue of *The New Yorker*.) Then there's the first-use parenthetical, allowing the reader to see both the spelled-out form of a name and its abbreviation that will be used throughout: "Committee to Re-Elect the President (CREEP)" at initial mention, but CREEP for the rest of the piece.

We think of censorship as primarily a First-Amendment issue, i.e., one of freedom of speech and of the press, often in the face of governmental attempts to squelch either or both: James Joyce's *Ulysses*, Roberto Rossellini's film *The Miracle*, the standup comedy of Lenny Bruce, Frederick Wiseman's 1967 documentary *Titicut Follies*, the Defense Department's "Pentagon Papers," and so on. The government usually contends that for reasons of state security or morality, public access to a given document or performance or work of art is pernicious on its face; the civil-liberties lawyers counter that in a supposedly free country with a valid First Amendment it is far more pernicious to suppress it. For the most part the courts have tended to side with the latter argument since World War II, at least till recently; during that war, on the other hand, the Office of Wartime Information, among others agencies, had kept a much tighter control on what the public could and couldn't see than in peacetime, and many people in Washington today would be pleased to enjoy similar privileges of informational control as a domestic weapon in their undeclared war against a transnational adversary (a classic instance of Pogo's bon mot "We has met the enemy, and they is us").

There have, of course, always been versions of classics edited for minds thought to be innocent and thus susceptible to corruption. Thomas Bowdler's ten-volume edition of Shakespeare, conforming to his stated objective that "those words are omitted which cannot with propriety be read aloud in a family" gave him a reputation more lasting than bronze in the eponymous term *Bowdlerize*. Bowdler would go on to apply the same principle to Gibbon's *Decline and Fall of the Roman Empire*, and he was hardly the only one at this game: W. S. Gilbert lampooned the "Family Edition" of an encyclopedia of classical mythology fashionable in his day in one of his Bab Ballads, "The Two Ogres" ("If you would learn the woes that vex / Poor Tantalus down there, / Pray borrow of Papa an ex- / Purgated Lemprière") as well as in his first full-length collaboration with Arthur Sullivan, the 1871 operetta *Thespis; or, The Gods Grown Old*.

More troubling is self-censorship, which the Hollywood studios practiced with sharply increased vigor after the House Un-American Activities Committee subpoenaed communist and left-leaning actors, producers, directors, and scriptwriters in 1947 and the loyalty-oath-and-blacklist era began in earnest. Writers who have been taught caution through bitter experience of what happens to the works of the outspoken may go to ingenious lengths in recasting their ideas in allegorical form; blacklisted screenwriter Albert Maltz's original script for *The Robe* was a relatively easy-to-read allegory of the left under fascism (and later came to be viewed by many as an allegory of the blacklist itself).

The pressure on public libraries to purge their own collections of material offensive to some members of the community has usually come to public attention when the librarians dig in their heels and say no. In the mid-1960s, public libraries sometimes kept books that were on their face controversial by reason of sexual content in a special area, often a case secured with a lock, partly as a way to make sure that minors could not get access to the material but also serving to keep such books in relatively safe storage.

Arguably this counted as a form of self-censorship too, as it made it more difficult for ordinary citizens to get at these books than at the rest of the holdings, but it also protected them from vandalism, of which they stood at higher risk. In the 1980s, for example, sneaking books out of the stacks with the collusion of an inside operative and then destroying them was a tactic successfully used by anti-Pagan vandals in their crusade to purge the library of Ohio State University of "satanic" content; much irreplaceable material was lost, dealing the folklore department in particular a serious blow.

For soldiers in wartime, inmates at prisons, and citizens conducting inquiries under the Freedom of Information Act, however, censorship often takes a different form: words which the censor thinks might compromise the security of the institution, whether an army, a jail, or a government spying agency that may have good reason to want to protect the identity of its sources of information (particularly when agents have actually been breaking domestic surveillance laws). In such instances one gets to see the document, but with parts of it blacked out and illegible.

In the same category might be considered the gray paint that municipalities use to paint over graffiti, on the not unreasonable theory that tagging public property with an illegible form of one's (nick)name is not an activity wholly protected under the First Amendment, particularly when the stuff is so dreadfully hard to read anyway. Graffiti artists counter by saying that what *they* are doing at least is art, not just speech. But then has just any private citizen a First Amendment right to decorate a public surface with his or her personal artistic vision, or do you really have to wait till the state arts council's jury awards you a Percent for Art commission? It's not too hard to guess where Jarry and the 'pataphysicians would come down on that one.

Censor comes from the Latin verb *censere*, "to offer an opinion, assess." The Censors were Roman magistrates appointed to 18-month terms every five years and charged with registering citizens (the *census*) and making sure they met the property and conduct qualifications appropriate to their class: If a member of the Knights (*Equites*), one had to be able to spend 5000 gold pieces (*aurei*) a year and have not committed any offenses sufficient to get one censured with a black

on the dot

mark next to one's name or earn expulsion from the order altogether. From *censere* also comes *recension*, the term for a text that results from comparing a number of available earlier copies and adopting the most plausible variants found in them.

Christian Rome had its own sort of censorship: The Vatican's *Index Librorum Prohibitorum* was first formally called by that name in 1557, though there had been plenty of precedent for it: *Brewer's Dictionary of Phrase and Fable* says that Pope Gelasius had issued a list of forbidden books over a thousand years earlier, in 494, and that his was by no means the first in the Church. Authors whose works were on the *Index* included Gibbon, Addison, Voltaire, Milton, Montaigne, Descartes, Copernicus, Chaucer, and even Dante.

The *Index* was abolished in 1966. It is not to be confused with the *Codex Expurgatorius*, a list of works available in editions from which the doctrinally objectionable bits had been removed. (The *-purg-* of *expurgatorius* is the same one in English *purge* and means "free from impurities.") For his own part, King Henry VIII exercised strict control on what was published in England during his reign through commissioners who vetted all books for doctrinally erroneous or otherwise seditious content. The idea that people could publish whatever they pleased so long as it was not libelous or caused a breach of the peace would not become a generally accepted notion for another couple of centuries. One who helped to make it possible was that devout Puritan, John Milton, who in 1644 published his *Areopagitica*, an eloquent and convincing argument against government-licensed publication in favor of a broadly interpreted freedom of the press.

●

"Where do my jokes go after I tell them?" wondered standup comic Demetri Martin. Where indeed? And where do the bits go that we leave out of the regular narrative, with or without replacing them with ellipses? Well, some of it isn't really left out so much as moved out of sight, or at least out of the line of fire: footnotes, endnotes (even farther from the front line), a URL in the front matter so that the reader can go to the computer to find the web page where the publisher has reproduced the notes rather than having to print them in the book at all. Of course, at each remove the likelihood that the reader will actually go there (bottom of page, end of book, off into cyberspace) diminishes, perhaps even by an order of magnitude; conversely, the closer the note is to hand, the more likely it is to get read. (Hence if one's notes are going to be available only on line, best to limit them to source citations and bibliography.)

In some instances, such as an academic symposium, when you read your paper out loud you're not supposed to read the footnotes, as Anthony Grafton points out in *The Footnote *A Curious History*. (What he doesn't mention, however, is that if you're a reader for Recordings for the Blind and Dyslexic, you do, bracketing each of them by saying "footnote" before you read it, and "return to text" when you're done.) On the other hand, there are some works in which this would be patently absurd, such as sociologist Erving Goffman's essay "The Insanity of Place," whose footnotes contain a great deal of substantive information and in some cases run to as many words as the body text from which they are called out.

In live broadcasting, the several-second delay between taping and transmission allows censors to bleep language thought to be too raunchy by community standards. (The visual equivalent used by the networks is digitally fuzzing the image, a technique resorted to when the mouth of the person saying the naughty word can too easily be lip-read.) *Bleep* is an instance of onomatopeia so commonplace as to be a household word, in its participial form credibly replacing (and not obscuring in the least) the taboo expletive: "I told him that if he let his bleeping poodle do her business on my lawn one more time, I'd personally rub his nose in it."

Bleeping and *do her business* are both euphemisms, a robust and open-ended class of utterances that allow the unsayable to be conveyed in less unacceptable ways, and traditionally a sign of successful upward mobility from mucker to middle class has been the shift from coarser terminology toward the more euphemistic: *died* is softened to *passed on, toilet paper* camouflaged as *T.P., What?* turned into *Pardon?*, and *pregnant* replaced by *expecting*—and here dwells *the f-word*, too.

Instances of euphemism on the part of government spokespersons are numerous enough that an anthology of them from antiquity to the present would make for a very fat book indeed. Sometimes such terminology is, to be sure, intended merely to present an unpleasant truth in a less unpleasant light, with the understanding that we will know what the missing words mean (or at least can hazard a pretty good guess, whether from the conversational "That bleeping son-of-a-so-and-so" or the wire service's "That [expletive] son of a [expletive]"). By the same token, we know that "surge" is the same thing as "escalation," and that both mean "send more and more troops over there." We may think such a strategy counterproductive, but at least anyone with any brains can see that this *is* the strategy. No substantive deception here.

But where goes the missing stuff whose absence we are intended never to notice? Sir Humphrey Appleby (played by Nigel Hawthorne), permanent secretary to cabinet minister Jim Hacker (Paul Eddington) in the BBC-TV comedy series *Yes, Minister*, tells his boss that the first principle in keeping a secret is to keep it secret that one has a secret to keep. If one's cover story is seamless, whatever got suppressed ought to stay that way, and such expressions as *he knows where all the bodies are buried* attest that there are indeed some tales not told out of school.

This is harder to do, of course, in countries with feisty journalists adept at bringing to light scandalous material hidden away in a filing cabinet or shoved in a drawer. (Watergate is a textbook example of this.)

Another category of what's not in the text turning up somewhere else: marginalia, those jottings at the edge of a book's pages that comment or amplify on the printed word. These can be reactive ("Ouch!" "Great!" "Is this true?"), erudite ("Archilochus's shield" "homoiousin" "Cf. Micah 8:11?") or hermeneutic ("Hawthorne is being coy here— clever purse = female sexuality"). In some older books such marginalia might also be supplied by the author, as in Samuel Taylor Coleridge's "Rime of the Ancient Mariner," whose opening three stanzas the poet succinctly glosses as "An ancient Mariner meeteth three gallants bidden to a wedding-feast, and detaineth one." (His marginal note on just a couple of lines about "the spirit that plagued us so," however, runs to 48 words, and is really much more in the nature of a footnote.) This can also be accomplished with brief running heads (in effect, headlines), which the King James Bible has at the top of every page toward the center, with the book and chapter numbers on the outer edge: The left page headed "St. Matthew 3, 4" is headed *Christ's Temptation in the Wilderness*; facing it on the right is "St. Matthew 5," whose running head reads *The Beatitudes*.

Apocrypha (from Greek *kryptein*, "to hide") are so-called hidden books that didn't make the cut for a canonical collection, such as those that were included in the Greek translation of the Old Testament (called the Septuagint from its panel of seventy scholars) but were never part of the Hebrew Bible. Because of Puritan objections they were left out of the King James Bible as well, starting in the 17th century. These books include two contributions to the robust tradition of wisdom literature (Wisdom of Solomon and Ecclesiasticus), three interpolations to the book of Daniel (Bel and the Dragon, the story of Susanna, and the song of the three Israelites Shadrach, Meshach, and

Abednego from the middle of Nebuchadnezzar's fiery furnace), the book of Judith, and the two books of Maccabees, among others.

There are New Testament apocrypha as well, such as an Apocalypse of Peter whose imagery of the trials and punishments of the afterworld owes a palpable debt to pagan Greek beliefs about Tartarus and Elysium, as might be expected in the Greek-speaking eastern part of the Roman empire. And—no surprise since Donne—we know that the bell tolls also for us: Our knowledge of the world to come is by definition elliptical, but most of us have at least *some* notion (if only a subtractive, falsificationist one), of whatever it is we expect will fill in the blanks.

81

stet

emendations of immortality

Despite their reputation as ruthless pursuers of deviations from ortho-
dox spelling, grammar, and usage, editors and proofreaders do make
mistakes. When they catch themselves having made one, however,
or wish to restore text someone else has edited with more zeal than
judgment, they put a line of dots under the marked word or phrase
and write *stet* (Latin for 'let it stand') in the margin. It is the inverse
to the three dots of ellipsis, marking something excised by chance or
design from the original text: *Stet* puts back into place the status quo
ante, restoring that which has been erroneously altered or deleted by
mistake.

He said, "If it hadn't ~~have~~ been for the honor I'd rather have walked." (stet)

Why a row of dots under a stetted item? This can be partly chalked
up to the technology of book manufacturing, in which proofreaders
have worked, within the constraints of their writing tools, much the

same way for the last six centuries: The marks are made by hand on hard copy; although there have been some recent proposals for conventions for editing on line beyond the editor's putting in the edits in another color or font or (heaven forbid) simply changing the text, proofreaders continue to work with actual physical typescript, galleys or page-proof, which they mark with a pencil (usually red).

What the computer *has* done, however, is to reduce sharply the number of errors that used to creep in between the author's typescript and publisher's typesetting. Nowadays it is expected that articles and books will be submitted as word-processor files from which (with some tweaking of format) electronic typesetting can be done directly. While eliminating this gap between the typesetter's eyes and fingers is in principle a good thing, it also means that if something is wrong in the manuscript, and the copy-editor fails to catch it, the error will persist into page-proof.

At that stage, the proofreader usually will be cold-reading—that is, without an earlier version of the text for comparison—and functioning primarily as a detector of typographic errors, although he or she may also flag phrases whose syntax is ambiguous or tormented and which threaten to be speed bumps that can be guaranteed to bring readers to a screeching halt in order to try to parse the sentence again. The proofreader is the final pass of the sieve, the fourth or fifth pair of eyes to give the author's work a close reading, and the last line of defense against some howler getting into print for malicious reviewers to pounce upon. All the more reason, then, that there should be a clearly understood inventory of signs that are understood throughout the world of publishing.

The row of dots under something to be stetted contrasts with the single underline (with *ital* circled in the margin, changing the text from roman to italics), the triple underline and double underline (with a circled *cap* or *sc* in the margin, respectively, depending on whether capitals in the body-text font or small capitals are wanted)

on the dot

and the wavy underline (with circled *bf* in the margin, signifying boldface).

Some signs deal expressly with punctuation: A period is represented by a dot with a little circle around it; an inserted comma is indicated by a caret with a comma under it; apostrophes and single or double quotation marks are inserted above an upside-down caret. (All of these signs appear both in the text and in the margin.) *Caret* is from the Latin verb *carere*, and means 'It is lacking,' the idea being that whatever is missing should go in the place indicated—at the point of the arrowhead, so to speak.

He said, "If it hadnt have been for the honor I'd rather have walked," ⌄ / ⊙

He said, "If it hadn't have been for the honor I'd rather have walked." ⌃⸴

He said, "If it hadn't have been for the honor I'd rather have walked," # / ⊙

He said, "If it hadn't have been for the ~~the~~ honour I'd rather have walked." ⌣/⌣

A sign may mean one thing in the context of proofreading and quite another somewhere else: A raised caret is used to signify a pointer in the Pascal programming language; in mathematics it signifies an exponent. In French, inverted over a vowel, it marks the historic loss of a preceding or (much more often) a following phonetic element or elements: Modern French *tête* ('head') came from Old French *teste*, itself from Late Latin *testa* ('pot'), and *âme* ('soul') from Old French *anme*, from Latin *anima*. The French call this an *accent circonflex*—from Latin *circumflectere*, 'to take a turn (around a thing),' a compound of *circum* ('around') plus *flectere* 'to bend, curve, turn.' Orthographically, it is like a monadnock poking its head above a peneplain, vestigial evidence of mountains whose less resistant rocks time and erosion have worn almost flat; phonologically, the circumflex lengthens or at least colors the vowel underneath it, at least in some modern-day dialects of French.

stet

The caret is one of several proofreaders' marks concerned with space, including the insertion of space itself (indicated in the text by a caret and in the margins by the sign variously known as the *pound sign, number sign, hash mark, double hash mark, sharp sign, octothorp,* or *octothorn* in English and as the *dièse* in French. *Diesis* in English, on the other hand, is another name for the double dagger [‡]). The *hash* of *hash mark* is a variant on *hatch* (as in *cross-hatch:* "These bogus $20 bills can be easily spotted: The engraver's cross-hatching is very amateurish—and come to think of it, isn't that Andrew *Johnson?*"), derived from French *hacher,* 'to cut up,' whence also *hatchet.* (It is unrelated to *hack,* however, which like *hooker, heckle, hacek,* and *Hakenkreuz*—German for 'hooked cross,' i.e., the Nazi swastika—comes from the Indo-European root **keg,* meaning 'tooth' or 'hook.') *Pound sign* seems to be gaining the upper hand as the popular name, thanks to its presence on the three-by-four array of buttons that replaced the old rotary phone dial and recorded messages telling us to "enter your PIN, then press pound," somewhat shorter and less confusing than the possible alternative, "Enter your PIN, then press the number key."

Of course, sometimes the hash mark *does* stand for 'pound(s), as in "20# flour, 5# sugar" on the baker's receipt. (Compare "Use a #2 pencil to fill in the dots," where the number sign precedes the number.) Of course, the telephone companies could just as well have called it a *sharp sign,* since the hash mark as an indicator on musical notation to raise the note that it follows a semitone has been around for half a millennium. By naming one of its products C#, Microsoft appeared to be asserting that it is a cut above the widely used programming language C. (Compare the name of the language C++ in which the ++ is the symbol for "increment.") The string *#include X* is the instruction in both C and C++ that means 'include the contents of the file "X" in this program.' In Perl, the hash mark is used to introduce a comment, i.e., an annotation that is readable by those who are looking under the hood of software at its actual source code (versus those who only see the program in its compiled/executable version), e.g., "#Cludge starts here." On the other hand, the pound sign that ends a variable name (e.g., *foo#*) in BASIC tells us that *foo* is a double-precision integer.

Then there is the converse, the sign for 'close this space up,' which is a pair of ligatures, a subscript ligature (like a tie in music between two notes—[⌣]) and a superscript ligature ([⌐]), which embrace the space to be removed. The close-space is often used in conjunction with the delete sign. On the next level up, the "run-in" sign eliminates a paragraph break, a line, usually forming what looks like a very large backward *s* from the last word of the previous paragraph to the first word of the new, with the circled abbreviation *ri* in the margin. This can also be used to show the splice within a paragraph where an editor has deleted some material (e.g., from the sort of copy-and-paste error that occurs all too easily if a phrase whose reiteration would spill over to the next line is inadvertently repeated, as if reiteration would spill over to the next line is inadvertently repeated, as in the present parenthetical): One long line with a loop in its tail deletes the extra words, and a ligature then connects the two loose ends.

The close-space marks frequently accompany a forward slash (/), which is also variously known as a *solidus*, *virgule*, or just plain *slash*, when the deletion of a single character is to be marked. The *solidus* was a Roman coin and is ultimately the basis for English *soldier*, the idea being that a soldier is someone who fights for money, or, as we might say today, a *mercenary* (from the Latin *merces* 'wages.') The solidus as slash is historically a straightened-out *S*, the abbreviation for the English shilling (as in 2/3—two shillings thruppence), the step from one coin to another being relatively easy. How we get from shilling to slash in its various other uses—as proofreader's strike-out mark, arithmetical sign of division, general separatrix, and so on—is rather more murky. The derivation of *virgule*, however, is straightforward: the term is from the diminutive (*virgula*) of Latin *virga*, 'switch, withie.' (In French, *virgule* is the name given to the comma, the semicolon being called *point et virgule*; a forward slash is a *barre oblique*, and a backslash is a *barre oblique inverse*.)

When marking proof, it's easy enough to insert a missing virgule, but it's only prudent to write it in the margin with a circle around it, to distinguish it from the vertical line used to separate two other proofreading marks—particularly if there is more than one typo in the line. This is even more advisable with the vertical bar itself, a character [|] in its own right sometimes referred to as a *pipe* because of its use as an operational sign in computer commands, *to pipe* meaning 'to take the output of one set of operations and use it as the input of another.' (The pipe is also used as a separatrix in marking proof.) Like the backslash, indispensable for naming DOS/Windows drives and files on or peripheral to our computers (e.g., "This file is c:\pubstuff\onthedot\chapters\stet.rtf"), the pipe is a newcomer to a keyboard subtly expanded since the typewriter era. So are the sideways carets (< and >, affectionately geeknamed *waka waka*) that tell your e-mail program to disregard the stuff displayed outside them and just send to the address within, e.g., "Prof. Philomena J. Birdsong <philbird@mail.markhopkins.edu>."

Some specialized uses of sideways carets: In the indexing program CINDEX, typing in "<The> Adventures of Robin Hood" means 'print "The" but ignore it when alphabetizing' so that this title will come between "Adler, Luther" and "*Advise and Consent*." <X> can also be read as 'we're interpolating X here,' while in mathematics "<" means 'is less than,' and ">" means 'is greater than.' This also goes for Computerese, in which double sideways carets (<< and >>) signify left shift and right shift, respectively, "<<" and ">>" being so-called *bitwise operators*, the idea being that you use them to change the value of a string of 1's and 0's by raising or lowering its value by one or more powers of two: e.g., 011 (3) << 1 results in 110 (6). In linguistics, "<" signifies 'derived from' as in *âme < anme < anima*, and ">" signifies 'becomes' as in *anima > anme > âme*. The sign is also sometimes used in computer manuals to represent a menu cascade (e.g., "File > Open"). And in French, the double sideways carets called *guillemets*—«...»—are quotation marks, a usage derived from the original *antilambdas* (so called because they looked like capital lambdas [Λ] turned on their sides) in medieval manuscripts, setting off passages that were being cited from somewhere else.

●

Proofreading practice prior to the invention of movable type is one of those shrouded-in-the-mists-of-antiquity aspects of everyday trade practice of which we see only occasional and partial glimpses, like Issa's cow. That someone (if only the copyist himself) at least occasionally proofread the work produced in the copying rooms of the monasteries we can infer from surviving manuscripts showing emendations, but in the main James J. O'Donnell is probably quite right to assert that "[p]roofreading was labor-intensive and wasteful in a manuscript scriptorium." However, references to proofreading turn up almost as early as printing itself. "Correctors," as proofreaders were first called, would be assigned by the master printer to work with the compositor—"some one that is well skill'd in true and quick Reading, to read the copy to him," says Joseph Moxon in his *Mechanick Exercises* of 1683—while authors read their own sets of proofs and might be obliged to make corrections by hand to pages already printed and bound. (In some instances, however, a missing line would be printed on a separate slip and pasted into the book, which is what Aldus Manutius the Elder did after dropping a line of Greek from Aristotle's *De Animalibus Historia*, which he printed at Venice in the late 1490s.)

A significant problem in early printing that has all but vanished today is the wide variation in English spelling. Compositors, while in principle charged with faithfully reproducing idiosyncrasies of spelling

89

and punctuation in authors' manuscripts, would often use their own judgment in setting type. Moxon says that though a compositor is supposed "strictly to follow his copy," adds that authors' ignorance and/or carelessness obliges "the *Compositer*...to discern and amend the bad *Spelling* and *Pointing* [i.e., punctuation] of his *Copy*, if it be English...." Hence, Moxon says, "it is necessary that a *Compositer* be a good English Schollar at least; and that he know the present traditional *Spelling* of all English Words, and that he have so much Sence and Reason, as to *Point* his sentences properly."

This problem would persist well into the next century; John Smith, in *The Printer's Grammar* (1755) would write scornfully of "the liberty which almost every Writer takes to display the talent which he has in Spelling." Given such variation, says Smith, his correctors need "to Spell and to Point after the prevailing method" and "fix upon a method to spell ambiguous words and compounds always the same way. And that the Compositors may become acquainted and accustomed to his way of spelling, the best expedient would be to draw out, by degrees, a Catalogue of such ambiguous words and compounds"— in other words, a style sheet.

●

A *proof* is a test. We have come to think of it in its narrower sense of producing results that verify our hypothesis (i.e., "proof positive"), distinguishing it from *disproof:* a test that falsifies, or one that leads to a contradiction. But the more general meaning is retained in such words and expressions as *100 proof bourbon* (a beverage whose alcohol content, when tested, *proves* to be 50%), *the proof of the pudding is in the eating,* and *it's the exception that proves the rule*—the last a source of epistemic confusion to those who think only in the positivist terms of a mathematical proof. (The set of mathematical proofs that don't work may not be a null set, but presumably nobody bothers to write them down, for the same reason chemists don't spend a lot of time learning phlogiston theory, astronomers Babylonian astrology, and biologists so-called creation science. To be sure, we can and do speak of the sort of mathematical proof that works by *reductio ad absurdum*; but the operative word here is *works:* It is not a failed proof, merely one that shows the failure of a certain set of propositions in order to bolster their opposites.) Most casual references to proof in everyday speech assume a positive outcome ("I know I can prove my innocence if I'm given my day in court." "If you're really God's Son, then for Heaven's sake prove it by saving yourself, and us with you!" "What's that drugstore cowboy in the White House think he's trying to prove, anyway?"). We can, of course, prove someone wrong, but nowadays we rarely if ever talk about just proving someone.

The noun *proof* and the verb *to prove* come from Latin *probare*, 'to test.' (*Test* comes from Latin *testa*, 'pot,' and in Middle English meant a *cupel*, a small cup—it's from the diminutive of Latin *cuppa*, 'drinking vessel'—made of a porous fire-resistant substance such as bone ash and used for assaying gold and silver and for separating base metals from them; compare *crucible*, from medieval Latin *crucibulum*, 'crucible; night light, cresset.' A cresset is a lamp in a pot suspended from a stick; the word comes [as does *crucibulum*] from Old French *croisuel*, which is in turn from *croceolus 'little lamp,' a diminutive of *croceus*, 'pertaining to saffron, saffron-yellow,' from Greek *krokos*, 'saffron.') Perhaps we may all be forgiven our inclination to read *proof* in its positive sense, for the Romans shared it before us: The other sense of *probare* is 'to esteem something to be good/proper/service-able (*probus*)'—compare *probity*—so what was *probabilis* could either be that which could be believed or assumed (what would pass the test) or what was commendable.

Probare has also given jurisprudence some terminology of the trying-something-out-to-see-what-happens variety: If you're on *probation*, you're living in an ongoing test of whether you can keep out of mischief if you aren't actually incarcerated; mess up, and they'll put you in jail. *Probate court* is where wills get examined and certified as valid or set aside (e.g., as having been made under duress or by a person of unsound mind or both). And government officials suspected of financial mismanagement may find themselves indicted as the result of a *probe* by a legislative committee, even as some other panel is debating whether to send to the floor a bill providing funding for exotic weapons whose prototypes were reported as performing adequately at some *proving ground* way off in the middle of the desert by a team of observers in a *blast-proof* bunker guarded by a platoon of unsmiling fellows in *bulletproof* Kevlar vests.

In printing, a proof is a test, too: a first impression that allows authors and editors (and the proofreaders working for both) to see what the printed page is really going to look like, and to fix whatever typographic errors (and others) may be there, prior to the actual print run of that edition. Originally, an *edition* was an act of promulgation or publication, *editio* being from Latin *ēdere*, 'to give out, put forth, publish' (a compound of *ē* [a preconsonantal form of *ex-*, 'out'] plus *dare*, 'to give,' not to be confused with short-*e̱* *ĕdere*, 'to eat,' as in *edible*, *comestible*, and *esurient*). *Edict*, on the other hand, comes from *ēdīcere*, 'to proclaim' (literally, 'to say forth'). French draws a distinction between the noun *édit*, 'edict' (as in the *Édit de Nantes*, by which the Protestant-turned-Catholic king Henri IV proclaimed religious tolerance for Huguenots), and the adjective *édit*, 'published,' the past participle of *éditer*, 'to publish,' digging into their Latin dictionaries and coming up with the verb *édicter* to refer to the giving of edicts.

Back-formation seems also to have been at work with the English verb *edit*, first attested in 1793 (nine years after the initial appearance of *éditer* in French) whereas *editor*, in its sense of 'someone who prepares work for publication,' had been current for most of the century, having been in print since 1712. A French copy-editor is called a *rédacteur*, an *éditeur* being a publisher instead; copy-editors in England are called sub-editors, presumably to distinguish them from acquisitions editors whose job description does not include comma-chasing and syntax repair. *Copy* is from Latin *copia*, 'quantity, abundance, plenty'—a *cornucopia* is quite literally a horn of plenty—which in the plural, *copiae*, meant 'troops.' In Medieval Latin, *copia* acquired the additional meaning of 'transcript,' presumably because if you had more than one copy of a book, in those pre-printing days of hand-copied manuscripts, you had an abundance of it. The -*op*- of *copy* is the same root as the *op*- of *opulent*.

Galleys (short for *galley proofs*) are the stage formerly between manuscript and page-proof, in which type was set in lines but often not in its final pagination. Although this intermediate stage has by now been virtually eliminated, thanks to the advent of computerized authors and typesetters alike, the word survives in the term *bound galleys* for uncorrected page proofs distributed to reviewers in advance of actual publication. A galley is a long tray, usually metal, in which the lines of type have been laid out and is so called because of its resemblance to the other sort of galley with rowers pulling two or more banks of oars, often under duress. Its source is Old French *galie* (which split in Modern French into *galée* for the printing term and *galère* for the boat), apparently from Medieval Greek *galeos*, 'shark,' in turn derived from Greek *galeē* ('weasel').

In French a proofreader is called a *correcteur*. Corrigenda, errata, and addenda are ways of getting around the fact that even the most sharp-eyed proofreaders will miss a thing or two by inserting a separately printed slip of paper in each copy after an edition has gone to press. For the most part, however, such corrections are best left to a second printing, if author and publisher are fortunate enough to sell out the first; such devices as adding an *appendix* and, of course, writing a *preface* to a second edition serve to atone for those things left undone

93

or that ought not to have been done in the first edition of the book, as well as an opportunity for authors to frame a reply to their critics.

●

Publishing is a business, and at least since the days of Henry James, one serious enough to require more than an oral agreement. And no contract is complete without the *dotted line* on the bottom for the parties' signatures. In some respects this resembles an ellipsis: Something is missing that wants filling in for the instrument to go into effect. A unilateral unsigned contract is hardly worthy of the name: If one of the parties holds what is in effect a dummy hand, the writer of the contract can interpret it quite freely, while the other parties can rightly say that it was not a contract of their making, and required no performance on their part. (Arguably of this sort was the Republican Party's "Contract with America," under which, since America never signed it, the GOP behaved as if at liberty to do pretty well anything it pleased so long as it had the votes, such as spending 46 million dollars to determine that its president and commander-in-chief was too intimate with an intern.)

Stevie Wonder, in the song "Contract on Love," urged his presumed girlfriend to "Sigh-igh-igh-igh-ign, sign on that dotted line" as a gesture implying the formalization of an otherwise vulnerable relationship; a more conventional formality is the signing of the marriage license by the two parties and the officiating cleric, justice of the peace, or notary. There is also the dotted line that's actually a row of perforations along which we are instructed to detach our paycheck from the cover sheet explaining what it is for, or the part of the bill we mail back with the check, retaining the upper portion for our records (often scribbling the check number and date we paid it in case our creditor's accounts-receivable department fails to credit our account properly). In the absence of a perforated line we may be asked to snip a dotted line with scissors, as when we clip a coupon to cash in for a store's discount or to redeem a bond's interest payment (whence the condescending term *coupon-clipper* for 'elderly person living partly on interest income').

Such lines are straight and straightforward; less so are the dots in numbered sequence that we are asked in our youth to connect in a puzzle, generating a metaphor for problem-solving applicable in a wide variety of situations (including the first chapter title in this book) for the rest of our natural lives. Crooked or straight, dotted lines have been with us for a long time: In the 1840s, war tax protester Henry David Thoreau wrote of his cabin in the woods near Walden Pond that "[i]n the deepest snows, the path which I used from the highway to my house, about half a mile long, might have been represented by a meandering dotted line, with wide intervals between the dots." (Best-selling author and sociologist Fr. Andrew Greeley, no fan of unjust wars himself, might well have replied to this with one of his favorite proverbs: "God draws straight with crooked lines.") In all these instances, the bottom line is that the dots serve to guide our hands and our eyes, even if it's only the proofreader telling us that what was tinkered with shouldn't have been: If it wasn't broken, it didn't need fixing, so stet it.

95

ninety-eight
point six
decimals and determinings

The cover of Martin Mull's record album *Normal* shows the singer-songwriter's face with a thermometer stuck in his mouth; the mercury in the thermometer is just at the 3/5 notch on the scale between "98" and "99." Outside the United States, this joke only works in Liberia and Burma (a.k.a. Myanmar); everybody else is on the metric system, perhaps the most far-reaching change wrought by the French Revolution, which replaced its cumbersome hodgepodge of standard measures with an ordered, rational, and ruthlessly decimal one. If the decimal point had not existed before, it would have been necessary to invent it in 1799, when the metric standard—*metros* is Greek for 'measure, mean'—was officially adopted by the French government. Napoléon Bonaparte's assumption of power in the coup of November 9–10 that year guaranteed that the new system, already in use and proving its manifest utility, now had the political clout of a dictator behind it.

Until recently, the standard meter was supposed to be equal to one ten-millionth of the distance from the earth's equator to its pole, or more tangibly the gap between two scratches on a platinum-iridium bar kept in a vault near Paris, with identical ones held elsewhere in the world such as the Bureau of Standards in Washington, DC. In the latter part of the 20th century, however, the meter was redefined as a set multiple of the wavelength of one of the spectroscopic excitation lines (the 605.8 nanometer one) of the inert gas krypton.

The principal advantage of a decimal system is ease of computation: If every quantity of real life can be expressed as a multiple of 10 or a decimal fraction (in exponential terms, X times some multiple of 10^2 or 10^{-1}), then all sorts of calculations from weighing birdseed or selling milk to measuring an inseam or breaking a fiver just got a lot simpler. The downside is that metric units are divisible by only two factors—2 and 5—while the units they replaced may have been a lot more forgiving of equal division. A third, for example, is an infinitely repeating fraction (.33333...), so if your fiver is in a metrical currency such as the dollar and you want to split it three ways, someone is going to come out a penny short of the game ($5/3 = $1.67 + $1.67 + $1.6\underline{6}$).

Not so for British money before its decimalization in the 1960s. Early in the decade, Britain still had paper currency for one pound and its multiples, with coins for everything smaller. The pound was worth twenty shillings (there was a snob unit of 21 shillings called a guinea, which was only used to express the price of certain high-ticket items such as a good tailor's suit or an automobile, but no surviving banknote or coin corresponded to it), and each shilling was worth twelve pence. The silver coins still in circulation at that time were the crown (five shillings), half-crown (two shillings and sixpence), florin (two shillings even), shilling, and sixpence; there was also a threepenny bit, made of brass, and the penny, half-penny, and farthing, all three of which were bronze. With four farthings to the penny, the pound was divisible into 960 parts, even subdivisions of which include 2, 3,

4, 5, 6, 8, 10, 12, 15, 16, 20, 24, 30, 32, and 40. By contrast, the dollar is divisible only by 2, 4, 5, 10, 20, 25, and 50, as is the new decimal British pound of 100 pence (abbreviated *p*, as in "Can ye lend me 30p until Thursday?")

So divvying up a pre-decimalized five-pound note was simple: Everybody would get three pounds thirteen shillings and fourpence (£3/13/4. In smaller amounts than a pound, the sign £ [from Latin *libra* 'pound of weight,' whence the abbreviation *lb.*] was eliminated, so that 2/6 would be read as 'two [shillings] and six[pence],' i.e., a half-crown). Indeed, most decimal fractions look sesquipedalian, even those that aren't repeaters, relative to their whole-number ratios: 1/9 is .11111..., 7/16 is .4375, 22/7 is 3.142857...(which is why it makes a quite adequate working approximation of pi [π], the irrational number representing the ratio of a circle's circumference to its diameter: 3.1415926...).

99

The decimal point cues the reader that to the left of it is the units place, and to the right the tenths, two places are hundreds to the left and hundredths to the right, and so on. A thermometer reading of 98.6 tells us that the human being in front of us is not running a fever; a thermometer that said 986 would be telling us something very different (that our low-temperature silver solder is just about warm enough to flow into the joints of whatever we're repairing) and a temperature of 9.86 (if our outdoor thermometer were that discriminating), something else again: that it's probably safe to go skating on our local pond. Of course, these are degrees Fahrenheit, named for Gabriel Daniel Fahrenheit, who in 1714 also invented the mercury thermometer to measure them; if it's 9.86 *Celsius* outside, that pond is thawed and then some (this being around 50° F). The "normal" 98.6° human temperature by mouth turns out to be a tidy 37° Celsius, named for Anders Celsius, the Swedish astronomer who thought up the centigrade scale in 1742, dividing into 100 degrees the difference between the freezing and boiling points of water.

To convert Fahrenheit to Celsius, consider the following: If between the freezing and boiling points of water there are 100 degrees Celsius and 180 degrees Fahrenheit, it follows that a single Celsius degree equals 1.8 Fahrenheit ones; conversely, a Fahrenheit degree is the equivalent of 5/9 (that is, 10/18) of a degree Celsius. So to translate 20° C into Fahrenheit, one must multiply by 1.8 (= 36) and add 32 (because 0° = 32° F), yielding a comfortably cool 68° F. To turn Fahrenheit into Celsius, on the other hand, first subtract 32, then divide by 1.8: On a hot summer day of 86° F, take away 32 to leave 54, which when divided by 1.8 yields 30° C. This may seem a bit unwieldy at first but one can get used to it.

The advantage of the Fahrenheit scale is that it permits finer divisions of scale without going into multiple decimal places; a difference of 1° F is about the smallest change the human body can detect without a thermometer. The principal advantage of the centigrade scale is that it *is* centigrade and accordingly ties in nicely with the rest of the metric system's ruthlessly base-10 algorithms. As the thermometric unit for the French metric reformers half a century after Celsius devised it, the centigrade scale was a conceptual shoo-in. It was only later, when dealing with extremely cold temperatures (far below −40° C, or −40° F, which is the same thing) that scientists came to refer to degrees Kelvin, i.e., above absolute zero, the temperature at which all activity stops cold, equal to −273.15° C. The Kelvin degree and Celsius degree are exactly the same size, differing only in their zero point; thus water thaws at 273.15° K and boils at 313.15° K. Astronomers are fond of referring to the "3° K hum," manifest as a faint background radio noise discernible from every direction in the universe and believed to be a relic of the Big Bang.

Other translations between metric and English measurement systems vary in untidiness: The inch is roughly two and a half centimeters, and the meter even more roughly a yard (39.37 inches as opposed to the yard's 36). A thousand cubic centimeters make a liter, which is very close to a quart (it's 1.056 of them, to be exact). American soft-drink manufacturers accordingly have begun selling soda pop in one-, two-, and three-liter bottles, while still retaining ounces for the smaller denominations. The kilogram, as any veteran of the 60s bulk-and-break cannabis scene may recall, makes for far more difficult conversions: At 2.2 lb = 1 kg it yields a clumsy 35.2 ounces in theory—and in practice tended to shrink during shipment (heh heh) unless purchased as an actual kilo brick brought from south of the border. (The slang abbreviation "key" allowed Arlo Guthrie to cobble together the felicitous rhyme "Coming into Los Angeles, / Bringin' in a couple of keys: / Don't touch my bags if you please, / Mr. Customs man," a scenario unthinkable in these days of heightened arousal on the part of Homeland Security agents and drug-sniffing pooches.) An ounce weighs 28.35 grams.

As of the turn of the 20th century, the *Century Dictionary* could report that the unit of volume was the *stere*, equal to a cubic meter (or a million cubic centimeters, take your pick), but nobody seems to use it much these days. Meanwhile, smaller units of measure have proven necessary for very small things such as viruses (measured in microns, i.e., millionths of a meter) and wavelengths of light (measured in angstroms, equal to one ten-thousandth of a micron and named for Anders Jonas Ångstrom, another Swedish astronomer and a pioneer in spectroscopic analysis, by which he discovered that there was hydrogen in the sun's atmosphere).

Unfortunately, there are no units in the metric system (or as it is now called, the International System of Units, or SI for short from its French name, *Système international d'unités*) for measuring very large lengths, the kilometer, at .62 miles (another not-great fit) being the largest. Instead, astronomers measure interstellar distances in light years, i.e., the distance light travels in a year (5.88 trillion miles/9.46 trillion kilometers). Such large numbers are commonly expressed as X times some exponent of ten: 9.46 times 10^9, for example. Prefixes to

101

metric units indicate notches of three in the exponents: *milli-* for one thousandth (10^{-3}), *micro-* for a millionth (10^{-6}), *nano-* for a billionth (10^{-9}); *kilo-* for one thousand (10^3), *mega-* for a million (10^6), *giga-* for a billion (10^9), and *tera-* for a trillion (10^{12}). The last two were virtually unheard outside of scientific circles until the advent of cheaper and cheaper memory for personal computers brought a gigabyte and even a terabyte of storage well within the budget of the ordinary user.

The dot as delimiter is a sine qua non of exponential notation; 9.46×10^9 takes up a lot less space than 9,460,000,000 as well as making it much easier to keep straight what the order of magnitude is (i.e., not dropping or adding a zero or two by mistake) when doing calculations. Nowadays we take for granted as a standard notational device the decimal point that sets off units from tenths, so it may come as a surprise that it has been around only since the late 1500s: Christoph Clavius, the head of Pope Gregory XIII's commission to reform the Julian Calendar, used it in a sine-function table published in 1593. It was in the mathematical treatises of John Napier, however, that it attained real currency.

Unfortunately, scientific progress is rarely the orderly march down the straight turnpike to which textbook glosses of the history of normal science would like to reduce it. Napier actually alternated between using a point and a comma as his decimal delimiter, and other mathematicians throughout Europe and in America would use other signs well into the 20th century (12 pages of Florian Cajori's *History of Mathematical Notations* are devoted to them), including apostrophes (forward and back), subscript wedges, a vertical slash (9|46) and the sign $\lfloor$ (9$\lfloor$46).

A further complication was the introduction of the dot as a multiplication sign (as in 22 · 43 = 946), in place of the X (as in 22 × 43 = 946) that had been casually introduced to English arithmetic by Edward Wright in his 1618 Napier translation, *A Description of the Admirable Table of Logarithms*, and advanced more conspicuously by

William Oughtred in 1631 in his *Clavis Mathematicae*. But one serious problem with X-for-multiplication is that it is too easily mistaken for *X*-as-variable in algebra. Using a dot for multiplication instead gets around this ambiguity but created a problem of its own in positioning it so it wouldn't be mistaken for a decimal point.

In America, thanks in large part to the recommendation of the National Committee on Mathematical Requirements' influential *Reorganization of Mathematics in the Secondary Schools*, published in 1923, we have settled on a baseline dot as decimal delimiter and a raised-to-center dot (sometimes called an *interpunct*) as multiplication sign; in Britain it is the other way around. (Elsewhere in Europe, people use a comma for the decimal delimiter, which at least avoids confusion with the multiplication sign but takes it out of the running as a means of breaking up very large numbers such as five billion— which, just to complicate matters even more, is 5×10^9 in America but 5×10^{12}, i.e., a million millions, in Europe.)

Because whole-number ratios generate fractions with repeating decimals, a method of indicating the period (that is, repeating part) is needed to show that it *is* the period. Easy enough to infer what the period is in a simple fraction such as 1/3 (.33333...); less obvious with one in which the period is very long (such as 11/29, whose decimal equivalent is .**3**7931034482758620689655172413793103**44**...; the initial and final digits are in boldface). The solution proposed by John Marsh in 1742 (in his optimistically entitled *Decimal Arithmetic Made Perfect*) was to write a dot over each end of the period (in this case the 3 at the beginning of the string 379 with which the decimal fraction starts and another over the 1 immediately preceding the next iteration of 379, in the 28th decimal place). A variant places the dot under the first and last number of the period (1/7 = 0.142857...).

Either way, the strings of numbers are kept as short as possible, though the 28-figure period above seems a visual thicket compared to whole-number fractions with a forward slash (*solidus*) or horizontal line (*vinculum*, Latin for 'bond, fetter') separating the two quantities and indicating that the left-hand or upper number is to be divided by the lower or right-hand one. (*Fraction* itself originally meant 'a breaking'—it's from the Latin verb *frango*, 'I break,' from which also comes the adjective *fragile*—but turns up in English in its mathematical sense as early as Geoffrey Chaucer, around 1400. The earlier meaning surfaces in the Anglican Church, which uses the term "fraction anthem" for the Agnus Dei, sung at communion immediately after the breaking of the consecrated host.) Fractions were extensively used in Egyptian mathematics, in which whole number proportions were of the essence. The Egyptian hieroglyphs for the binary fractions ½ through 1/64 were all components of the standard iconography of the *wedjat* eye, the eye of falcon-headed Horus, which according to the Osirian myth cycle was torn out and apart in a fierce hand-to-hand combat between Horus and his father's murderer, his evil uncle Seth, but later restored to Horus and put back together again. An exhaustive discussion of Egyptian math—whose divine patron, the ibis-headed Thoth, was also the conductor of the dead—can be found in R. A. Schwaller de Lubicz's monumental two-volume book *The Temple of Man*, largely drawing on the Rhind Papyrus, a mathematics textbook in hieroglyphic script thought to date from the 17th century B.C.E. If the papyrus represents an accurate sample, working a problem in Egyptian arithmetic often amounted to translating it into a geometry problem and then solving that.

The Babylonians, on the other hand, understood fractions as reciprocals: The reciprocal of 3 is one over 3, i.e., 1/3. If Egyptian math seemed happiest with what could be readily represented geometrically, Babylonian mathematicians were most at home in the realm of numbers whose computation rested firmly on a combination of our familiar base 10 and a greater base of 60 (a number conveniently divisible by 2, 3, 5, 6, 10, 12, 15, 20, and 30). It was from the Babylonians that the Greeks got the idea of dividing the circle into 360 degrees; no coincidence that the Babylonian year had 360 days in it (with five more of "sacred time" off the chart, so to speak, at the New Year festival, during which the entire creation epic was recited from start to finish).

Filling the gap between the easily subdivided calendar year and the actual solar year was all of a piece with another Babylonian innovation: the use of a null sign in place notation. It was not exactly a zero (it had no function in calculation, for example) but a placeholder between two real quantities that added together made up the number and were themselves two orders of magnitude apart (much as we would write, "That's who was the terror of Highway 101"). This Babylonian quasi-zero usually appeared as a pair of short-lined wedge marks (visible in the inscription on a Babylonian full-moon table from late in the second century B.C.E.) but sometimes there were three and sometimes only one—barely more than a dot, as writing on clay with a stylus goes.

105

In fact, the dot and the zero seem to have played tag with each other throughout much of history. (After all, a mere empty space is ambiguous: It could be a placeholder or just a space, or those could be two separate numbers on either side of it. So what's going on?) Moreover, calculation wasn't just in one's head: The counting board with sand on it and pebbles for counters was the ancestor of the abacus, and the Greek word for such a board, *abax*, may well be derived from a Semitic word for dust (*abq*); one appealing but probably fanciful candidate for the ancestor of zero is that it is the shape left on the sand when a pebble is removed. (For what it's worth, the original form of the zero in India, once its mathematicians got around to deciding they needed one, was a dot.)

The common use of the abacus throughout much of the Far East notwithstanding, it appears that the Orient got the device from the West instead of vice versa. Examples of Roman abaci survive to this day: slotted plates with bronze calculi instead of stone ones, and even in some cases extra slots on the side for fractional amounts. Although the abacus fell into disuse in the Western world during the Dark Ages, it continued to be employed in the markets of bustling Islamic Africa and the Near East, which is how Leonardo of Pisa, better known as Fibonacci, came to learn to use one while working in his father's trading company in Bugia, on the North African coast (today's Bejaia, Algeria). What's more, he also learned how to use the local number system, which had spread throughout the Islamic world from India, and found it far less cumbersome for calculations than the Roman numerals in which Italy's business had been transacted for the preceding millennium and more. His *Liber Abaci* (whose title is variously translated as "Book of the Abacus" and "Book of Calculation"), published around 1202, went beyond its stated purpose of instructing people in computation with an abacus to make the case for the adoption of Hindu-Arabic numerals.

For better or worse, Hellenic mathematicians did not adopt Babylonian place-notation; in Greek, numbers were assigned to letters of the alphabet (as also in Hebrew). Greek geometry, on the other hand, owes a good deal to Egyptian mathematics, in part due to an accident of history: After Philip of Macedon had brought all of Greece under his sway, and his son Alexander then set out to conquer the rest of the world known to the Greeks and very nearly succeeded, the latter's penchant for founding new cities to consolidate his administration bore conspicuous fruit at Alexandria, at the mouth of the Nile, which under the descendants of his general Ptolemy came to have the largest lighthouse (the Pharos, considered one of the Seven Wonders of the ancient world) and the largest library collection in antiquity.

●

A library needs a coherent system for organizing its inventory so that its contents can be logically arranged and easily retrieved. One

on the dot

happy use to which decimalization has been put in our time to this end has been the invention of the method of classifying information for libraries known as the Dewey Decimal Classification system (commonly known as the Dewey Decimal System). Perhaps "Harris-Dewey" would have been fairer, because when coming up with a taxonomic system for the publications in the library of Amherst College in 1873, Melvil Dewey drew on the categories already formulated by W. T. Harris at the St. Louis Public Library. But it is Dewey, who first published his system in 1876, who gets the credit and the brand name: "Dewey" and "Dewey Decimal Classification" are today trademarks of Online Computer Library Center (OCLC) of Dublin, Ohio, which bought them from the previous owner, Forest Press, in 1988. Dewey had turned over ownership of this valuable intellectual property to the Lake Placid Club, of which he was a member and Forest Press a subsidiary.

107

Under this scheme all knowledge can be divided into 10 major branches, and to each of these a hundred numbers are assigned to denote subdivisions within them. So every book can be assigned a three-digit number defining its subject matter with some precision, and further refinements are possible within even those subcategories. The 10 main headings include a catch-all "general knowledge" category (numbers 000–099), followed by philosophy and psychology (the 100s), religion (200s), social sciences (300s), language (400s), natural sciences and mathematics (500s), technology (600s), arts (700s), literature and rhetoric (800s), and history, biography, and geography (900s). Dewey put these categories in this order because he believed that they represent the order in which humanity acquired them. Under this scheme the authors' *A B C Et Cetera: The Life and Times of the Roman Alphabet* is classified as "Languages (400s)—Latin (470s)—writing systems, phonology, phonetics (471s)—alphabet (481.1)."

Further subdivision is always possible, both into subcategories and, thanks to the Cutter-Sanborn author tables, to distinguish among different authors in the same field, a necessity for a library with a sizable collection. In addition to the Dewey number, the call letters on the spine of a library book will include a second line starting with the first (or first two or sometimes three) letters of the writer's last name plus a number, often followed by a lower-case letter that is usually the first initial of the first word in the title. Thus 471 H883a is the catalogue number for *A B C Et Cetera* at the Cambridge (Mass.) Public Library, the H̲ in H883a being for Humez and the final a̲ for *A B C*. However, a given book may not need as extensive a set of call letters at a smaller library, nor as fine distinctions from other Dewey categories, as at a large one.

In practice, it's never so simple, and variations in the call letters for *A B C* at libraries in several other Massachusetts cities and towns display some leeway in cataloguing: 471 H in Somerville and 471.1 HUM in Belmont (no Cutter-Sanborn tables at work here); in Newton, *A B C* is 470 H88a (that is, it's under "language—Latin" without differentiation) while in Acton it's 472 H992 (472 is "Latin—etymology). All safely within the 470s, one might suppose—but then at the Cary Memorial Library in Lexington, *A B C*'s call letters are 411 H (much like Leominster's: 411 Humez), 411 being "language—writing systems." Still other libraries classify *A B C* primarily as a history book, e.g., the Springfield City Library, where it's 973 H883a (973 is "history—ancient Rome"); Arlington and Sudbury give it this Dewey number as well (admittedly there *is* a lot of Roman history in there). Different cataloguer, different mind-set.

But what if your library is full of scrolls rather than books with spines with accession numbers on them? Alexandria's contained some 700,000 papyrus volumes (*volumen*, the Latin for 'scroll,' is from *volvere*, 'to turn'), making up some 30,000 complete works. These holdings were continually being augmented by customs officers' confiscating every book in the possession of anyone who entered Egypt so that the great library's scribes could make copies, which were given to owners when they left the country (the library kept the originals). The entire collection was catalogued by a Greek scholar named Callimachus during the reign of the second Ptolemy (called Philadelphus). His annotated bibliography of the Alexandrian collection, which ran to 120 papyrus rolls all on its own, was called the *Pinakes* (*pinax* is Greek for 'writing tablet, chart, map'), and though it is no longer extant, it is known to have replicated the physical location of works within the actual collection, as well as functioning off-site (e.g., in educated circles at Rome) as "an overview of the classical heritage, of genres and subject categories, and of individual works," according to Christian Jacob, who adds that "[t]he Alexandrian catalogue gave rise to a scholarly tradition in which bibliography became independent from the library itself and became meaningful on its own."

This greatest and best of libraries in its time was unfortunately all too vulnerable to serious fires and other disasters: in 47 B.C.E., collateral damage from Julius Caesar's attack on the Egyptian fleet; burned in 272 C.E., supposedly on orders from the short-lived Roman emperor Aurelian; razed to the ground in 391 C.E. by command of another Roman emperor, Theodosius, who was on a mission to stamp out paganism. The last of its books were burned in 640 during the reign of the Prophet Muhammad's friend and advisor Caliph Umar I, on the theory that writings that disagreed with the Qur'an were heretical, while those which agreed with it were superfluous.

109

dot com

computation punctuation

The dot has a wide variety of uses in the ever-expanding world of the computer—in file names, commands for navigating among file directories, Internet addresses, programming language syntax, the representation of fractions as fixed-point or floating-point numbers, the printers that render files as hard copy, down to the version of the software that actually lets you do your plugged-in work or play. All of these uses of the dot will be visited here. In most cases, the examples that follow are system-agnostic, though the assumed context is generally a personal computer of some sort. Some examples are specific to the Personal Computer (PC) and the DOS/Windows operating systems, though with a few tweaks, these examples would work just as well on a Mac or under UNIX.

Computers are everywhere, a fact so commonplace that to say it elicits little more interest than remarking how perpendicular the walls seem nowadays. Your ATM, cell phone, automobile, microwave oven, camera, CD player, digital watch—digital anything, in fact—is apt to have a computer as part of its hardware, each such embedded device smaller and more powerful as the technology of miniaturization improves and the price of memory falls.

So pervasive is computerization in our tools of literacy (hands up if you've used a manual typewriter at any time in the last year? Decade? Generation?) that we easily forget that computers began as nothing more than calculating machines. The concept is simple enough: processes that act on input with predictable results can be automated; all one needs to do is come up with a bit of hardware that will replicate faithfully whatever algorithm one was planning to apply to the input. The properties of whole numbers and the rules for manipulating them in basic arithmetic are quite simple (an abacus, correctly used, will work every time), and it is possible to construct a device with cranks and gears that will perform an arithmetic operation on even a very large number and produce a correct result, in far less time and with more reliability than someone doing it by hand with a pencil and paper (let's see, carry the ... er ... was that a three or a four?).

Indeed, as far back as 1822 the mathematician Charles Babbage proposed to build just such a machine, which he called the "Difference Engine," to run the calculations necessary to produce mathematical tables; Moreover, he proposed an even more radical machine, the "Analytical Engine," which would be able to tailor subsequent calculations to reflect the results of an initial run. (Although Babbage died in 1830, before such a device could be built, two Swedish engineers, Georg and Edward Schuetz, would construct a modest version of the Difference Engine in 1834.) Toward the end of the century Herman Hollerith came up with a machine to tabulate the 1890 U.S. census using the punched cards that are still known by his name.

The big push in computerization, however, came with the electronics made possible by the development of the vacuum tube—the first computers' binary switches—at the turn of the 20th century. The first British computer, the Colossus Mark I, was developed to do the number-crunching required in decoding messages created by the German Lorenz SZ40/42 encoding machine by coming up with probable matches for the encoder's settings; it became operational in 1943, the same year the University of Pennsylvania's ENIAC (short for "Electronic Numerical Integrator and Computer") began calculating artillery tables for the U.S. Army's Ballistic Research Laboratory at Aberdeen Proving Ground, Maryland.

The Bureau of the Census once again provided the impetus for a milestone "electronic brain" when it installed its UNIVAC I in 1951; this would be the first commercially marketed computer, with nearly 50 of them sold by Remington-Rand by 1957 to such clients as the Prudential Insurance Company, ratings maven A. C. Nielsen, and New York City's Consolidated Edison. (The company also donated them to Harvard, the University of Pennsylvania, and Cleveland's Case Institute of Technology, now part of Case Western Reserve.) Not to be outdone, **113** IBM, building on its development of the Mark I Automatic Sequence Controlled Calculator at Harvard in 1944 and its own Selective Sequence Electronic Calculator (SSEC) four years later, rolled out the first of its new series of vacuum-tube scientific computers in 1953, the IBM 701; it would be followed in 1955 by the IBM 650, of which the company would make close to 2,000 in the next seven years.

But it was the development of the semiconductor industry that made possible the computers (and the industry attached to them) that we know today. Vacuum tubes are switches; but so are a set of elements and compounds with the curious property that when you try to pump a small electrical current through them they act as resistors, but turn up the juice and they become very compliant conductors. Such components can be made very, very small, and cheap enough that a state-of-the-art microprocessor can contain well over one and a half billion transistors (of which a simple logic gate requires about 20). Transistors were already in use in a number of wildly successful commercial applications, such as the transistor AM radio, of which one of the earliest was made by Texas Instruments in the early 1950s; they replaced vacuum tubes and computers got smaller and cheaper (the first UNIVAC machines had sold for up to $1.5 million; the IBM 1620, a solid-state, 20-kilobyte-core computer introduced in 1959 and manufactured until 1970, sold for about $90,000 at the company's educational discount). And the development of the integrated-circuit chip brought size prices down even more: The 1620's much-touted successor, the System 360/40, had the same amount of memory—64 kilobytes—as the Commodore 64 desktop computer ordinary consumers were buying for home use just a few years later: The revolution in desktop computing was starting and would transform computers from something understood only by specialists into an everyday commonplace household object used by the whole family.

●

How is it possible, given the variety of manufacturers of computers and software, to have a computer-literate society functioning as a unified system that allows Mary on her Mac to talk to Dennis on his Dell? This is the result of a nesting of languages within languages: The deep structure of any computer's functioning lies ultimately in a machine language of binary digits ("bits" for short)—that is, the strings of zeros and ones—that any computer actually "reads." A programmer can give any given device its input as machine language (and in the earliest days of the "big iron" computers such as UNIVAC I and ENIAC there was no choice), but a computer's assembly language is a meta-language that allows the programmer to say consequential things about machine language, including instructions for common operations, with codenames such as ADD or MULT. This saves a good deal of writing out binary numbers (and lessens the opportunity for error).

Machine language and assembly language are specific to a type of computer; you cannot input the assembly language for your Gateway

PC into a Macintosh and expect results, at least not meaningful ones. (The first axiom in computers is GIGO: garbage in, garbage out.) And in any case, assembly language is still pretty tedious stuff and not particularly user-friendly. Higher-level languages solve this problem; one writes a program in COBOL or FORTRAN II or BASIC or C++ and then runs another program called a compiler, which translates the higher-order language into machine language (sometimes though not always via assembly language) for one's particular device. This allows a much less tedious and more programmer-friendly programming environment and gets everyone through the day without having to crumple up too many sheets of wonky code and throw them in the wastebasket with a colorful oath.

More important is the fact that high-level languages have made possible the sorts of operating systems and accompanying software that are user-friendly to the point of requiring very little sophistication on the user's part as to how a computer actually works. An operating system is control software; it manages the way operations stipulated by other programs are sequenced and mediates access to peripheral devices such as printers and disk drives. The IBM PC, which broke onto the personal computer market at the start of the 1980s, hard on the heels of the Apple IIC (1977) and Hewlett-Packard HP-85, came with an operating system called MS-DOS (or just DOS for short). Acquired by Microsoft from Seattle Computer Products (its original name was QDOS, for "Quick-and-Dirty Operating System), it was retooled to work on IBM's PC. DOS-based software for the PC burgeoned as independent developers saw the potential for business applications given IBM's already strong position in this market. Apple's Macintosh offered a more user-friendly graphic interface, with icons and mouse clicks in place of command-line instructions and carriage return; nevertheless, the business applications for DOS far outnumbered those for the Mac (many banks would still be using them well into the '90s), and Microsoft further widened the market share gap with the introduction of its first Windows operating system in 1985, offering a look and feel similar to the Mac environment while retaining the option to go into DOS for operation of its existing software.

Fundamental to the operation of DOS and Windows was its filing system, 5 to 8 characters+ dot+extension of up to three characters having been the SFN (short file name) convention in DOS prior to support for LFNs (long file names), which eases this constraint. The 5-to-8 part is the *base file name*, and the up-to-three part is the *file extension*, e.g., `autoexec.bat`, `myfile.txt`, or `whatsup.doc`. The 8+3 file name is a feature of the FAT (file allocation table) system design, a file allocation table being a structure supported by various operating systems (including DOS) that contains a variety of information about the files you've written to some storage medium—such as your hard drive, a floppy disk, a CD—that allows the system to locate the file in that medium. Think of an entry in the table as a set of fixed-length fields: For example, in DOS/Windows, these fields include name, size, file type, and modification date and time. The length of the name field in the SFN FAT system is 11 (the dot doesn't count as a character). Long file names can be more than 8 characters for the base file name and more than 3 characters for the file extension.

So, why 8.3? This constraint on file names is a function of the format in which information is represented—stored, accessed, and processed—internally by a computer, the smallest unit being the binary digit (bit), access usually being by the byte (a block of binary digits) or by the word. Nowadays, a word is typically 16, 32, or 64 bits, which may be subdivided into 8-bit bytes. (The term *bit* was credited by Claude F. Shannon in a 1948 paper to John Tukey of Bell Labs who apparently coined the term in 1947; *byte* was coined by Dr. Werner Buchholz of IBM in 1956, a prudent respelling of the originally proposed *bite*, which looked too much like *bit*.) The characters that make up a file name (or any other piece of text) are represented in bits, the conventional encoding system being the American Standard Code for Information Interchange (ASCII); this system's canonical inventory runs from binary 100000 (decimal 32), the space character, to 11111111 (decimal 255, i.e., 2^8-1), the character ÿ—where, reckoning right to left, each digit is an increasing power of 2, starting with 2^0, which has a decimal value of 1. (ASCII inventory has subsequently been extended above decimal 255 to accommodate additional characters. For example, extended ASCII 10000000—decimal 256—is used to represent Ā.)

In the days before IBM's System/360 computer promulgated the 8-bit byte and 16-bit word, and the 8.3 file name length became standard, different computer architectures had supported a variety of word lengths and, as a result, a variety of permissible file name lengths. So a system whose native word length was 36 bits could accommodate base file names of five 7-bit characters (with a bit left over), or base file names of six 6-bit characters plus a 3-character extension. The 6-bit solution entailed some electronic legerdemain: The trick was to subtract 32 from the 7-bit ASCII value before processing (and put it back when the processing was done); this was fine for the uppercase characters (100001 to 1011010—decimal 65 to 90—minus 32 yields 100001 to 111010—decimal 33 to 58) and the characters with lower ASCII values (space, !, $, and so on), but not workable for the lowercase letters, which run from 1100001 to 1111010 (decimal 97 to 122) and which still use 7 bits even when you subtract 32. But since printers of this era could only print uppercase characters and some marks of punctuation, this limitation wasn't really a hardship.

IBM's Systems 360 computer, however, promulgated the 8-bit byte and 16-bit word and the 8.3 file name format, which eventually became standard. Once the word was standardized to 16 bits, it was possible to accommodate an 8-character base file name in three and a half words (8 characters times 7 bits = 56, three and a half words = 56 bits) and a 3-character extension in a word and a half, with a few bits left over for other information about the file. This would continue to be the convention for early versions of Windows and its File Manager module; longer names would be truncated at the seventh character with a tilde for the eighth. Hence the annual Christmas epistle-general ("Ashley graduated with a summa from Dunkin' Donuts University in June and we're all very proud of her; Porcius Cato, our poor old Vietnamese potbelly, having rooted out a bad truffle in March, was called home to Piggy Heaven, sadly missing the graduation," &c.) would either have to be saved as christms.doc or, if one attempted to name it in full, would be automatically renamed christm~.doc. Fortunately, later versions of Windows have abandoned this restriction, and LFNs are now AOK.

Files reside in directories, which may contain subdirectories. Let's suppose we have a file called myfile.doc stored in a subdirectory we'll call otd, in a directory we'll call projects, a subdirectory of a directory we've named mystuff, whose parent is the root directory, C:\ Thus: c:\mystuff\projects\otd\myfile.doc. But DOS provides a number of short-cut mechanisms (borrowed from UNIX) to allow you to navigate up a directory tree toward the root so that you don't have to type such strings any more than necessary: Typing the command chdir (or just plain cd) at the DOS prompt will move you to whatever directory or subdirectory you choose to specify: For example, cd c:\mystuff\projects will take you to the projects subdirectory of the mystuff directory. But if you just want to go to a directory or one or two up the tree, typing cd .. changes the directory to the next one up the tree; cd ../.. will take you two directories up, and cd \. will take you all the way up to the root directory (in this case, C:\).

But why, one might ask, use plain DOS rather than the handy Windows graphical user interface to navigate among files? Well, for one thing, you can execute a set of commands in a file (called a *batch* file) from DOS, something that you simply can't do from the

on the dot

Windows interface. For example, you might use a batch file to compile a report consisting of data stored in multiple files in different directories. To navigate among these directories to those files, you'd use cd dot/slash commands.

●

The retrieval and manipulation of files on one's own system is the key to the difference between actually being able to use one's computer and merely staring at the screen in glassy-eyed bewilderment. But what of other worlds beyond one's desk—our e-mail correspondents, our IM buddies, our newsgroup sparring partners, not to mention our favorite sites on the Internet? Not surprisingly, the dot also plays an important part in the syntax of finding one's way around the Net.

URIs (Uniform Resource Identifiers—originally, Universal Resource Identifiers) and URLs (Uniform Resource Locators—originally, Universal Locators) are sometimes confused because of the similarities in what they are and what their dots delimit. A URI consists of a scheme name (a protocol), such as HTTP, URN, FTP, mailto, or the like, that identifies a set of rules for conveying information over the Internet. The scheme name is followed by the address of the resource—a document, a graphic image, a sound clip, or the like—that you want to locate and possibly additional information about the resource.

A URL is a particular type of URI. In canonic form, a URL consists of the scheme name HTTP—HyperText Transfer Protocol—followed by a colon and two forward slashes (://) followed by the address of the resource to be displayed, liberally sprinkled with dots. This address consists of a domain name possibly followed by the path name to the resource of interest possibly followed by a query (? <keyword> = <value>) or a tag specifying, for example, a particular section of the document that you are trying to locate.

For example, if you enter `http://whatis.techtarget.com/` in your browser's search box and then enter "URL" when the page is displayed, the page defining a URL is displayed at the following URL: `http://searchnetworking.techtarget.com/search/ 1,293876,sid7,00.html?query=url`

Under certain circumstances, you can omit parts of a URL and still locate the resource you want. For example, the system will typically fill in the HTTP:// scheme if you don't include it in the URL. If you don't specify a particular file to locate, the system will typically display the home page for the domain that you have included in the URL. For example, if you type `ibm.com` in your browser's search box, the system will fill in the `HTTP://` scheme, the `/us/` domain, and throw in the prefix `www.` for free (`http://www.ibm.com/us`), and display the IBM Welcome page.

The suffixes of URLs look a lot like filename extensions, and do serve the purpose of distinguishing among types of entities: commercial sites are suffixed `.com` (`.co` in the UK)—and more recently, `.biz` as well; academic institutions are `.edu` (in the UK, `.ac`), and nonprofits generally `.org`; in the United States, at least, governmental entities are suffixed `.gov`, and military ones `.mil`. Pornographers, for whom the Internet has provided audience access unimaginable in the days of printing-press reproduction and nosy vice squads, have sought (so far without success) the creation of a new suffix, `.xxx`, specifically for naughty bits; this terminology originated with the movie rating system under which films considered wholly unsuitable for children and other innocents got rated X.

To locate a networked device or document or send someone e-mail on the Internet, you need to specify an address for that device, document, or e-mail recipient. The concepts of *domain* and *subdomain* come into play with all of these. A *domain* (or subdomain) is a named node in the hierarchical Domain Name System (DNS) tree. For example, in the e-mail address `my_name@us.ibm.com`,

on the dot

com identifies the primary domain under which subdomains designate such a commercial organization, e.g., International Business Machines (ibm), and geographical areas, such as the United States (us); so (DNS root →) com → ibm → us is what the tree looks like in descending order. (A further subdomain might be the Internet node that identifies a given PC; see below.)

Hence the basic format for an electronic mail (e-mail, or, variously, email) address is addressee@subdomain.(subdomain.)domain, so the following examples are correctly formatted e-mail addresses: humezn@mail.montclair.edu, zobi.lamouche@mcgill.ca, or my_name@us.ibm.com. E-mail addresses can also include a name (that the e-mail system doesn't actually use) to remind recipients who the addressee is in case that person's e-mail name is not transparent—for example, "The Rev. Hezekiah Cardinal Pilkington-Thomas" <spintrian@earthlink.net>.

Most e-mail programs these days will let you send e-mail to a list of addresses, which you can either enter by hand on the fly or list in a group in your e-mail address book. However, because of the vexing growth of spam—those unsolicited messages touting everything from someone's new CD recording to myriad forms of sexual gratification—most legitimate servers will limit the number of people you can list in the header of a single message.

It would be a simple matter to retaliate against spammers were it possible to trace them back to their own desktops and mail-bomb them with thousands of copies of their own message. This sort of libertarian vigilantism is officially frowned upon, but a well-founded fear of retaliation has nevertheless led spammers to be increasingly crafty (with the help of increasingly sophisticated software) at the shoot-and-run tactics that have always characterized the guerrilla (whether "insurgent" or "freedom fighter") in an adversarial relationship with an institution (real-life or virtual or a hybrid of both).

In theory, one ought to be able to trace the sender of a message through its header information back to his or her Internet protocol (IP) address, a 32-bit number that uniquely identifies a networked device such as your PC or a VOIP phone. For example, the IP address 192.158.1.91 (= binary 11000000.10011110.00000001.01011011) could uniquely identify one of the authors' PCs (but actually doesn't, because we changed a couple of digits). The address can be static or dynamic—typically, a PC capable of connecting to the Internet is assigned ("leased") a dynamic IP address. A dynamic IP address is so called because it depends on, among other things, the PC's physical location. So, for example, if you're running your laptop at home in Boston, it will be assigned one IP address, but if you fly to Cleveland, it will be assigned a different IP address.

An IP address is typically displayed not in binary notation but, rather, as four decimals separated by dots (*dotted decimal notation*) for easier readability. An IP address is divided into two major components, the Network address and the Host address, that is, the address of the network to which your local device is connected and the local address of the device itself. Which portion of an IP address designates the network and which the local device depends on what used to be called *IP address classes* and are now a function of what's called the *natural mask*. (The nomenclature has changed, but the rules for determining which part of the IP address identifies the network and which the local host are basically the same.) All of this is determined by what's known as a *network prefix*, which can be one, two, or three bits (binary 0, 10, 110), identifying an address as class A, B, or C, respectively. Thus, depending on the prefix, the first byte, the first two bytes, or the first three bytes of the IP address 192.158.1.91 might designate the network address, and the remaining byte(s) would designate the local host address. Bits can be "borrowed" from the local host part of an IP address to identify a *subnet*, which, as the name implies, is an extension of the network portion to accommodate additional host addresses.

on the dot

You can ascertain your PC's IP address by opening the DOS window and typing ipconfig. For example:

```
C:Documents and Settings\zobi lamouche\ipfonfig
Windows IP Configuration
Ethernet adapter Local Area Connection:
Connection-specific DNS Suffix . : cable.rcn.com
IP Address. . . . . . . . . : 192.158.1.91
Subnet Mask . . . . . . . . : 245.245.245.0
Default Gateway . . . . . . : 192.158.1.1
```

The ipconfig command returns four pieces of information about your PC:

- The connection-specific DNS suffix, which identifies the domain that should be searched in the Domain Name System (DNS) for your IP address when you start your PC.

- The PC's IP address, which consists of four eight-bit components, conveniently displayed as decimals separated by dots.

- The subnet mask, which specifies the portion of the subnet address belonging to the network address and the portion set aside for local host addresses.

- The Default Gateway, which identifies a computer (a *node* on the network) that mediates between networks.

123

You can display additional information about your IP configuration by typing ipconfig /all at the DOS prompt. One of the pieces of info that ipconfig /all returns is your PC's Host Name, which is an alphanumeric name that you can use instead of the dotted-decimal

IP address, e.g., the Host Name `zobilamouche` can be used instead of the dotted decimal IP address `192.158.1.91`.

Now if you know a computer's IP address, you can "ping" it to see if it's up and running. The term *ping* is from sonar, onomatopoeia for the sound a detector makes when the signal it sends out bounces back and is received by the sender; the program to do this was written and named by Mike Mauss at Berkeley in 1983.

For example, if you ping the computer whose IP address is 192.158.1.91 and that computer is up and running, you should see the following:

```
C:\Documents and Settings\zobi lamouche\ping
192.158.1.91
Pinging 192.158.1.91 with 32 bytes of data:
Reply from 192.158.1.91: bytes=32 time=68ms
TTL=128
Reply from 192.158.1.91: bytes=32 time=1ms
TTL=128
Reply from 192.158.1.91: bytes=32 time=12ms
TTL=128
Reply from 192.158.1.91: bytes=32 time=2ms
TTL=128
Ping statistics for 192.158.1.91:
Packets: Sent = 4, Received = 4, Lost = 0 (0% loss),
Approximate round trip times in milli-seconds:
Minimum = 1ms, Maximum = 68ms, Average = 20ms
```

A *packet* is a block of bits constituting a segment of a longer block. A message (such as a request to ascertain whether a computer is up and running) is broken up into packets for faster transmission and then reassembled at the message's destination. Occasionally, one

on the dot

or more packets may go astray, in which case, you'll be so informed, and you can try again. Ditto if you ping a networked computer that is not up and running: your request will return a message that your request has timed out.

•

The various travel times that a ping returns are all integers—for example, the time it took the first packet to make its journey in the preceding example was 60 milliseconds. This is not to suggest that a computer's central processing unit (CPU) is incapable of representing and manipulating fractions in binary form—presumably, you don't really care if a packet took 67.7 milliseconds to travel, 68 being close enough. There are, of course, plenty of situations in which you *do* want to deal with fractions. Modern computing offers a number of ways of handling fractions, two of which—fixed-point and floating-point arithmetic—are worth a quick look here.

The fixed-point representation of a fraction (or, more properly, a *real* number) is so called because the position of the character that separates the integer part from the fractional part of the number is fixed. (In English decimal notation, this character, known as the *radix point*, is a dot; in countries where a comma separates the integer part from the fractional part, the radix point is a comma.) The integer and fractional parts are also fixed in the sense that each has a set number of bits allocated to represent it, but that's a constraint shared by other representational systems and not peculiar to fixed-point notation (see below).

In fixed-point binary notation, a number consists of a series of bits representing the integer part of the number, the radix point, and another series of bits representing the fractional part of the number (called the *mantissa*). The position of the radix point determines the

125

degree of precision you'll get when you add two numbers together. For example, if your system allocates enough storage space for a 10-digit number, the radix point is between the eighth and ninth digit, so if you want to add 100,000.257 to 25,000.989, you'll get 125,001.25 (rather than 125,001.246). If you had been dealing with dollars and cents, placing the radix point before the last two digits would have been fine and dandy, as indeed it was for many early users who were not dealing with large sums or minute fractions. Floating-point representation was subsequently devised for those users who needed more flexibility—and greater precision—in dealing with very large and very small numbers.

The concept of the floating point was introduced to the world of computers very early, but it took a while to become widely adopted. Konrad Zuse, a German engineer working for Hermann Goering's Air Ministry, constructed a computer called the Z4, which used binary numbers and electromechanical switches (laying hands on the requisite 2000 vacuum tubes in wartime Germany was impossible). Its input was punched movie film (analogous to the punched tape used by Harvard's Mark I and a number of the other "Big Iron" machines well into the '50s). It could multiply two numbers in three and a half seconds, and add them in a third of that. The Z4 also could deal with infinite values without crashing and included a null operation as one of its commands, which turned out to be very handy later on as programming became more sophisticated. But by far its most interesting feature from a programming standpoint was its use of floating-point decimals.

Floating point arithmetic takes the desired number of significant digits of a number and expresses them as multiples of some exponent of the base in which the calculations are to take place. This allows the manipulation of numbers in a wide range of sizes expressed exponentially: "1,705,000 times .003145" becomes $.1705 \times 10^7$ times $.3145 \times 10^{-2}$. The advantage to this sort of notation is that a number can be expressed parsimoniously in the form $\pm M \times R^e$ (where R is the *radix*, or base: We use base 10; computers use base 2), the first bit indicating whether the non-exponential part of the number, called the *mantissa* (*M* for short in the formula above), is positive or negative; a second set of bits (a fixed number of them) gives the exponent, and the third set of bits is the mantissa, to however many places it has been allowed (also fixed). If the latter has four digits, then the value for π we'll get by with for the duration of this calculation is going to have to be $.3142 \times 10^{-1}$, but if everything else we're working with is down to four significant digits too, that's not going to present any serious problems—and the resulting calculations just got a lot faster, because fewer actual bits are needed. A supercomputer can perform over hundreds of millions of floating point operations per second (called FLOPs for short).

•

No matter how they handle fractions (nowadays mostly as floating-point), it is now common for programming and scripting languages to use dot notation to show that one type of entity belongs to another—*x.y* signifies that *x* is a member of *y*. For example, the C language uses a dot to signify that what follows is a member of a *structure*. A structure is a compound data type consisting of a set of members. Some brief examples follow.

A program in the language C might contain the declaration of a `structure` template to describe information about books:

```
struct books
    {
    char author
    char title
    float listprice
    }
```

The program would presumably then declare "books" variables, that is, instances of the "books" template, store them in a collection (called an *array*, which may be likened to a filing cabinet with a drawer for each "books" variable), and assign the members of each variable a value using the format *variable[index].member = value*:

```
struct books
    {
    char author
    char title
    float listprice
    }
main()
    {
    struct books inventory[100];
    inventory[0].author = Galván and Teschner
    inventory[0].title = Dictionary of
    Chicano Spanish
    inventory[0].listprice = 12.95
    inventory[1].author = Humez and Humez
    inventory[1].title = Latina Pro Populo
    inventory[1].listprice = 13.95
    inventory[2].author = Musciano and Kennedy
    inventory[2].HTML: The Definitive Guide
    inventory[2].listprice = 34.95
    /* and so on */
    /* code to manipulate these values goes
    here. */
    }
```

The Java programming language makes somewhat more elaborate use of dots in identifying members of a package hierarchy (for example, java.lang.String), a *package* being a collection of Java classes (such as the String and Character classes, which are contained in the java.lang.String package), a *class* being a template which, when instantiated, provides an object for a Java program to manipulate. Classes typically contain member variables and procedures (called *methods*) that perform a variety of functions.

In the following code snippet, the integer variable len is declared, an instance (firstthree) of the String class is created, and the String class's length() method is invoked to assign the number of characters in firstfive to len.

```
...
int len;
java.lang.String.String firstfive = new String
("abcde");
len = firstfive.length();
...
```

Actually, instead of writing out the full name of the package in which the String class resides, the Java programmer would use the shortcut provided by the import keyword:

```
import java.lang.*;
.........
public int len;
String firstfive = new String("abcde");
len = firstfive.length();
............
```

The *scripting language* JavaScript is not, whatever its name might imply, a simplified version of the Java *programming language*, though the two languages share a number of concepts and terms, such as *object* and *method*, and the use of dot notation to show membership hierarchy. For example, to close the current window using JavaScript, you use the `close()` method of the Window object: `window.close(self)`. To determine the date on which the document in the current window was most recently modified, you can retrieve the value of the Document object's `lastModified` property and assign it to a variable:

```
moddate = document.lastModified
```

●

130

And then there is the dot in the naming of software versions—e.g., SoftWeasel 1.0, 1.0.1, 1.0.1.1; 2.0 (initial release; a fix-'em-up release/a point release; a further fix-'em-up to the previous fix-'em-up/point release; new version). A good rule of thumb is never to buy any software that begins with a 1, as it is bound to be really buggy and you'll have the heartbreak of upgrading later (assuming that the product is still supported). Lots of folks in business get the 1.x version to play with but are usually smart enough not to use it for serious production work, especially as the company that created the product may dump it if it turns out to be a dud (or the company burns through its venture capital and goes belly-up). We had such an experience in the days when Radio Shack was selling its Tandy 386 series (it ran Windows 3.x) and we bought one, along with the desktop publishing software with which we were to produce the quarterly newsletter for a small nonprofit we were helping to get up and running.

Marvelous software it was, too, easy to use and producing pages that quite credibly emulated the look and feel of the daily papers. The only problem was that the program crashed very easily, sometimes taking down the current Windows session with it. Finally we called the manufacturer's 800 number for support, only to find that the product had been sold to another company. We called *that* number and got a friendly and eager-to-help support technician who asked us what version of the software we were running. "One point Oh," we answered. There was a hear-a-pin-drop silence of about two seconds at the end of the line, and then the voice came back, this time with a calming tone such as might be used to coax a person of unsound mind back indoors off a window ledge: "Ah...why don't we just send you Version 3.2?" And he did.

131

bang!

The dot meets the family

The dot is an indispensable component of more punctuation marks than just itself alone (the subject of our final chapter). Conventional signs that include a dot are the colon (:), semicolon (;), ellipsis (...), question mark (?—and, for Spanish, its upside down version, ¿), and exclamation point (!—and its inversion in Spanish, ¡). (There are some unconventional signs as well, current out to the edges of a given epistemic community but not yet in general use beyond the pale; we'll get to them a little later on. For everything you ever wanted to know about the ellipsis, turn back to "Dot Dot Dot.")

Colon is a Latin transliteration of Greek *kōlon* (κωλον), 'limb, member, clause of a sentence.' The Latin equivalent is *membrum*, which Roman grammarians and rhetoricians used more or less interchangeably with *colon* in all its senses above. Grammarians for centuries tried their hands at offering a clear definition of just what a *colon/membrum* was as a unit of discourse and how it differed from its two companions, the *comma* and the *periodus* (borrowings of the

Greek rhetorical terms κόμμα and περίοδος, respectively), the three terms forming a boxed set describing the sentence and its rhetorical constituents.

Aristophanes of Byzantium, a librarian at Alexandria around 200 B.C.E., is credited with inaugurating the practice of marking accents on the words in Greek manuscripts (indicating correct intonation and stress for an increasingly non-Greek-speaking readership, including newly Hellenophile upper-class Romans trying to write properly scanned Greek poetry). But more important, he also put dots in the text to indicate short, medium, and long pauses—in effect, the three types of *distinctiones* adopted by the Romans as well. The raised center-position dot—we would nowadays call it an *interpunct*—thus served in place of the semicolon, there being no colon mark as such. It was only a millennium later—in the eighth to ninth century C.E.—that the semicolon symbol was introduced as the Greek form of the question mark (see below).

134

Three centuries later, in his nuts-and-bolts how-to book for Roman public speakers, the *Institutio Oratoria*, Quintilian would write that a *comma* was part of a *membrum*, and a *membrum* was contained by a *periodus*. The Roman term for what we call punctuation marks is *positurae* ('the things that are going to be placed,' i.e., in your text), by no means a bad way of describing them; hitherto texts were written without any punctuation at all and often with the words run in and no spaces between them. (The Romans experimented with putting middle dots between words—a feature surviving in public inscriptions and in the legends around the rims of coins in at least some countries down to the present day—but gave it up after a couple of centuries.)

The argument for punctuation raised by two treatises of about 350 C.E., both entitled *De Posituris* (one was by Diomedes, the other by Donatus), was that at least that way you knew where to take a breath. (Reading, after all, was something one did out loud, even if nobody else was listening; in the next century, St. Augustine of Hippo could write, with obvious admiration, of the singular ability of St. Ambrose (d. 397) to read without moving his lips.) Diomedes taxonomized the divisions of sentences into *distinctio*—today's equivalent would be our sentence proper, with a full stop at the end, indicated by a high dot—the *media* ('middle') *distinctio* or *mora* ('delay'), followed by a middle dot, and the *subdistinctio*, with a dot at the base line where our period would be today. Donatus likewise observed the threefold division and explained it very clearly, too: "*Distinctio* is when a sentence completely terminates: We place this dot above the last letter. *Subdistinctio* is when not much of the sentence has been completed but it's necessary to mark a certain separation: This dot is placed at the level of the base of the letter. *Medio distinctio* is when much of the sentence has been said, and it is necessary to breathe: The dot is placed at the level of the middle of the [last] letter. In reading, the complete sentence is called *periodus*, and its parts are the *cola* and the *commata*."

As a mark of punctuation, the colon as we know it evolved from the *media distinctio*. The system of dots for marking the ends of the *comma*, *colon*, and *period* eventually gave way to a new system of punctuation, which began to evolve in the 14th–15th century (and is still arguably still evolving). One of the new marks of punctuation was the *punctus elevatus* which, in one or another of its forms, gradually replaced the *medio distinctio* as the sign of the end of a *colon/membrum*. With little effort, the *punctus elevatus* eventually morphed into the colon that English and other modern European languages use today. The German for colon is *Doppelpunkt* ('double-point'); in French it's *deux-points* (treated, interestingly enough, as a singular), and in Spanish, *dos puntos*.

Ben Jonson's posthumously published *The English Grammar* tackled what he called "the Distinction of Sentences." Jonson contrasts *perfect sentences*—that is, sentences that can stand as complete—with *imperfect sentences* and says that the latter can be subdivided into

135

subdistinctions and *commas.* "A subdistinction," he writes, "is a mean breathing, when the word serveth indifferently, both to the parts of the sentence going before and following after, and is marked thus (;)." He goes on to say that "[t]he distinction of a *perfect* sentence hath a more full stay, and doth rest the spirit.... A pause is a distinction of a sentence, though perfect in itself, yet joined to another, being marked thus with two pricks (:)."

A number of things have happened to the colon since then. First, it has crisscrossed the semicolon in usage, so that either mark can now be followed by an incomplete sentence, and has come to mark a descending hierarchy of importance, such that in standard English what comes after a colon is now expected to be derived in some way from what came before. (Examples might be "Please don't touch that dial: Our sponsor has an important announcement" and "I'll tell you what he's getting for Christmas: a lump of coal.") Second, as the literacy of the English-speaking world has generally risen, there has been a concomitant drift away from thinking about punctuation as a mere aid to pronunciation and toward viewing punctuation marks as syntactic indicators that might or might not have corollaries in spoken discourse.

Third, the colon has been borrowed for a number of uses that are distinctly *not* uses of punctuation (unless we define "punctuation" rather loosely). In arithmetic, a colon can denote a ratio, such as 3:2, or by extension, 2:4::4:8—whence its adoption beyond mathematics to represent various sorts of analogies: gold:sun::silver:moon, woman:man::fish:bicycle, *ellbeejay*:Indochina::*dubya*:Mesopotamia, or *chant*:song::*mer*:sea. Unicode allows you to distinguish between the sign used in a mathematical ratio and the regular colon (∶ [U+2236] vs. : [U+003A]) should you care to do so.

The colon turns up in Computerese as well; three examples may be mentioned, the first two of which are drawn from the Pascal programming language. In Pascal, a colon is used when you declare a variable—as in variable: data type, e.g., VAR COST : REAL; (the semicolon is part of the declaration), which declares the variable COST as a decimal fraction. The subsequent statement COST := 2.5 (variable := value) assigns the value 2.5 to the variable COST.

In the C programming language, however, the colon has a rather different function: Here it signals the final clause in a conditional expression. In the following example, if the statement some_integer_variable > 0 (is greater than zero) evaluates to "true," print the string "Greater than zero." and otherwise print the string "Zero or less." That is, if the statement some_integer_variable > 0 evaluates to "true," make "Greater than zero" the second argument of the printf() function (the first argument being the specification "%s," which signals that the other argument is to be written as a string), and otherwise make "Zero or less" the second argument of the function. So:

```
int some_integer_variable;
some_integer_variable = some number;
printf("%s," (some_integer_variable > 0) ?
"Greater than zero." : "Zero or less.");
```

Note the use of the question mark (?) to mark the first result. (We shall say more about question marks below.)

Not really a colon (though in 12-point type it looks like one): the International Phonetic Alphabet marker for vowel length (Unicode U+02D0), as in [aː], though a colon is what you'll see in pre-Unicode transcriptions. The upper triangle without the lower one is used to mark vocalic half length.

And the comma? Not a spinoff of any of the three heights of dots at all, it arose in medieval textbooks from the substitution of the *virgule* (/) for the high dot, the slash gradually getting smaller until it was just

bang!

a dot with a left-trailing tail hanging from the base line. (Not for nothing is *virgule* the French word for comma to this day.) The apostrophe, which looks for all the world like a comma except for being in high position rather than low, is actually much older—the librarian Aristophanes mentions it—as a curve or squiggle to indicate elision. In English it would come in handy when the possessive ending -*es* (as in *Goddes son*) ceased to be pronounced as a separate syllable (>*God's son*)—compare its use in such contractions as *can't*, *I'm*, and *it's*.

As the only obvious remnant of the original English case system outside the pronouns (where the distinctions of nominative, possessive, dative, and objective case remain hale and hearty: *I* was told to clean out *my* desk by the Human Resources hatchetperson who handed *me* my pink slip, but I'm sure someone will hire *me* tomorrow), the apostrophe has been the source of confusion for children and grown-ups alike who understand well enough that it signifies possession but aren't exactly sure where a particular apostrophe should go, or whether there should be an *s* after it. (Let's see, is that *Socrates'* or *Socrates's?* And what about the possessive plural of *Humez?* Oh, yes, and what about *its?*)

In addition, the apostrophe has been dragooned into service as the marker before final s to indicate the plural of words that don't usually have one, where there would be confusion without it (as in *o's*), perniciously giving rise (particularly in vernacular outdoor signage) to spurious plurals that are all too easy misread as possessives instead: the roadside mailboxes for *The Carter's* or *The Jones'* at the homes of the Carters and Joneses or the city whose parks departments posts notices reading *Do Not Feed the Pigeon's.*

●

Editors tend to pounce on sentences with *semicolons* and ruthlessly red-pencil them; both teachers and professional proofreaders may grind their teeth when confronted with strings of phrases separated by semicolons where ordinary serial commas will serve quite unambiguously: "the Trojan War; the War of Thonder-ten-Tronck; the War of the Spanish Succession; the War of Jenkins's Ear; the War of 1812; the Spanish-American War; the Gulf War." But a semicolon can be used quite properly to separate two halves of a sentence each of which could stand as a sentence on its own, but of which the second follows logically from the first. The French for semicolon is *point et virgule* ('period-comma'; compare Spanish *punto y coma*); the German is *Semikolon* or *Strichpunkt*. (*Strich* has a variety of meanings: 'stroke,' 'line,' 'dash,' 'mark,' 'nipple' [in Swiss German], and "compass point.")

Semicolon literally means 'half a colon'; it's the mark of punctuation that offers a compromise between the comma and the colon in terms of both oral pause and syntactic subdivision. While the sign had been in use for five hundred years as a question mark for Greek (see above) and Old Church Slavonic, the pioneering printer Aldus Manutius (Aldo Manuzio) the Elder was the first printer to use it (in an edition of Pietro Bembo's *De Ætna* he published in 1494) for its present Western European purpose as a separator of statements dependent on each other (as in "The prayers ascend; the excrement falls down"). Its first use in English is 1591 and as noted above, its systematic use was explained by Ben Jonson in his book on English grammar published half a century later.

The semicolon has been playfully described as "a comma on steroids," and in its defense it must be said that it can be a helpful tool in setting boundaries between phrases that require their own internal commas: "My freshman roommate claimed that he got pulled over seven times for speeding—in Albion, Maine; Rochester, New Hampshire; Athol, Massachusetts; Thomaston, Connecticut; Haverstraw, New York; Somerville, New Jersey; and King of Prussia, Pennsylvania—within a single weekend, and got off with no more than a warning each time." Nevertheless, semicolons are best reserved for parallel constructions, as in "*Veni, vidi, vici* means 'I came; I saw; I conquered'" or the classic bogus syllogism "That which you have not lost, you have; you have not lost a horn; therefore, you have the horn." While three or more such "perfect sentences" (in Jonson's parlance) may be separated by semicolons, the usual number is two, making it a valued component of many a binary gag: "I'd like to help you out; which way did you come in?" "In God we trust; all others pay cash." "My cousin likes work; he can sit and watch it for hours." "Jane runs the marathon; Dave runs the dishwasher." "Jesus saves; Moses invests."

In mathematics, a semicolon can be used to separate variables from parameters in the argument part of a function, as in $f(x_1, x_2, \ldots; a_1, a_2, \ldots)$; here it is a delimiter not unlike the semi between recipients in the address fields of some e-mail programs. The symbol also turns up in differential geometry: A semicolon before an index indicates a covariant derivative of a function of the coordinate associated with that index. Here the semicolon is being used as a symbol in its own right rather than a syntactic marker.

Several programming languages use the semicolon to mark the end of a statement, as in the following Java example, where statements declaring the integer variables year_of_birth and year_of_hire are terminated by semicolons:

```
Class myClass
{
        public static void main (String args[])
        {
                int year_of_birth;
                int year_of_hire;
                //etc.
        }
}
```

on the dot

Here's another example, in Perl:

```perl
#! /usr/bin/perl-w
#Elicit input from the user by printing a
#request for same.
print "What is your home town?";
#Assign user input to the variable $town.
town$ = <STDIN>;
#Remove the newline character (\n) that comes
#as part of the user's input.
chomp($town);
#Print "You said your home town was" + whatever
#the user typed + a newline character.
print "You said your home town was $town.\n";
```

The first line beginning with the comment character (#) announces that the following is a Perl script that should be compiled with the −w switch, which turns on extra warnings about potential problems in the script.

•

The *exclamation point*—colorfully called by printers in America a *bang* or *screamer*, and in the United Kingdom a *pling*—is said to have been invented by Iacopo Alpoleio da Urbisaglia, and there is at least an apocryphal tradition that it is simply a superimposing of the I and O of the Latin exclamation *Io!* (as in the Roman end-of-the-year Feast of Fools cry, *Io Saturnalia!*), though a tamer alternative has been proposed: that it is shorthand for *interiectio*, "interjection." It was formerly known in English as *note* or *mark of admiration* (a straight-forward translation of Iacopo's term *punctus admirativus*), acquiring its present English name in the middle of the 17th century.

bang!

For the most part this sign is used pretty much the same in all the European languages—that is, to mark surprise or astonishment, or as the final mark of an actual exclamation or sudden noise ("Gee, Dad, it's a Wurlitzer!" "Oh look—a ship, in the air!" "Whoah, Nellie!" "Ka-POW!") but there are some subtle variants: In German, an exclamation point may follow the salutation in a letter, where English would use a comma, colon, or dash: *Liebster Fritz!* ('Dearest Fritz—'); and in German and French it follows imperatives that would not necessarily have an exclamation point in English: *Wachet auf, ruft uns die Stimme!* ('Wake up; the voice is calling us.'); *Allez-vous-en!* ('Go away'). Note the space between the last word and the exclamation point; this is also standard French practice with the question mark, semicolon, and colon. As with the question mark (see below), an inverted exclamation point has been standard punctuation introducing Spanish interjections since the 18th century.

The fact that dialogue balloons in comic books may seem to have an awful lot of exclamation points in them says at least something about the whiz-bang nature of plot and dialogue in this artistic genre, but a more practical reason is that printers in the early 19th century, using the workaday offset presses of the time, found that periods by themselves tended to disappear, while exclamation points remained largely legible. As a speech or thought balloon item by itself, the exclamation point serves to indicate surprise (as the question mark alone can indicate perplexity). For what it's worth, punctuation maven Lynn Truss (*Eats, Shoots, and Leaves*, p. 135) reports that women use more exclamation points in writing than do men.

The International Phonetic Alphabet uses what looks like an exclamation point for the so-called tongue click (strictly speaking, a postalveolar click) of such speakers as the !Kung people of the Kalahari desert in southern Africa, of whose language it is a conspicuous feature. (To distinguish this from the ordinary exclamation point—alt-0033 or Unicode U+0021—this character has its own Unicode formula, U+01C3.) The exclamation point was also formerly used to represent a glottal stop, but nowadays this is represented by an apostrophe or a raised glottal stop symbol itself (ʔ).

The exclamation point is also used as the sign meaning "factorial" in mathematics ($4! = 1 \times 2 \times 3 \times 4 = 24$), while some programming languages (e.g., C and Java) use $! =$ to mean "not equal," and the mark-up language HTML uses it as part of the mark-up element that introduces a code comment (thus: <!--My comment goes here and ends here-->). In chess—as pastimes go, a perennial favorite in the technological community—"!" after the notation of a move indicates that it was a good one ("P × Kt!") and two of them an exceptional one ("Kt × Q!!").

●

The *question mark* (a.k.a. *query sign*) was until the 19th century exclusively called an interrogation point (Latin *punctus interrogativus*). Its origin has been variously given as (1) the abbreviation q° for *quaestio*, (2) a neume derived from medieval music notation indicating the intonation with which a question concludes, or (3) a point with a slated tilde-like curve (or "lightning squiggle") tacked on, first appearing in the manuscripts of Charlemagne's close adviser, the scholarly monk Alcuin of York. Whatever its provenance, the question mark was in general use by the ninth century.

The upside-down question mark that introduces a question in Spanish (and the upside-down exclamation point that introduces an exclamation) "developed in the second half of the 18th century," according to Sebastián Mediavilla: "In books printed before that time, the general practice was followed of putting a question mark only at the end of a sentence. At its meeting on March 5, 1739, the Real Academia Española decided to establish some general rules of Spanish orthography and, in 1741, published a treatise on that subject." The Academia took up the question of punctuation as well, declaring in the second edition of the treatise (1754) that

> "after lengthy examination, it has appeared to the Academia that one can use the same sign of interrogation, inverting it before the word that has the first interrogative intonation, in addition to using the regular question mark to signal the end of the clause, thereby avoiding the ambiguity resulting from a lack of any sign that poses a common problem when reading long sentences...."

The *punctus exclamativus* or *admirativus* was treated the same way. Following its own prescription, the Academia put this into practice in the books published under its auspices, and other publishers eventually followed suit.

In computing, ? can be used as, among other things, a wild card typically meaning "single or no character" as in the following Lotus-Script script fragment, which elicits your last name and uses the wild card ? to ascertain whether your surname is Manuzio or Manuzius (or, actually, *Manu* + [any character or no character] + *i* + [one, two, or no characters]), such that if there's a match, the number of publishers is incremented by 1:

```
Sub Click(Source As Buttoncontrol)
    Dim yoursurname As String
    Dim publisher As Integer
    yoursurname$ = Inputbox$("Type your last
    name.")
```

on the dot

```
If yoursurname$ = "Manu?i?? Then
     Publisher% = Publisher%+1
```

•

Conventional in one of its functions, but decidedly on the fringe in another, is the *point d'ironie* (first promulgated in 1899 by a French poet, Alcanter de Brahm, in his *L'ostensoir des ironies*) for expressions not meant to be taken at face value. It is virtually identical to the existing character for the question mark in Arabic (؟), whose mirroring of the Roman-alphabet query mark is a logical consequence of the language reading right to left.

Other Gallic proposals for new punctuation marks have been more far-fetched. Jacques Rouxel's animated TV series *Les Shadoks* proposed the *point d'appréciation*, an exclamation point whose top **145** has ballooned out to an open triangle standing on its vertex with a dot underneath, while Hervé Bazin, in his whimsical book *Plumons l'oiseau* ('*Let's Pluck the Bird*'), made a case for rational spelling (why, for example, shouldn't the French for "bird," *oiseau*, be spelled *wazo*, he wondered) and more context-sensitive punctuation, such as the *point d'amour* ('love mark'), "two question marks looking at each other that form a sort of heart," *point de certitude* ('certainty mark')—an exclamation point whose top forms a tiny cross)—*point d'autorité* ('authority mark'), which he says "settles onto your sentence like a sultan's parasol," and *point d'acclamation*, which looks like two exclamation points sharing a common dot, with one slanting forward and the other back, "the stylized representation of the two flags they stick on top of buses when there's a visiting head of state."

Probably the oddest work on punctuation ever written is Julien Blaine's *Reprenons la ponctuation à zéro (0)*, which has much more the look and feel of a dada/surrealist book of the Paris "banquet years" than the sober appearance of a scholarly monograph, but which

bang!

promotes some signs plausible enough to be taken seriously, such as the "poetry mark" (*point de poésie*). A sign that started out unconventional but has advanced into some sort of respectability is the *interrobang* (‽) the hybrid of exclamation point and question mark first published by its inventor, Martin K. Speckter, in the magazine *TYPETalks* in 1962. (It is most useful—Mr. Speckter might argue, indispensable—in such expressions as would formerly have been punctuated thus: "What the—!?" or "You want it *when?!*") Despite being panned by one national magazine as the silliest punctuation mark of the year and being adopted willy-nilly as the title of an Oberlin College humor magazine in the 1970s, it has now become at least conventional enough that there are extended-ASCII and Unicode symbols for it. It has also been adopted as the logo of the Partnership for a Drug-Free America.

146   Likewise unconventional, but at least drifting well into mainstream use, are emoticons, the combinations of characters that draw the little icons we insert in our text to signal the emotion that one would detect in a face-to-face interaction, drawing on pitch, stress, facial expressions, and other body language, evidence that is either completely absent from type-based electronic communication or may be ambiguous of interpretation, such as the original *smiley*, originally represented sideways as a colon plus a closing parenthesis—:)—and subsequently formalized as an ASCII character all its own in certain fonts (in Wingdings ☺ is what you get when you type the capital letter J, and is one of three smileys offered in the font, the others being properly a frownie and a straightie, i.e., neither smiling nor frowning). The list of ASCII emoticons has spread like a stand of bamboo to include specialty characters for particular online communities and their areas of interest, such as __/)- for '(gone) sailing,' (_:-(|) and @@@@ :-) for 'Homer and Marge Simpson,' .\/ for 'duck' (the bird, not the verb), (oYo) for 'Wonder Bra bosom,' : /) for 'not amused' (i.e., 'nose out of joint'), and (#(# | for 'spanked bottom.'

on the dot

Although *emoticon* has also come to refer to the actual icons of smileys, a wide variety of which are available as free downloads for use in html-friendly e-mail programs, it seems unlikely that the creation of new images from combinations of keyboard characters will stop any time soon.

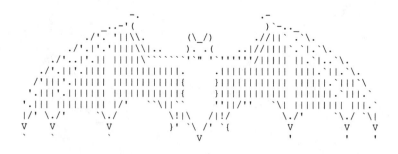

period

the end point

The dot as period pervades our writing, inconspicuous in itself but decisive in the way it marks the end of declarative sentences and tells us, when we're reading them to other people, when to let our voices drop and take in some air. Making written thoughts more intelligible to readers and their listeners is something all punctuation marks do, as we have seen in the previous chapter, but this is especially true for the period. Remove the first five periods from this chapter and this paragraph becomes a syntactic thicket in whose tangles we can no longer easily guess where one sentence ends and another begins. With the periods in place, the meaning snaps into much sharper focus. And the text on the page now cues us when to pause (and for how long) if the text on the page is to be spoken out loud.

Since Roman manuscripts usually had no punctuation and little if any space between words, once the practice of writing dots between words fell into disuse by the end of the first century C.E., most texts for the next four hundred years were in what the Romans called *scripta continua* (*theeffectofwhichmaybeseeninthisparenthetical*)—which hardly made for easy reading, as Quintilian noted in his *Institutio Oratoria*. Not surprisingly, errors of sense were legion; even so skilled a grammarian as Donatus could (and did) misread Vergil's phrase *collectam exilio* ('gathered in exile') as *collectam ex Ilio* ('gathered from Ilium,' i.e., from Troy).

Nevertheless, educated Romans knew about Aristophanes of Byzantium's little marks (see previous chapter), or at least grasped the idea behind them, and occasionally would annotate their own copies of manuscripts for easier reading aloud. Such a text was called *distinctus* (that is, one in which the *distinctiones* were marked, showing where one should make a short pause, a medium pause, or a long one); a letter from the second-century orator and philologist Marcus Cornelius Fronto promises his correspondent, one Volumnius Quadratus, copies of some of Cicero's works punctuated (*distincti*) by Fronto himself. Yet for Fronto to make a special point of saying this underscores the fact that in his day, such texts were the exception rather than the rule.

We have already seen in the previous chapter ("Bang!") how the period, colon, and comma came to be distinguished from one another as the marks signifying Donatus's three types of *distinctio*. More to the point, punctuation itself by Isidore of Seville's day (i.e., the seventh century C.E.) had come to be accepted as a necessary evil at worst, and at best a great help to intelligibility. The term *periodus* for the mark of punctuation, as distinct from the quantity of text it terminates (that is, the sentence) does not turn up in Latin for another five hundred years (its first appearance in a British manuscript is in 1267), and in English the earliest attestation in the *Oxford English Dictionary* is 1609.

At that time *period* was still being used interchangeably with 'sentence,' a word current in English in its modern grammatical meaning since mid-15th century; *sentence* in all its senses comes from Latin *sententia*, 'maxim, sentiment, saying,' derived from the verb *sentiire*, 'feel, think, sense.' The French word for 'sentence' is *phrase*, whose

English cognate designates instead a part of a sentence—such as a *clause*, from Latin *clausula* (in turn from the verb *claudere*, 'to close'), the term for the ending of a periodic sentence or a line of verse, especially when talking about its rhythm.

As previously mentioned ("Bang!"), *period* comes from Greek—*peri* ('around') plus *hodos* ('road, way')—and originally meant a circuit that one traveled around. It is in this sense of a path that returns to its starting point that *period* has amassed its wealth of figurative meanings in English (and in other European languages as well): the period of a decimal fraction (e.g., 1/24, whose decimal equivalent is 0.037037...and whose period,...037..., repeats ad infinitum); the periodicity of variable-magnitude stars (such as the Cepheid variables), whose cycle from brightest to dimmest and back is a function of their absolute magnitude; the periodic table, in which atoms of elements in the same column have the same number of electrons in their outer shells; the menstrual period, which usually comes to women of reproductive age in sufficiently consistent intervals month to month that they may regard a significant deviation with joy or alarm, depending on whether they are hoping to get pregnant or not.

In the examples above, the subtext seems to be that what goes around comes around, and predictably so. But we also use *period* to refer to an isolated interval of time of some consistent nature throughout, whether cyclic or just a one-shot deal sandwiched between two periods of a different character: Pablo Picasso's Blue Period (as distinct from his Rose Period); the decreasing frequency of King George's periods of lucidity; a period of peace between the two World Wars; the speculative period abruptly terminated by the stock market crash of 1929; the period of liberalization under *glasnost* ushered in by Mikhail Gorbachev. All of these share the characteristics of having a limited time span and a recognizable finish (like a well-formed sentence), even if one cannot necessarily pin down the definitive starting point.

Point is French for 'period' qua punctuation mark; like its English cognate, it comes from Latin *punctum* ('pinprick'), itself the neuter form of the past participle of the versatile verb *pungere*, 'to prick, stab.' *Punctum* had a variety of analogous meanings as well, such as 'mark resembling a puncture, dot, or spot,' 'spot (pip) on one of a pair of dice,' 'geometrical point, especially the center of a circle,' 'point marked on a scale,' and 'speck or other infinitesimal portion of space'—*puncto* (the ablative case) having the adverbial sense of 'by a hair's breadth.'

In geometry, a point really is infinitesimal: It has no dimensions. It does, however, occupy (and occupy exclusively) a place in n-dimensional space that can be stipulated in reference to a particular graph in a two-dimensional space; we could say, for example, that the parabolas graphing the equations $X^2 = Y$ and $2X^2 = Y$ share a single point with coordinates $X = 0$ and $Y = 0$—that is, the origin, the point where the X axis and Y axis cross. An infinite number of points side by side make a *line*, stretching straight to infinity in either direction. A *half-line* starts with a given point and goes to infinity in only one direction; it is to be distinguished from a *ray*, which is a half-line minus its initial point. The Scholastics' proverbial question about how many angels could dance on the end of a pin was talking about just this sort of point.

In fact, the medieval cathedral universities had lots of pointy bits: Just down the hall from the theologians, we might find the cathedral singers wrestling in the chapel with a tough little bit of choral counterpoint—*punctus contra punctum* meaning 'point against point,' i.e., note against note. In the background, the wall glistens with fresh plaster over which a draftsman has laid a cartoon whose thin paper has been pricked through along the lines of a drawing to be transferred to the wall by *pouncing*—tapping the cartoon lightly with a little porous sack with colored chalk, and leaving a dotted-line sketch

on the dot

as a guide for what the artist will paint when he comes to do that section of fresco later that day.

Glaziers use *glaziers' points* to hold glass into a frame before applying window putty; in their simplest form they are triangular, one vertex being shoved or tapped home and the other two corners and one side flat against the glass they overlap. We speak disparagingly of religions that seek to convert infidels *at the point of the sword*. When Benjamin Franklin and others first proposed putting lightning rods on steeples and other eminences in Boston in the mid-18th century, the idea met with surprising resistance from those who thought that the "little points," as they were called, sought to frustrate God's will in sending lightning to strike wheresoever it might please Him. Any place on a shoreline where the land sticks out into the water a bit is apt to be called a *point*; a count of such names along the Maine coast turns up more than two dozen named points between Blue Hill and Prospect Harbor alone (including two Haynes Points in Trenton and two Old Points in Lamoine!). And we may wish an interlocutor who tells us that what will follow is a long story, and then amply demonstrates it, to "get to the point."

Here the common theme is sharpness (the flat of the sword has won few converts, and it is difficult to imagine a pane of glass being held in its frame with some other shape: **glaziers' spheres?*). Sharpness is also the meaning of *pungency*, and to arrive at 10:15 sharp is to arrive punctually (in German, *punktlich*; *Punkt* means 'point', 'dot', and 'period'). The Latin word *punctuatio* in the sense of 'punctuation' was in use by the 14th century; its English gloss 'pointing' was the term used for punctuation in English through to the end of the 1700s.

It may seem a little surprising to see *pugnacious* and *poignant* in the same sentence, but in fact both are relatives to *point*: Latin *pugnus* ('fist'), like *punctus*, comes from the Proto-Indo-European root *peuk-/*peug-, meaning 'to prick,' some of its other derivatives being *impugn, pygmy, poniard, bung,* and *spontoon.* (*Prick* is from Anglo-Saxon *prica,* 'dot, point, puncture,' cognate with Icelandic *prik,* 'dot, little stick' and Middle Low German *pricke,* 'point, sharp implement.')

Pointillism is the method of painting that produces an image as an assemblage of tiny dots; the style was characteristic of the postimpressionist painter Georges Seurat, who introduced it to the French art world toward the end of the 1800s. By this time the clumping of silver halide molecules to form the grain in a black-and-white photograph was already a familiar phenomenon, but neither the photographers nor the painters could have anticipated the conversion of images to arrays of pixels in the computer-assisted photography now common just a century later. With all three of these reductionist techniques, our perception can be counted upon (assuming we don't come too close to what we are looking at) to average out what we see so as to make a continuous wash of form and color out of many discrete points.

•

What Americans call a *period,* Britons call a *full stop.* (So do Canadian anglophones, with *period* as a synonym.) A subtle difference between British and American punctuation style is that in the former, when a quotation ends a sentence but is not a complete sentence in its own right, the quotation mark comes first and the full stop after it. American telegraphers abbreviated *full stop* to *stop* and used it in place of the more ambiguous "period," and one paid for it as for any other word: the feckless student wiring home DEAR DAD SEND MONEY STOP would be charged for five words, not four.

We make a full stop at a corner when the vehicle we are driving is at rest—as distinct from the "rolling stop" (i.e., just slowing down) we may make at a corner to allow us to see that nothing's coming at us.

on the dot

The latter plays fast and loose with the primary meaning of the noun *stop* as given in the *OED*: the action of stopping. Thus we are at pains to keep awake on the train trip home at the end of a long day so as not to *miss our stop*; the politician assures us that if elected he will *put a stop to* the corrupt practices that have characterized the previous administration; we instruct our bank to put *a stop on our account* after we discover that our checkbook has been filched.

A stop can also refer to the interruption of wind in our vocal apparatus (as in a *glottal stop* or the stop consonants [t] and [d]) or to the mechanism that allows air to flow from a organ's wind chest to the pipes of a particular rank (thus: "Double reed stops include the cromorne, nazard, and canardo d'amore"); hence, by analogy, a harpsichord may be said to have several stops, i.e., ranks of strings (as an 8′ and a 4′) whose jacks can be engaged or disengaged by the pulling of levers, or a lute stop (or buff stop), which applies a row of felts to the edge of one of the ranks of strings close to the jacks and dampens the sound. (Moreover, a string, if lightly *stopped* at one of its even divisions of length, and sounded just as the stopping finger is released, will produce a harmonic at the octave if stopped at the middle, another at the twelfth—an octave plus a fifth—if stopped at a third of the way, and so on.)

Specialized meanings of *stop* and compounds containing it include the *rabbit stop*, a hole in the ground where the female rabbit makes a nest for her young; the *stop bath* in photography, generally a weak solution of weak acetic acid that almost immediately neutralizes the effect of the developer before submerging the film or print in a fixative bath; *stop-action* photographs, made much easier in the middle of the 20th century by Harold Egerton's invention of the strobe-light; the *stopwatch*, which allows the user to measure elapsed time; a *stop-drill*, which is a drill with a collar or other impeding attachment that allows drilling only to a particular distance; the *stopway*, the part of an airport runway where a plane that has made an aborted takeoff can be

155

period

stopped; and of course the familiar hue and cry, in Britain obliging all citizens to assist the chase: "*Stop thief!*"

•

The period signifies a sentence's end. Closure is as syntactically important as it is emotionally; one of the many startling things about James Joyce's last and arguably greatest book, *Finnegans Wake*, is that its last sentence trails off with no ending—or, rather, without a warning that you have to go back to the beginning of the book to get to the end. We expect things to have a beginning and an end: Our vernacular is full of such expressions as *wait for the other shoe to drop*, and at least one animated film (*Who Killed Roger Rabbit?*) draws on the supposed irresistibility of answering the final two raps (the "two bits") of what H. Allen Smith somewhere calls the "wise guy knock" (the one that begins "shave-and-a-hair-cut...") as a device for flushing a character from his hiding place.

As a basic metaphysical concern, our need for closure may explain our appetite for *teleology*—that is, the exploration of whether there is a purpose, an end-toward-which (Greek *telos*) to existence in general and human life in particular. Some belief systems satisfy this urge with a definite eschatology (*eschatos* is Greek for "last") and one or more written apocalypses (in Christianity, the book that made the cut was the Book of Revelation attributed to the "beloved disciple" John, son of Zebedee; in Norse mythology, some passages in the Icelandic Eddas describe the end of the gods and the world as we know it in the final battle of Ragnarok).

On a less cosmic scale, we all give some thought at some time to the end of our lives, if only to make sure that Great-Aunt Liz's old Slazenger goes to someone in the family who will truly appreciate it. But those who believe in an afterlife will have even more pressing concerns, since this usually entails some sort of judgment and reward/punishment payoff with at least some connection to one's earthly conduct. For the Egyptians, giving the right answer to Osiris and the Forty-Two Judges got you admitted to the West Country with all its blessings. (Those who flunked their orals, on the other hand, got eaten by the crocodile-headed monster Amemait.) The Greeks and Romans believed in a tripartite afterlife, in which the especially good and virtuous got to go to the Elysian Fields, the so-so went to the Asphodel Fields, and the real baddies went to Tartarus, where they were obliged to endure an existence that was unpleasant and eternally repetitive, often tailored to their sin: Tantalus's gustatory transgressions (the worst being serving up his son Pelops in a stew to the visiting gods) earned him perpetual thirst and hunger, tethered within sight of water and fruit that receded coyly from him whenever he reached for it; Ixion, for the heat of his lust for no humbler a love object than Zeus's wife Hera, queen of Olympus, got bound for eternity to a fiery wheel; Sisyphus, for being too smart for his own good, was sentenced to do something *really* stupid and pointless, involving a boulder and a hill, forever and ever, world without end.

157

Adherents of the Abrahamic religions (that is, Jews, Christians, and Muslims) share a good deal of theology, but their views of the afterlife differ, in places markedly so. Islam has a journey that includes a bridge over a terrible abyss; as a clear alternative to dreadful punishments for the wicked it offers a paradise for the virtuous, as does Christianity. (Sheol, the place of departed spirits in Judaism, is a pretty bland place for all the dead, irrespective of prior virtue, though in later antiquity there would be added Gehenna, a place for the wicked dead to go to be punished.)

We employ an astonishing array of euphemisms to speak of our life's end (or someone else's): Contemporary Americans often say that a person has *passed on* or *passed away* (or simply *passed*), reflecting our need to call death or its trappings by other than their own names in order to spare, as we suppose, the already raw nerves of the bereaved by putting a face on mortality that will somehow make it seem less harsh a fact. Thus we may say that someone is *no longer with us* or *departed*—this last sometimes expanded by sympathetic outsiders to *dear departed*, presumably to temper the bereaved person's sense of loss with a reminder of the affection of *the loved one* but perhaps also (at least unconsciously) to placate the spirits of those *gone before*.

There is theological periphrasis to cushion death's impact as well: *to go to one's reward, to meet one's Maker, to cross the bar, to be called home*, or in the case of nonhuman decedents, *to go to Kitty/Doggy/ Trombone Heaven*. Other biblical and literary euphemisms include *put on immortality, crossed over Jordan, climbed the Golden Stair, went to the bosom of Abraham*, slept *the Hamlet sleep* (Thomas Gray) or *that dreamless sleep* (Byron), *paid the tribute due unto nature* (Laurence Sterne), responded to *kind nature's signal call of retreat* (Samuel Johnson), or have *shuffled off this mortal coil* (Shakespeare)—all combining a softening of death's brutal reality with a touch of class.

A second, very rich source of death euphemisms is in gallows humor that allows us to joke about death with a levity that may be proportional to the unease we feel about it. In the "Dead Parrot Sketch" (immortalized in the Monty Python film *And Now for Something Completely Different*), John Cleese achieves this effect in a litany of clichés (the bird *is deceased, has ceased to be, it's a stiff, bereft of life, has rung down the curtain and joined the choir invisibule* [*sic*], *is pushing up the daisies*...) as shock therapy for a pet-shop owner in denial. Often such phrases can seem to bend over backward to be in bad taste, as an antidote to the first two types of euphemisms above, by making explicit reference to the mechanism of extinction of life and the decomposition of our mortal remains thereafter: *croaked, turn up one's toes, kicked the bucket, snuff it, take a dirt nap, six feet under, worm food, made dust like all our bodies*, and so on.

Stephen Andrew Chrisomalis, an anthropologist at the University of Toronto, is the host of a website that lists over two hundred euphemisms for death and dying, many of them sardonic in this way. Some are peculiar to, or at least had their origin in, particular epistemic communities, such as chefs (*basting the formaldehyde turkey, cooking for the Kennedys, sleeping with the quiches, marinating in soil and worms, pushing up parsley, put in the crisper, got 86'd* or *donated the liver paté*, has *reservations at the Chateau Eternity*, is *peasant under grass* or *fettucine al dead-o*), computer wonks and technical writers (*bought the disk farm, cached in his chips, got formatted with black borders, gone to the big glass house in the sky, inspired a new warning message, had his/her 80-column card punched, mailed in his/her warranty card, moved into upper management,* or *got struck out by the Big Blue Pencil, printed white on white, reformatted by God,* or *exported to a flat file*), the armed forces (*it's Taps, he answered the last call, the bullet had his number on it, he got wasted, he went home in a box*), and gangsters and prisoners (got *bumped off, knocked off, pasted,* or *whacked, rode the lightning* [the electric chair], *went to a necktie party, danced on air,* or *went up the long ladder and down the short rope* [hanging], *wore cement overshoes* [murder and/or disposal of the body by submersion]).

A third source of death euphemisms is arguably a variant of the first: propriety (or political correctness) carried over the top or even around the bend. The medical profession is on the whole tactful, sometimes to a fault: The dying are *terminally ill* (or, even more delicately, are in *a condition non-conducive to life*) and death is *negative patient care outcome*. The temptation to parody this sort of discourse is sometimes irresistible; the authors' current favorites in this line are *living-impaired, permasleep,* and *metabolically challenged*.

Useful as death-and-dying metaphors may be in the social interactions of everyday life, decoding them is a journalistic imperative. The former obituary writer for a northern New England newspaper tells us that "[i]n newspaper style, people...do not pass away, go to their reward, meet their Creator, rejoin their beloved relatives, close their eyes forever, go to be with Jesus, join the saints, or engage in any

159

other euphemistic exit from this life; they just plain die. Changing 'passed away' to 'died' is my most frequent editorial task."

●

We cannot end this book without mentioning the use of the word "period" to mean "This is the long and short of it." An elegant example is offered by Ann Patchett in her novel *The Magician's Assistant*: "'Dead is dead,' Parsifal had told her. 'Period.'"

afterword and acknowledgments

As the preceding pages attest, the roles of the dot in English and beyond have been as many and varied as those of a thespian in a touring company, and our own tour has by no means exhausted the possibilities. Three additional players may serve as a representative sample:

- *Dots as diacritical marks* are used in a variety of non-Roman scripts and in the transliteration of those scripts. For example, the Hebrew writing system uses dots (points) to represent vowels in what is basically a consonantal script, and to distinguish between pairs of otherwise identical letters (e.g., *beth* [בּ] and *veth* [ב], *sin* [שׂ] and *shin* [שׁ])—Arabic uses dots in this latter fashion as well (contrast *beh* [ب], *teh* [ت], and *theh* [ث], which are distinguished solely by their dots). In addition, Hebrew uses combinations of dots to indicate how to intone text when declaiming (cantillating) it to the congregation. A dot is used in Sanskrit and Hindi to stand in for a nasal consonant and, in transliteration, dots are used to signify that a consonant is to be pronounced retroflexively (e.g., ṭ[ट] versus t [त], as in Hindi ṭan [टन] 'chime' versus tan [तन] 'body').

- A *dotted-line reporting structure* in an organization denotes a relationship in which A, who officially reports to B, also unofficially reports (dotted-line) to C—Gene is the Documentation manager to whom I report directly and who writes my annual performance review, but Martha is the manager of the project to which my services have been lent and to whom I currently report along a dotted line.

162

- And where would the moviegoing public be without *Dots*, the candy that you buy at the refreshment counter before the show to make sure that the popcorn will properly adhere to your teeth?

Other examples abound, but a book can be just so large, and in any case we are confident that our readers will by now have a pretty good sense of how to spot them where they lie and to mine the wealth of stories beneath the surface. If so, we may be satisfied that we have done our part, and here must pay tribute to those without whom we could not have done so.

But for publishers, authors would write in a vacuum, their words as unheard as the tree that falls in the wilderness. We owe a deep debt of thanks to Erin McKean, who during her time at Oxford University Press coaxed us into floating a proposal for this book at a period in our lives when all of us had many competing distractions, and to Oxford's Casper Gratwohl, without whose enthusiastic reception to the notion this book might still be merely a fancy in the Cloud-Cuckoo-Land of conceptual art. To our senior editor, Peter Ohlin, and our copy-editor, Patterson Lamb, we shall be eternally grateful for the close reading and dialectical nuts-and-bolts tweaking without which even the best of books would go into print with spinach between its teeth.

Our heartfelt thanks go out to the goodly fellowship of personal sources, expert witnesses, and eggers-on who have supplied us with many of the cheerful facts and enlightening suggestions that have gone into the making of this book: John Adams, Andy Adler, Karen Bjorkman, Bruce Harris Bentzman, Carol Borthwick, Michelle Buchanan, Mario Capasso, Jane Cates, Charlotte Cooke, Ronald D'Argenio, Jo Diggs, Alan Delozier, Malcah Yaeger Dror, P. Matthew Edwards, Sheila Fischman, Rob Flynn, Jean Humez, Leslie Edwards Humez, Bob Harwood, Jennifer Holan, Tim Kassinger, Sherri Linn Kline, Jan Willem Maessen, Joseph Maguire, Teresa Nielsen Hayden, Robert Nowicki, Timothy Renner, Célinie Russell, Valentine M. Smith, Roger Staum, Guy Steele, David Weinstock, and Fr. Augustine Whitfield. We have endeavored to reproduce their contributions faithfully, but human nature being fallible we've probably not got it *quite* right every time; and insofar as we didn't, freely and frankly own that such errors were our fault and not theirs.

163

notes

accurate enough clocks: See David S. Landes's *Revolution in Time: Clocks and the Making of the Modern World;* for the story of how a clock was invented that could withstand the rolling of a ship in even the roughest passage from England to the West Indies, see Dava Sobel's *Longitude.*

railroads: Landes, *Revolution* (p. 286); for Grandfather's first train ride, see Adams, *Grandfather Stories* (p. 50).

monotonous regularity: The only slightly hyperbolic wording by the coauthors (John C. Alden et al.) of a railfan book, *The Central Mass.*, published in the mid-'70s shortly after the line's final abandonment. A ghastly military blunder popularly attributed to allies running on different clocks would also take place in World War I at Gallipoli on April 7, 1915, during an attack on Turkish positions by the Australian Light Horsemen, when, according to T.H.E. Travers ("Gallipoli: the Allied Failure" http://www.worldwar1.com/neareast/gallfail.htm), "the artillery ceased firing seven minutes before the attack and condemned many hundreds to death," but Travers goes on to suggest that notwithstanding the film "[i]t seems likely that the problem was not so much poor synchronization of watches but naval and field artillery fear of hitting their own men plus poor staff work."

pile ou face: The website http://fesrouge.free.fr/neologismes_fessologiques.htm, a sub-page devoted to new word coinages by frequent visitors to a website for French spanking enthusiasts, gives the punning *pile ou fesse* ("tails or buttock"); the same contributor (identified only as "Felippe2003") also suggested *Fessecequ'ilteplait* (literally, 'spank what it please you'), probably intentionally reminiscent of Rabelais's slogan *fay ce que vouldras* ("do as ye please"), inscribed over the door of the Abbey of Thélème (François Rabelais, *Gargantua et Pantagruel* I:57). Another interesting wrinkle on *pile ou face* for francophone computer users is to be found at www.dice.ucl.ac.be/crypto/introductory/pileouface/pof.html, where the authors discuss strategies for playing *pile ou face* by e-mail and strategies to avoid cheating.

pile *comes from Latin* pīla *('pillar, column'):* Classical Latin distinguished between long and short vowels (e.g., ī vs. ĭ), a distinction lost as the language evolved into Medieval Latin. We will mark Classical Latin vowels for length only where the distinction is relevant (as in the story of *pīla* and *pĭla*). We will mark vowel length in transliterating the Greek letters *eta* (η) and *omega* (ω)—ē and ō, respectively—as these are distinct orthographically from their short counterparts, *epsilon* (ε) and *omicron* (o).

face...*sovereign:* Leo Braudy, *The Frenzy of Renown*, p. 41. Over two thousand years later, an English gold coin called the sovereign was still being minted and circulating during the reign of Queen Victoria.

Etruscan...*make sense of it:* See, for example, the exuberant hypothetical reconstructions in Zacharie Mayani's *The Etruscans Begin to Speak*.

China: For an article discussing the paper-scissors-rock algorithm in contemporary China, see Paul Cabana's article "The Rock Heard Round the World" (*Boston Sunday Globe*, December 8, 2002, pp. D2–3), which also points out that the Japanese version, Jan Ken Pon, "appears in the written record as early as 200BC." A popular form of divination in China was scapulomancy, the interpretation of fissures formed in a shoulder blade (or sometimes a turtle shell) thrown into a fire and heated until it cracked.

Suetonius...*Seneca...:* See "Claudius" in Suetonius, tr. Robert Graves, *The Twelve Caesars*. A translation of Seneca's acid lampoon was appended by Graves to the end of his own historical novel *Claudius the God*, another translation, by J. P. Sullivan, appears in *The Satyricon and the Apocolocyntosis* (pp. 221–42), felicitously offering first-century Rome's two best-known Menippean satires—one spoofing Claudius, the other thought to lampoon his successor, Nero—as a boxed set, with some little-known poems and fragments of Petronius thrown in for good measure. (See bibliography under Petronius.)

Coyote tricked Old Man Thunder: This story appears as "Coyote Steals Fire" in a collection of Native American trickster stories compiled by Richard Erdoes and Alfonso Ortiz. Tricksters are fire-bringers in the myths of other societies as well, e.g., the Greeks credit the ingenious swiping of fire from Olympus and its distribution to humanity to Prometheus—one of the offenses that got that benign Titan chained to a rock on a mountain face with a carrion bird sent every day to peck at his liver.

Pass the Pigs: The manufacturer (Milton-Bradley) credits David Moffat Enterprises for the rulebook inserted in a package (designed by Hasbro International) that also includes two pigs, two pencils, and a scorekeeping tablet, all in a thin black plastic case. "A good game to take on a camping trip," according to former Girl Scout troop leader Jane Cates, it fits neatly in a 3"×6" pocket and weighs just three ounces.

fuzzy dice: Sometimes called hairy dice. The search engine Google lists over 61,000 entries for this popular item, ranging from the websites of manufacturers (e.g., http://www.blackballcorp.com/catalog/fuzzy_dice_281204_products. htm, offering seven different varieties, including one in fake zebra) to a site giving instructions on how to make your own (http://www.tackyliving. com/crafts/fuzzyDice.html). For a history of dice, fuzzy and other, written by a stage magician who claims to have collected "[t]housands of dice over a period of decades," see Jay, Ricky, and Rosamond Purcell, *Dice: Deception, Fate, and Rotten Luck.*

no longer making qualitative distinctions: Jan Huizinga, *The Waning of the Middle Ages* (p. 164).

lares and penates: Romans also might feel a particular closeness to lesser but generally accepted deities, such as the emperor Claudius's devotion to the nymph Egeria.

Tony, Tony, turn around: The Ohio informant (Leslie Edwards) who brought it to our attention added that most (though not all) pious adults in her childhood frowned on the easy familiarity, not to say impertinence, of this popular incantation.

denarius...libertas: This coin was used by way of illustration in a lecture on Roman coinage and its propaganda value delivered at Montclair (N.J.) State University by Dr. William Metcalf of the American Numismatic Society on February 22, 2002. Excellent examples of the denarii commemorating the deification of Antoninus Pius, touting Nero's brief era of peace, and paying off Marc Antony's legions are in the D'Argenio Coin Collection at the Walsh library on the campus of Seton Hall University in South Orange, New Jersey (personal conversations with the curator, Alan Delozier, and the donor of the collection, Ronald D'Argenio, January 2005). For an illuminating discussion of the coinage of imperial largesse, see Jeannine Diddle Uzzi, *Children in the Visual Arts of Imperial Rome* (pp. 35–41).

blow one's stack: One of the earliest conceptual problems proponents of steam-powered industrialization encountered was the public's apprehension about boiler explosions; see Julie Wosk's *Breaking Frame: Technology and the Visual Arts in the Nineteenth Century,* particularly pp. 33–46. The popular metaphor has long outlived the time when steam was considered perilous: A Three Little Pigs animated cartoon of the 1940s, for example, contained the

nursery rhyme burlesque "A tisket, a tasket, / The wolf will blow a gasket...."
(*Pop one's cork*, on the other hand, alludes to a risk still run by anyone rash
enough to mishandle bottled champagne, whose stopper, as warning labels
nowadays are at pains to tell us, can be discharged with sufficient force to
put out an eye.)

CHAPTER 2

one small step for a man: Note the "a," a 35 millisecond monosyllable that was
the subject of debate for nearly forty years until Peter Shann Ford, an Australian using the Canadian high-tech sound-recovery software GoldWave,
managed to extract proof positive of it from the tapes of radio communication between the lunar astronauts and Mission Control. Armstrong, who
has always maintained that he "didn't intentionally make an inane statement,
and...certainly the 'a' was intended, because that's the only way the statement makes any sense" was naturally pleased by evidence he characterized
as "persuasive," adding that "I would hope that history would grant me leeway for dropping the syllable and understand that it was certainly intended,
even if it wasn't said—although it might actually have been."

What Hath God Wrought: A Bible quotation, Numbers 23:23, supposedly suggested to Morse by a friend's child named Annie Ellsworth. The question
mark with which this sentence should end (and does in most versions of the
story) was a later addition to the code, being represented by the six-pulse
character *dit dit dah dah dit dit* (·· – – ··). For tables of World Standard Morse
now in use, as well as for Greek, Hebrew, Arabic, Cyrillic, Japanese, and
Korean, see http://homepages.cwi.nl/~dik/english/codes/morse.html; for
more on Morse, for whom telegraphy was a serendipitous second career—
he was already a respected portrait painter—see http://lcweb2.10c.gov/
ammem/today/may24.html, and for his partner Vail, see http://en.wikipedia.
org/wiki/Alfred_Vail (accessed August 7, 2007).

Farmacias Benavides, a Mexican drugstore chain: According to a press release
dated July 26, 2007, accessed on http://ir.westernunion.com/press/news.
cfm.

eye-blink the word "torture" in Morse code: The event is described in detail in the
entry for Jeremiah Andrew Denton, Jr. at the Denton genealogy site (http://
dentongenealogy.org/Jeremiah%20Andrew%20Denton.htm).

hillbilly said to the schoolma'am: The comic hillbilly stereotype, often exploited
by Southern and Appalachian entertainers themselves such as Uncle Dave
Macon, was a staple of the vaudeville stage, radio, and the funnies for much
of the first half of the 20th century, with a long pedigree: Mark Twain and
Artemus Ward, Royall Tyler's comic-Yankee servant Jonathan, the *valets*

fourbes of Beaumarchais (Figaro) and Molière (Scapin, Sganarelle), all the way to the trickster slaves of Roman comedy (Terence's Phormio, Plautus's Sosia). Big-band-era solo vocalist Dorothy Shay's singing career took off in the late 1940s, when during an extended engagement she ran out of encores one evening and trotted out an obscure song spoofing Appalachian kinship and marriage customs, called "Uncle Fud." The audience loved it and soon she added other numbers such as "Feudin' and Fightin'" and "I've Been to Hollywood," repackaging herself as "the Park Avenue Hillbillie" [*sic*]. See www.bigbandsandbignames.com/shay.html.

ostensible errand to one's kinsman in Ionia: Herodotus tells this story of Histaeus, who had been detained in the Persian capital, Susa, by King Darius. The message, which safely reached his son-in-law Aristagoras, governor of Miletus, advised the Ionians to raise a revolt, which they did. The difficulty of suppressing it, and the Athenians' role in having helped to bankroll it, persuaded Darius that his provinces in Asia Minor would never be secure unless he subjugated the mainland Greeks as well, which led to the first of the Persian Wars. See Aubrey de Sélincourt, tr. *Herodotus: The Histories* (pp. 350–51).

plausibly innocuous-seeming: For those who'd like to experiment with a little quick-and-dirty steganography of their own, the website www.spammimic. com can take your (short) plaintext message and turn it into (much longer) quasi-spam, which anyone else using the same site can then decode into your original message. However, if after encoding it you then delete a portion of the fake-spam message, what's left of it will be gibberish when decoded by the site's "decode" algorithm. But if you send the deleted part under separate cover to your correspondent, with exact directions as to where to paste it into the quasi-spam, presto! the restored message will decode to your original one. (Thanks to Theresa Nielsen Hayden for bringing this site to our attention.

Jack Kelley: Later dismissed from the newspaper for his role in the fabrication of other news stories.

the tell-tale 'signature' of steganography: Andrew Glass, "The War on Terrorism Goes Online," a December 2001 paper from Harvard's Kennedy School of Government (http://www.ksg.harvard.edu/presspol/research_publications/ papers/working_papers/2002_3.pdf), where Glass was a Shorestein Fellow that fall. Glass gives the URL for the Michigan researchers' report as www. citi.umich.edu/techreports/reports/citi-tr-01-11.pdf.

the krypt- *of* kryptonite: In the early 1970s an enterprising fellow named Michael Zane began manufacturing bent-bar bicycle locks made of a tough steel compound under the trade name of Kryptonite, and selling them to bicycle shops all over the country from the back of his VW Microbus. Since 2001 his company has been owned by Ingersoll-Rand. (See www.kryptonitelock. com/OurStory/History.aspx.) The Greek verb *kryptein* means "to hide," whereas *lanthanein* means "to escape notice," which is what steganography is all about. The element *lanthanum* was so named from having been first discovered hiding in a sample of what was mostly cerium oxide; it gives its name to the *lanthanide* series of so-called rare-earth elements such as erbium, terbium, and ytterbium, all of which were teased (along with yttrium) from what at first appeared to be samples of a single element first found at a Swedish town named Ytterby.

scratch their heads over: Unless they lived in Judea, where a variant on this sort of cipher had been around for centuries: For the first letter of the Hebrew alphabet (aleph) was substituted the last (taw), for the second (beth), the next to last (shin) and so on, whence *Athbash*, the name by which the cipher is known. See Alexander D'Agapayeff, *Codes and Ciphers—A History of Cryptography* (pp. 19–20).

George Washington: He was first referred to as "Father of His Country" as early as 1778, well before it was a foregone conclusion that the former colonies would win their independence and actually *be* a country of their own. (By contrast, Augustus had to wait until he had been in power for over a quarter-century before the Roman Senate voted him the title *pater patriae* in 2 B.C.E.)

an organist, and composed... music: Most of this paragraph draws on Paula Kimbrough, "How Braille Began," at www.brailler.com/braillehx.htm. Organist-composers Louis Vierne and Jean Langlais also got their training in the school's organ program. Another alumnus, Claude Montal, wrote a book about piano tuning and began teaching fellow students as well; this would also become a strong part of the curriculum at American schools for the blind, such as Perkins Institute in Watertown, Massachusetts.

plain English disguised in Greek characters: In a similar vein, during a term when he was studying Greek at college in the 1960s, the composer John Adams put a sign over his desk admonishing his roommates to "κεεπ ψουρ κραπ οϕϕ μυ δεσκ."

zydeco fans: As Carol Borthwick once pointed out to us, *zydeco* also makes a good six-letter computer password since it's not so common as to be easily guessed, and when you're entering it, your hand blocks most of the keys readily visible to someone looking over your left shoulder so it's hard to see what you're typing.

Most ham radio operators use Q code: A comprehensive listing of Q codes may be found at www.kloth.net/radio/qcodes.php.

Titanic's *radio operator sent out both:* Germany had enacted SOS into law as its official *Notzeichen* (distress signal) effective April 1, 1905; the Second International Radiotelegraph Convention, which adopted it, was held in Berlin the following year. For a more detailed summary (with bibliography) of the derivation and use of SOS, see http://en.citizendum.org/wiki/SOS.

notes

a sign that what follows is code: An interesting variation of this convention is found in Hebrew, where certain numbers (such as the year) can be represented using letters of the alphabet, each letter being assigned a numerical value. To distinguish a date so written from the surrounding text, a marker is inserted before the last letter in the date. For example, 2007 C.E. = 5767 of the Hebrew calendar = (from right to left) ת (*thav* = 400) ש (shin = 300) + ס" (samekh = 60) + " (marker to show that we're dealing with a number) + ז (zayin = 7) = ז " ס ש ת = (5)767, the 5 being understood. Malcah Yaeger Dror adds (personal communication), "In incunabula, and some more modern books, the date is not done that way. The author/redactor/whatever picked a quote that's relevant, and then put dots under or over the letters that can be added up to the date."

code for sexual and racial transgression: A point persuasively made by Sean McCann in his essay on jazz in postwar cinema, "Dark Passages," in Frank Krutnik et al., eds., *"Un-American" Hollywood: Politics and Film in the Blacklist Era*, see especially page 120.

sign indicating Christians: The ichthys fish icon has recently been revived as a bumper sticker, sometimes with "Jesus" inscribed inside it. To this some anti-fundamentalist wags have responded with their own sticker, in which the fish has grown legs and frames the name "Darwin."

chalked on the sides of houses: Our favorite being a large triangle with three small ones next to it, meaning "tell pitiful story."

used it publicly at every opportunity: Desmond Morris et al., *Gestures* (p. 227). The two-finger V sign has had a checkered history; the backward V (that is, with the back of the hand facing the viewer) has been documented as a sexual insult at least since before the First World War: Morris et al. reproduce a 1913 picture of a crowd of soccer fans, one of whom is displaying it, and give literary evidence that it had been current in the British Isles at least three centuries before that (p. 228).

specifying the day's settings: The quotations are from Hans Peter Bischof's www. cs.rit.edu/~hpb/Lectures/20042/AdHoc/all-inOne-19.html.

those with the right key: As Alexander D'Agapayeff neatly puts it (*Codes and Ciphers*, p. 96), "The ideal cipher is one that is simple for those who use it and difficult for anybody else." In 1883 French cryptographer Auguste Kerckhoffs published six specifications for a system of encoding: It should be in practice indecipherable to anyone without the key, its method should not have to be kept secret and not have disastrous consequences if the enemy gets hold of it, and its key should be communicable and memorable without written notes as well as changeable at will by the users; it must be adaptable in telegraph communications, readily portable, not require multiple persons (other than sender and recipient) to make it work, and be usable without great mental exertion or the need of memorizing a long series of rules. This set of requirements is collectively known as Kerckhoffs' Law. (See Bischof lecture.)

key selected from the first 256 ASCII characters: That is, the characters between ASCII 0 (the null character) and ASCII 255 (ÿ). For all practical purposes, if you restricted your choice of character combinations to the standard ASCII character set, you'd use the characters between ASCII 32 (space) and ASCII 255. With support for 8-bit character encoding, the original 7-bit ASCII character set has been extended to include an additional 128 characters, thus adding to the possible inventory of ASCII-based encryption keys. For an accessible and lucid treatment of data encryption in general, see the "Data Encryption" article at www.britannica.com/eb/article-9002217.

send a reply (also secret/encrypted)... and so on: See the entry "Alice and Bob" *in The Jargon Dictionary,* http://info.astrian.net/jargon/terms/Alice_and_Bob.html.

A French website: See J.-M. Boucqueau et al., "Comment jouer à pile ou face sur l'Internet sans tricher?" Tech. Report CG-1997/1, UCL Crypto Group (http://www.dice.ucl.ac.be/crypto/tech_reports/CG1997_2–1.ps.gz).

tell her I love her: We are indebted to Jo Diggs for bringing this Aerosmith song to our attention. Polyphonic pieces that juxtapose syllables that are perfectly innocent by themselves but make scurrilous words when all the parts are sung together are called catches, a genre whose musical steganography was much in fashion in England at the end of the 17th century. Examples include Atterbury's "Hodge Told Sue" and Cranford's "Mark How These Knavish Rests" and "Here Dwells a Pretty Maid," all of which can be found, along with a dozen other .mp3 files made from the recording *Catches and Glees of the English Restoration* on the website www.drinkingsongs.net/mp3s/1600s/1600s--1950s-catches-and-glees-of-the-english-restoration-(LP)/index.htm.

CHAPTER 3

Frank Zappa: In the mini-operetta "What Kind of Girl Do You Think We Are," recorded on the vinyl LP *The Mothers Live at the Fillmore East.*

books of lists: The most celebrated is surely the book so titled that was created by Irving Wallace and his children David Wallechinsky and Amy Wallace, and published in 1977 by William R. Morrow. Its latest version, *The New Book of Lists*, was published in New York as a Canongate paperback in 2005 and dedicated by the two offspring to the fond memory of their father, now deceased. Many of their lists are apparently random, including "Walter Matthau's 10 favorite Comedies" (p. 66), "10 Famous Insomniacs" (pp. 151–53),

notes

and "5 of the World's Most Oft-Sighted Lake and Sea Monsters" (pp. 190–91) while others are in a definite sequence, such as "12 Places with More Sheep than Humans" (sheep population, in descending order, pp. 191–92), "10 Animals That Have Eaten Humans" (alphabetical, pp. 181–83), and "13 People Who Succeeded after Having a Stroke" (chronological by year of birth, pp. 130–32).

spaghetti Western: While Italian fascination with plots set in the American Wild West has been lively ever since Giacomo Puccini's *The Girl of the Golden West* (*La Fanciulla del West*, 1910), a case could be made that this phenomenon is rooted in an orientalist tradition traceable all the way back to Greco-Roman antiquity (e.g., Plautus's comedy *The Little Phoenician* [*Poenulus*], or the popular Greek novels of the first century B.C.E.) As with the appropriation of Slavic folkdances by urbane Viennese composers such as Brahms and Dvořak, however, Italy's cinema Westerns—variously dubbed *spaghetti Westerns, Westerns all'Italiana,* or (in Japan) *macaroni Westerns*—transcend the genre that inspired them, with their arias and stage business arguably owing a great deal more to the grand opera house tradition than to the Hollywood production lot. The launching of the Italian Western is widely credited to director Sergio Leone, whose collaborations with composer Ennio Morricone include the seminal *A Fistful of Dollars* (1964) and *The Good, the Bad, and the Ugly* (1966). In addition to DVD re-releases of many of these films, there are also now a number of CD anthologies of their music, e.g., the eponymous *Spaghetti Westerns Vol. I,* a two-disk set with no fewer than 67 cuts characterized (as All Music Guide reviewer Richie Unterberger put it) by "galloping rhythms, tear-jerkingly sad melodies, overwrought melodramatic vocals, low twangy guitars, indescribably oddball orchestral flourishes of mariachi trumpets, lonesome harmonicas, tinny organs" (http://music. msn.com/album/?album=41639439&menu=review, accessed 6/30/2007). For an interesting cross-cultural spinoff anthology, recorded between 1968 and 1972, see *The Big Gundown: Reggae Inspired by Spaghetti Westerns.*

tree houses: Janet Podolak, "A Place Where Kid Is King," *Lake Chatter* (Lake County, Ohio), June 25, 2007, p. 2. The sub-headline is "■ Backyard tree houses challenge young imaginations" in which the square bullet appeared in the original sub-headline.

1056 B.C.E.: Butehamun himself almost certainly was the maker of the inscriptions as well, probably a few years earlier; as for the pharaohs whose tombs he helped build and adorn, even a middle-class artisan preparing his own postmortem habitation would spread it out over several orders of magnitude more of his adult life than is the case today. See John Romer, *Ancient Lives* for this story (p. 200) and much else about this next-to-last scribe from the twilight of the community of Valley of the Kings tombworkers, including the text of a poignant letter to the spirit of his wife that he wrote on a shard of rock and deposited in her coffin (p. 187).

on to the next thing: At a memorial service for the composer and choir director Francis Judd Cooke, his eldest daughter recounted that when she asked him to give her advice on what she ought to do with her life, he laconically replied, "Get on to the next thing."

number one: American troops encountered this formulation both during the Korean War and earlier in occupied Japan, where it was simply a straightforward gloss for Japanese *ichi-ban.* There are, however, many exceptions to the ordering of best/not so best 1-to-10, such as the judging at the Olympic games (in which higher number equals better score) and the movie *10,* in which 10 is the best—a "perfect 10." (A *perfect 10* among dressmakers, however, is not an extreme but rather a golden mean between a waiflike 8 and a fuller 12, a size about which we have heard women of more mature years reminisce with no little nostalgia.) Of course, if the desideratum is lack of deviation from a mean, on a scale of one to five the optimum number is three.

manual override: The lethal implications of not being able to power a window if one's car has gone off a bridge and submerged and the electrical system is shorted out become all too clear when one realizes how much strength is required to open a door in a car still full of air against the water pressure outside. Probably the only preventive is always to travel with a brick in one's glove compartment.

Ten Commandments...an ordered list: A rare exception to this rule is Tuli Kupferberg's eponymous musical setting, recorded in 1965 on the *Virgin Fugs* album, in which the order has been changed to meet the demands of scansion. It may be argued, however, that in this song the Fugs treat the Decalogue less as a theological statement than as an *objet trouvé.*

Vote for one person for mayor: In some municipalities, of course—e.g., Cambridge, Massachusetts—the mayor is elected not by popular vote but from among themselves by the members of the newly seated city council. Cambridge also differs from many places in having adopted some decades ago an electoral algorithm called *proportional representation* whereby voters are asked to rank-order their council preferences (1 being the favorite) in the citywide elections. The surplus of "#1" votes over a given threshhold drawn by the leading candidate gets redistributed proportionally to the other contenders. The process is then repeated for the second highest "#1" vote-getter, and so on down the list until all the available seats are filled. An advantage of this system is that it offsets the tyranny of mere numbers over small-constituency candidates. Drawbacks are that the election nearly always takes two or three days to tally and that voters apparently need to be constantly reminded to play by these moderately complicated rules, whence the city election commission's didactic slogan "Ballot, don't bullet!"

province of mobsters: But hit lists go much further back in history, at least to the time of the proscriptions of the Roman Civil Wars in the first century B.C.E. and persisted under at least the nastier of the emperors. The historian Suetonius records that after the assassination of the mad Caesar Caligula (41 C.E.), "two books were found among his papers entitled *The Dagger* and *The Sword*, each of them containing the names and addresses of men he had planned to kill" (Robert Graves, trans., *The Twelve Caesars*, p. 178).

kill, harm, or knock out cold: Susan Saulny, "On Hit Lists, Anger Finds an Outlet" (*New York Times*, Thursday, March 22, 2007, pp. E1–2). Or simply give a noogie to? But perhaps the degree of animus toward such people is so close to background-noise irritation as not to make any list. The origin of noogie (also spelled newghie in a 1976 play by Israel Horovitz, *The Indian Wants the Bronx*) is, according to the *Random House Historical Dictionary of American Slang*, unknown, but the entry adds that in the plural it refers to testicles; see also the note on *bollocks/bollix* at *bawd* below.

hurled by auxiliary soldiers with slings: Slingers such as the Roman *velites* ('fast guys') were a standard part of the military mix in the armies of antiquity; like the throwing stick (also called an *atlatl*, from the Nahuatl verb *atla*, 'to throw'), a sling extends the arc of a thrower's arm, allowing the projectile greater exit velocity than if lobbed by arm alone. According to Edwin Tunis's *Weapons: A Pictoral History* (p. 30), Roman cast-lead balls for slings sometimes bore for good measure images of thunderbolts or motivational inscriptions such as "Take [this]!"

ballein, 'to throw': Surprisingly, this *is* the source of "ball" in the sense of an event at which people get together and dance: Late Latin made a first-conjugation verb out of it, *ballare*, 'to dance' (i.e., to throw one's legs about), borrowed into French *baller* (cf. *ballet*). The naughty sense of *ball*, however (as in the refrain of the Little Richard rock'n'roll classic "Good Golly, Miss Molly") derives ultimately from PIE **bhel-*, not *gʷel-*; see next note.

bawd: Other **bhel-* words include *phallus* and *bollocks*, whose variant *bollicles* is better known to British speakers of English than to American ones, particularly veterans of the Second World War familiar with the coarse eponymous ditty of "Bollicle Bill the Sailor" (plausibly bowdlerized to "Barnacle Bill" in the United States). The variant spelling *bollix* (sometimes followed by *up*) is defined by the *American Heritage Dictionary* as "throw into confusion, muddle," a usage it lists as merely "informal," though candid in giving its derivation. *Pellet*, however, is from Late Latin **pilotta*, the diminutive of *pila* (Classical Latin *pĭla*), "ball," whose other diminutive, *pilula*, is the ancestor of English *pill*.

175

clay tokens: This discovery and the literacy origin theory based upon it are in large part the work of archeologist Denise Schmandt-Besserat, who has published a number of articles about them, notably "The Earliest Precursor of Writing" (*Scientific American* 238, no. 6 [June 1978], pp. 50–58) and "The Envelopes That Bear the First Writing" (*Technology and Culture* 21, no. 3 [July 1980], pp. 357–85). For a photograph of a bulla from the ancient Persian capital of Susa, dating to 3300 B.C.E., see *Past Worlds: The HarperCollins Atlas of Archaeology* (p. 125).

standard character meaning "donkey": And pronounced *anshu*, which Ernout and Meillet's *Dictionnaire étymologique de la langue latine* (p. 51) advances as a plausible ancestor of Latin *asinus*, Old French *asne* and modern *âne*, and English *ass* and its more learned adjective, *asinine*. Few if any English words can claim so long a pedigree in so easily recognizable a form: five millennia, all the way back to civilization's cradle in the Fertile Crescent. The Greek cognate is *onos*, from which is derived the name for the wild ass, *onager*—a term borrowed by the Romans for a variant of their *ballista*, or catapult, no doubt on account of the formidable kick of both. Mesopotamia's first war chariots were pulled not by horses but by asses; a lost-wax copper casting from around 2700 B.C.E. found at Tell Agrab, near the confluence of the Tigris and Diyala rivers, shows a warrior on a chariot drawn by four onagers (*Past Worlds*, p. 121).

Bill Cosby: On his 1967 Warner Brothers LP *Why Is There Air?* (W-1606), Cosby recalls that in contrast to his college girlfriend, a philosophy major, who posed it, he thought the answer to this question an obvious one: "to blow up basketballs with." Scholars of humor will recognize in this a version of the trope of theory versus pragmatism familiar from a host of research-scientist-vs.-engineer jokes.

lawn bowling: A more genteel equivalent of "Lie down with dogs, get up with fleas" is "They who play bowls must expect to meet with rubbers." *Brewer's Dictionary of Phrase and Fable* explains that a rubber is the name lawn bowlers give to a collision of two balls.

... and if I die I'll spit in your eye: Or, in some other variants, "Jesus tells us: Never lie," or "hope the cat will spit in your eye" or "stick a needle in my eye." Rhyme and stress are probably the overriding consideration here, as with jump-rope chants—and, of course, children making such a declaration don't *really* hope to die in any case.

Der Freischütz: The collaboration of *metteur-en-scène* Robert Wilson, writer William Burroughs, and composer/lyricist Tom Waits in the 1990s produced a memorable reworking of the folktale on which *Der Freischütz* is based: *The Black Rider: The Casting of Magic Bullets.*

lead's molecular weight: When it comes to the shoot-'em-up, all other things being equal, the heavier the bullet for its volume the better—hence the use of spent uranium for certain types of bullets by the U.S. armed forces. But one might think a golden bullet (gold has a molecular weight of 196.9, just 5% less than lead) would serve, as well as being more in the grand tradition of alchemy. This connection was pleasantly made in John Gay's *Beggar's Opera* (1728), whose posse, sent to arrest the picaresque highwayman Macheath, sings (to the tune of the march from Handel's *Rinaldo*), "See the ball I hold! / Let chemists toil like asses; / Our fire their fire surpasses, / And turns all our lead to gold!"

Rossini's *William Tell:* The Lone Ranger's chief competitor for the hearts and minds of American youth, Roy Rogers, rode off into the sunset singing "Happy Trails to You" to be met when he arrived home by his faithful dog, Bullet.

bullet that you bite: Before anesthesia, this was something for the patient to clench between the teeth while being operated on; it prevented chomping off one's own tongue. By extension *bite the bullet* has become a catchphrase in all sorts of situations where there's nothing for it but to grimace and bear it.

CHAPTER 4

concert polonaise: Such as the one Mussorgsky wrote for the courtship scene between Marina Mnishek and the pretender Dimitri in his opera *Boris Godunov*. Intended to give a particularly Polish flavor to the scene—Marina was the daughter of the Voevod of Sandomir—this stirring polonaise owes much to Chopin's revisionist ones of three decades earlier, described by Arthur Jacobs's *New Dictionary of Music* (p. 289) as "of an ardent, even martial, nature," the original dance being rather more stately. (For J. S. Bach's take on this earlier form, see the second interlude of the last movement of *Brandenburg Concerto No. 1.*) Other Russian composers experimented with the form as well, notably Tchaikovsky in the finale to his *Third Symphony* (called the "Polish" for this reason) and Rimsky-Korsakov with his "Procession of the Boyars."

plainsong: Benedictines of Solesmes, eds., *The Liber Usualis*. In the edition of 1962 the "Rules for interpretation" are on pp. xvij through xxxix, with a general introduction to plainsong notation from the Vatican edition preface on pp. xj–xiv.

adds to the note…the neighboring part: Anonymous V, *Ars cantus mensurabilis*, cited in "Notation," *New Grove Dictionary of Music and Musicians*, Vol. 13, p. 365. The roughly contemporary (ca. 1340) *Libellus cantus mensurabilis* (*"Little Book of Measured Song"*) by Jehan des Murs also says that an "imperfect" note may be made "perfect" by adding half its value.

David Fuller points out: In "Dotted rhythms," in Stanley Sadie, ed., *The New Grove Dictionary of Music and Musicians* (New York: Macmillan, 1980), Vol. V, p. 582.

classic treatise on flute-playing: Johann Joachim Quantz, *On Playing the Flute,* trans. Edward R. Reilly.

t-k-t for a triplet: See Laszlo Boehm's concise and invaluable *Modern Music Notation,* on which we have relied here.

Come in two sexes: "Or else," as they might say who would insist on grounding the construction of gender in biological essentialism. The assiduousness with which children born with ambiguous genitals are surgically "assigned" to one sex or the other is poignantly documented, and pointedly critiqued, by Suzanne J. Kessler in her book *Lessons from the Intersexed.*

listen in on his thoughts anyway: A situation examined at some length by several psychiatrists in training and their mentor, Dr. Sidney Tarachow, in his *An Introduction to Psychotherapy* (pp.161–63).

simplistic binaries... reinforce existing power structures: A prominent discourse throughout 19th-century literature, painting, and opera is orientalism, which posits an exotic eastern Other that is a stand-in for all sort of things Western society disapproves of but desires, from dusky skin and powerfully feminized eroticism to outlandish intoxicants (hashish, opium) and music filled with gestures and tonalities imitative of the East; see Edward Said's classic *Orientalism* and Lisa Lowe's commanding study of French and British orientalisms, *Critical Terrains.* The orientalizing tendency is by no means confined to dominant white males; the term applied to bebop by traditional jazz musicians who couldn't get their heads and chops around it was "Chinese Music."

One cannot imagine oneself...: H. G. Wells, Julian Huxley, and G. P. Wells, *The Science of Life* (p. 222).

something like a five-armed starfish: Naomi Mitchison, *Memoirs of a Spacewoman* (p. 20), cited in Susan Squiers, *Babies in Bottles* (p. 181).

spectacular successes: So described by mathematician-philosopher Murray Code in his 1995 epistemological critique *Myths of Reason.*

by a mortal man and a god: The theme of doubling, and the mistaken identities that result, are the engine that drives Plautus's comedy *Amphitryon,* starting from the proposition that Heracles' and Iphicles' mortal father comes home with his valet, Sosia, before the departure of Jupiter and Mercury, who have been impersonating them in order for Jupiter to impregnate Amphitryon's wife, Alcmene.

your Majesty does not do things by halves: This exchange between Strephon and the Queen will be found on pp. 242–43 of *The Plays and Poems of W.S. Gilbert.* The Centenary Edition of *Brewer's Dictionary of Phrase and Fable* defines *To do a thing by halves* as "To do it in a slapdash manner, very imperfectly" (p. 521), but there is not a single example of this phrase in *Bartlett's Familiar Quotations,* and we know of no instance of it ever being published without a *not* somewhere in it.

notes

usually referring to a two-way division: Hence the school-yard joke: A: "We'll divide the candy bar even-Steven." B: "Hey, you only gave me a third. I thought you said we were going to divide it even-Steven." A: "Right. A third for me; a third for you; and a third for my cousin Steven."

semiautomatic is less than fully automatic: But semiotics are *not* a quarter of what gets killed off by antibiotics. This *sem-* root means "sign," the same *sem-* in *semaphore,* literally "sign-bearing,"—an apt name for communicating a message a letter at a time by waving flags. The familiar "peace symbol" of the 1960s is a superimposing of the semaphore-flag positions of N̲ (for nuclear) and D̲ (for disarmament). The first peace march at which it was displayed was British (Aldermaston, 1958). The sign is generally thought to have been invented by Bertrand Russell, who was at that time head of the Campaign for Nuclear Disarmament and who emphatically denied any connection to death (in pre-Norman days symbolized by *yogh,* the last in the Nordic alphabet of runes, to which the peace symbol bears a superficial resemblance when turned upside down).

Ernout and Meillet say: Their entry for *sēmi-* argues a connection with the root **sem-* "one" that appears in such forms as *simplex.*

as in digamma: The Greek letter *digamma* (ϝ), so called because it looks like the letter *gamma* (Γ) sitting on top of another *gamma,* had a phonetic value somewhere between [w] and [v] and was eventually discarded, though not before it was borrowed by the Greeks' Italic neighbors to form our letter *F.*

the Petit Larousse *describes it:* At *demi-deuil* (p. 285), where lower in the same column can also be found a very lucid little diagram of the sort of star-fort projection called a *demi-lune* ("half-moon").

the mid- *of such compounds:* It is not the *mid-* in *midden,* however. This comes from Middle English *mydding,* which according to its entry on page 575 of the *Oxford Dictionary of English Etymology* is "identical with Da[nish] modding, earlier *møgdyng(e),* f[rom] *møg* muck + *dynge* heap (cf. dung)."

whose pipes sound a fifth higher: But the sesquialtera's distinctive color results from its sounding an *octave* and a fifth higher than the predominant tone. This is because a 4-foot sesquialtera is added as part of a registration at whose core are 8-foot stops, an octave down. As a result, its fifth actually reinforces the second harmonic of the lower pipes as well, at least if the organ is in reasonably good tune. For an unusually lucid article on how harmonics work, see "Harmonic Series" in Jacobs, *New Dictionary of Music* (p. 160).

two and a half asses: An *as* was originally worth a pound of copper but shrank over time; four *sestertii* made a *denarius,* the "penny" of the "Render unto Caesar" story in Matthew 22:21, Mark 12:17, and Luke 20:25. (So why 2½ asses to the *sestertius?* This makes more sense in light of the original unit being duodecimal, and the later system decimal, much as the British equivalent of the old sixpence would be 2½ New Pence.) A thousand *sestertii* made a *sestertium*, and probably for some confusion as well when writing about either denomination in other than the nominative singular.

Halb drei *(literally, "half three"):* Compare German *Drittenhalb*, "two and a half."

one-third human and two-thirds divine: The Standard Version of the Gilgamesh Epic (the one found in the ruins of Assurbanipal's library at Nineveh) states this quite clearly at line 48 of the first tablet. See Andrew George, tr., *The Epic of Gilgamesh* (New York: Penguin, 2000), p. 2.

Asimov told a story: This droll reminiscence introduces his article "The Imaginary That Isn't," in *The Magazine of Fantasy and Science Fiction*, March 1961.

CHAPTER 5

have in common: Apart from their being fictional, of course. Cartoonist Robert Crumb created the nightshirted, white-bearded guru *Mr. Natural. Dr. Doolittle*, who could talk to the animals (and unlike Owen Glendower's spirits from the deep, they would talk back), was the protagonist of a series of children's books by Hugh Lofting. *Mrs. Malaprop*, whose inexhaustible fund of malapropisms gave rise to that eponym, is a character in Sheridan's play *The Rivals. Ms. Airychord, Capt. Dandelion, Sen. Dreckslinger, Sr. Dymphna-Joseph, Prof. Mamamouchi, Fr. Feeley*, and the *Rev. Byron Frimstone* are our own inventions—though we owe a hat-tip to Molière, from whom we took *Mamamouchi*, the title that went with the rank of nobility to which Monsieur Jourdain, the eponymous protagonist of *Le Bourgeois Gentilhomme*, believed he was being elevated to be worthy of marrying his daughter off to a bogus son of the Grand Turk.

Tanya Erzen wrote: In a 2006 *Boston Globe* article, "Partners in Prayer."

Proletarian Cultural and Educational Association: Or rather its Russian cognates, which started the same way. Unfortunately, one of its noblest goals fizzled: Only one bona fide "proletarian novel" came out of the project, Fyodor Gladkov's *Cement*. See Edward J. Brown, *Russian Literature since the Revolution* (Cambridge: Harvard University Press, 1982).

Winston Smith's day job: Orwell's Newspeak was replete with semi-acronyms of this sort, such as *MiniTrue* for the Ministry of Truth. See the appendix "The Principles of Newspeak" at the conclusion of *Nineteen Eighty-Four*, serving both as a glossary to terms mentioned in the preceding narrative and as a parody of academic essay-writing under a totalitarian regime.

Ph.D.: Why not P.D.? Granted that the original *ph-* of *philosophia* was one letter—Greek *phi*—one would think Latin orthography would have trumped that. For the French, at any rate, the answer is a no-brainer: They pronounce the letters *P.D.* as *pay day*, slang for *pédéraste*, a term used interchangeably with *homosexuel*. (In northern Ohio, however, *P.D.* stands for Cleveland's largest-circulation newspaper, the *Plain Dealer*.)

the first six keys on the standard English typewriter: Compare, for example, the pronounceable French and Belgian *AZERTY*, Lithuanian *ĄŽERTY*, and German/Austrian *QWERZ*. Italian *QZERTY* does not trip so easily off the tongue and (according to the "QZERTY/QWERTY/QWERZ" entry in pc-facile.com's glossary, "Nowadays, computers sold in Italy have adopted a modified QWERTY format, derived from the keyboard layout of the original IBM PC." As for the keyboard invented by August Dvorak (a distant relative of Czech composer Antonin Dvořák), any attempt at acronymic pronunciation is pretty much out of the question: the top line of alphabetic characters begins with three sets of non-alphabetic characters—(" '), (< ,), and (> .)—before moving on to P, Y, and so on. So people just call it the Dvorak keyboard instead, pronouncing the r̲ in the inventor's name in the American fashion (no [-zh-] sound).

backronym: See the "acronym" entry at whatsis.com for a lucid summary of what is meant by *backronym, acronym, abbreviation,* and the more exotic *anacronym* and *apronym.*

Compiles Only Because of Luck: Compare the facetious derivation of the programming language BASIC (Beginners' All-purpose Symbolic Instruction Code) from 'Bill's Attempt to Seize Industry Control,' a reference to the crucial role that Bill Gates and Paul Allen's early version of the language played in the explosive growth of the personal computer industry (much to Microsoft's subsequent profit).

friend(s) of Bill: Either Bill W., founder of Alcoholics Anonymous (A.A. for short, but always pronounced as two letters and never like *aʻa*, the geologists' term, borrowed from Hawaiian, for a type of lava common to the islands' shield volcanos) or Bill Clinton. Wikipedia's disambiguation page for F.O.B. (http://en.wikipedia.org/wiki/FOB) gives more than a dozen alternative meanings, such as Fresh off the Boat (a euphemism for "recent immigrant") and the military term Forward Operating Base.

F.T.A.: Also the abbreviation for Future Teachers of America, considered one of the more sedate student organizations at the authors' high school, in marked contrast to the Fretted Strings Instrument Club where all the folkies and hipsters hung out. (Well, it *was* the early '60s. You had to be there.) The movie *F.T.A.* was a documentary squarely in the Red Hollywoood tradition, produced by Francine Parker (its director), Donald Sutherland, and Jane Fonda. Its release in July of 1972 coincided with Fonda's visit to Hanoi, which probably didn't help its dismal box office gross (in its first week it earned just $11,500) and almost certainly bolstered American International Pictures' decision to pull it from circulation the following month.

181

notes

See Mark Shiel, "Hollywood, the New Left, and *FTA*" in Frank Krutnik et al., eds., *"Un-American" Hollywood: Politics and Film in the Blacklist Era* (pp. 210–224).

OICU: Compare Marcel Duchamp's scandalous "Readymade" of the *La Gioconda* (the *Mona Lisa*) with a thinly penciled mustache and goatee, *L.H.O.O.Q.*— homophonic for *Elle a chaud au cul*, roughly translatable as 'She's got hot pants.' A further irony of this picture may lie in recent assertions that *La Gioconda* is actually of a man: a self-portrait of Leonardo himself, or at least some of him. The artist and art historian Giorgio Vasari identified its subject, some fifty years after Leonardo's death, as Lisa Gherardini, the wife of a merchant named Francesco del Giocondo. (*Mona* is a contraction of *Madonna*, i.e., "M'lady"). But Joseph Harris, in a 1999 *Smithsonian* article entitled "Seeking Mona Lisa," reports that computer mapping of a Leonardo self-portrait onto *La Gioconda* reveals that the forehead, eyes, nose, and mouth of both pictures are so close a match that the artist might indeed have drawn hers from his looking-glass. It is possible that del Giocondo's wife stopped sitting for Leonardo before the painting was finished and he simply filled in the details as best he could, but there are far more extravagant theories, the most what-iffy being Dan Brown's mischievous suggestion in *The Da Vinci Code* that not only is the lady manifestly Leonardo in drag but that her name is an anagram of *L'Isa* (far-fetchingly interpreted as "The Isis") and *Amon*, and hence that she is a hermetic (and hermaphroditic) representation of the mystic union of male and female.

published his apocalyptic sci-fi short story "FYI": In Frederik Pohl, ed., *Star Science Fiction Stories #2* and reprinted in Clifton Fadiman, ed., *The Mathematical Magpie.* Sci-fi is itself a syllabic abbreviation, and (unlike *FYI*) sounded out: *sigh-fie.* (So is *fanfic,* i.e., fiction written by [sci-fi] fans themselves, increasingly for Internet publication. The genre called *femslash* started out as a spinoff of this.) Like *A.S.A.P.* ('as soon as possible') and *P.D.Q.* ('pretty damned quick'), *F.Y.I.* was probably already in wide circulation by the end of the Second World War.

ROTFLMAO: This is one of the few Cybershorthand standards that could conceivably be pronounced (the result would be something like *rotfull-mau*), but the authors have never heard it tried. Indeed, the majority of such acronyms never occur in oral form at all, being reserved for written communications, and overwhelmingly electronic ones at that. The coarseness of the expression is reminiscent of another acronym well known from Computerspeak, usually as an exasperated response to a bewildered newbie seeking guidance through a not-so-user-friendly program: RTFM ('Read the Fucking Manual'). Given the murkiness of most software manuals, this is usually not very helpful advice.

182

notes

from one's francophone friends: Cul is French for 'arse' and 8 is *huit* (pronounced "weet") and hence *8r* would probably be pronounced as if it were *cul-huitre*, 'arse-oyster,' along the lines of *b8* for *bonne nuit* ('good night'). *Cul-huitre* might indeed be a viable French insult whose time has come, save for its resemblance to the other quaintly worded deprecations with which the French sentry taunts King Arthur from the battlements of the Castle Aaagh in the film *Monty Python and the Holy Grail.*

computer elite: The origins of this term are murky, but its truncated form *Puter Leat* appears repeatedly in Russell Hoban's post-apocalyptic novel *Riddley Walker.* For more details on L33t Speak, see the "133tspeak" entry in the online Urban Dictionary (www.urbandictionary.com).

Boston Phoenix: Once described as a former underground periodical "that has at least risen to sea level." We have been unable to trace the writer of this zinger, but it is alluded to by John Domini in his 2003 novel *Talking Heads: 77,* the first chapter of which is downloadable as a commendable teaser from www.redhen.org/files/pdf/1888996463.pdf. The *Phoenix,* an advertising-supported giveaway tabloid founded by theater afficionado and small-press publisher Larry Stark, was originally called *Boston after Dark,* or *B.A.D.*, but changed its name after it bought the rival *Cambridge Phoenix* following the latter's two-week writers' strike in 1969.

a tad less scary than SM: Michelle Buchanan, "Identity and Language in the SM Scene," in Erin McKean, ed., *Verbatim* (p. 163).

example of a real estate ad: From the real estate section of the *Boston Globe,* May 13, 2006. A second reason that such ads may tend to be laced with abbreviations is that they may have been placed not by the seller but by the real estate agent, who is working on commission and paying for such advertising out of pocket.

and the unabbreviable Miss: Also sometimes in the southern United States *Missy* (as in, e.g., *"Listen here, Missy"*). *Missy* is attested as a nickname as well.

litigation in England's medieval court at York: Charles Donahue, Jr., *Law, Marriage, and Society in the Later Middle* Ages (p. 112). Although the guiding legal principle (as articulated by Alexander III, pope from 1159 to 1181) was that marriage contracts made under duress were void, in 1332 Alice de Brantrice succeeded in winning her suit to enforce hers with William Crane, made some eight years earlier when both parties were in their early teens, despite witnesses' testimony that his godmother, Elizabeth Crane, "told him that if he did not come along and marry Alice, she [Elizabeth] would cut off his ear" (Donahue, p. 99).

old ones should be married: Judith Martin, *Miss Manners' Guide to Excruciatingly Correct Behavior* (p. 565). Earlier in the same work (p. 298), Miss Manners, in discussing the various terms one might use in referring to the person with whom you form a couple but to whom you are not married, rejects *mistress:* "This suggests some financial arrangement favoring the lady, and what, pray, is the corresponding term for the gentleman involved?"

used with young ones: Martin, *Miss Manners' Guide. Madam,* of course, has also been used for well over a century to mean "proprietress of a house of ill fame," as in Madam Cyn, the London entrepreneur whose £25 "luncheon vouchers" entitled the bearer to a bit of crumpet for dessert (Adrian Room, ed., *Brewer's Dictionary of Modern Phrase and Fable,* p. 421), and Mayflower descendant Sidney Biddle Barrows, whose top-of-the-line Manhattan escort service was shut down in 1984 and who went on to write a bestseller, *The Mayflower Madam,* later made into a TV movie of the same name.

sometimes shortened to 'Ster: We are obliged to Joseph Maguire for this observation (personal conversation, 1992).

didn't do his homework: An example quoted from his college Russian instructor by Roger Staum while a roommate of one of the authors (NH) during their freshman year.

monsieur: The plural is *messieurs,* the abreviations are *M.* and *MM.,* respectively. (Compare *SS.* for Saints, as in SS. Perpetua and Felicity, and the Spanish EE.UU or EEUU for *los Estados Unidos*—the U.S.A.) *Madame* is *Mme* (or *Mme*) and *Mademoiselle* is *Mlle* (or *Mlle*): French generally doesn't seem to bother with periods in abbreviations, though *M.* for *monsieur* and *MM.* are exceptions to this rule. For some reason, French or French-English/English-French dictionaries tend to be fairly cavalier about including the abbreviations for the plurals of *Madame* and *Mademoiselle*—the *Petit Larousse grand format* gives neither. Francophone publications seem to favor *Mmes* and *Mlles,* while Anglophone dictionaries (such as the fourth edition of the *American Heritage Dictionary*) tend toward dot madness—*M.M., Mme., Mmes., Mlles.*

The fundamental appeal... is that they are brief: As Maurice Grevisse so aptly put it in *Le Bon Usage* (7th ed., Éditions J. Duculot, Gembloux, 1961) (§152), "The spoken language naturally resists words that are overly long, especially those whose appearance [*physionomie*] reveals them to be of learned or pedantic origin, and so it abbreviates them. This betokens a tendency towards economy of effort which has been manifest since the very beginnings of the French language, though it is since the end of the XIXth century that abbreviation has considerably extended its reach."

terse: Joseph Maguire again—an apt answer to a silly question. One of the authors (AH), asked for the same sort of one-worder to describe a six-foot-and-over friend who had given him as a reference, replied, "Tall," with the explanation that from the author's perspective (5'5") this was indeed his most salient characteristic.

notes

You lose: Coolidge might well have approved of the sentiment expressed in the final line of "Our Photos," a terse poem by Laurel Speer: "The really pithy don't want to know you."

CHAPTER 6

Nine tailors make a man . . . : And six make a woman—the "tailors" being teller-strokes on the parish church bell to indicate death and having nothing to do with needles and thread, a droll one-liner by Queen Elizabeth I notwithstanding. (She once greeted a delegation of 18 tailors from the guild with "Good morning, gentlemen both!") The bell was struck nine times for a man, six for a woman, and three for a child, and after a pause a series of strokes equal to the number of years the deceased had lived. Dorothy Sayers, in *The Nine Tailors*, describes Tailor Paul, the tenor bell at fictional Fenchurch St. Paul, as inscribed with the couplet "NINE · TAYLERS · MAKE · A · MANNE · IN · CHRIST · IS · DETH · ATT · END · IN · ADAM · YAT · BEGANNE." The Anglican church of St. Mary's Bluntisham, where Sayers's father had been rector, recently got its bells rehung, and with a boost from the Dorothy L. Sayers Society, a newly cast bell with the motto above on it. See "For Whom the Bells Toll," *Ely Ensign* 182 (January 2005), pp. 1 and 10–11 (online at http://archive.ely.anglican.org/ensign/e2005pdf/e0501.pdf).

185

and three dots make an ellipsis: Actually, while this is the truth, it's not the whole truth, for in fact *four* dots sometimes make an ellipsis—see, for example, the 15th edition of the University of Chicago Press *Manual of Style* (§§11.51–11.65)—and, at least in French, two may suffice—see Jacques Drillon, *Traité de la ponctuation française* (pp. 405 *ff*).

I want the erasure to show: Suetonius, *The Twelve Caesars*, "Claudius," §16 (p. 195).

damaged cuneiform tablet: In Andrew George, tr., *The Epic of Gilgamesh* (p. 36); these are the lacunae-laced lines 159–161 from Tablet IV of the Standard Version, most of which was unearthed at Nineveh in 1850 and 1853. For a lively account of the rediscovery of this Mesopotamian classic, see David Damrosch, *The Buried Book*.

blurb: A term coined in 1907 by Gellett Burgess, better known for his verse about the purple cow. A formal definition followed seven years later in his *Burgess Unabridged* of 1914: "1. A flamboyant advertisement; an inspired testimonial. 2. Fulsome praise; a sound like a publisher" (quoted in Room, ed., *Brewer's Dictionary of Modern Phrase & Fable*). Unlike some other neologisms in this now-forgotten work, *blurb* caught on and has been with us ever since.

falls short of being a circle: From a mathematician's viewpoint, a far-too-elliptical gloss. The *American Heritage Dictionary* offers a more rigorous one: *Ellipse* is from *elleipsis* (as is *ellipsis*), in the specific sense that this type of conic section "fall[s] short (from the relationship of the line joining the vertices of a conic and the line through the focus and parallel to the directrix of a conic." The term *ellipse* was first used in this sense by the Greek mathematician Apollonius Pergaeus, a contemporary of Archimedes, who like him had studied at Alexandria.

A Void: *La Disparition* literally means *The Disappearance*—but that has three *e*s in it. The Adair translation, *A Void,* obeys the no-*e* rule even in its title, which felicitously puns on *avoid* as well.

book on French punctuation: Jacques Drillon's *Traité de la ponctuation* discusses various sets of multiple dots on pp. 136–37. The original French of the quatrain—*Espérez!... Plus d'espoir!/Trois jours, leur dit Colomb, et je vous dô. . o. .nne un monde. / Et son doigt le montrait, et son œil pour le voir / Scrutait de l'hô. .o.o.rizon l'i. .mmen-si... té prôo. .fonde...*—consists of three and a half lines of alexandrines whose sonority the typographic plausibly reproduces even as it tests anew the limits of print in transcribing real-world utterances.

You saw it here first....: This is not an instance of the four-dot ellipsis mentioned earlier but, rather, a period followed by an ellipsis. How you're supposed to punctuate an incomplete sentence ending in an ellipsis seems to be with three dots, though the United States Government Printing Office's *Style Manual,* which prefers asterisks to dots when it comes to ellipses, addresses this issue with the following example (p. 125): "He called *** and *** he returned the ***."

f***-letter word: At "Full Stop," in Torbjörn Lundmark, *Quirky Qwerty* (p. 145).

T*m, D*k, and Ha*: The UNIX operating system supports two slightly different uses of the asterisk as wild card, one of them as described here and the other in the grep command, which you use to search for text strings in a file or set of files. Here, the asterisk matches zero or more characters preceding a specified item marked with a leading apostrophe. For example, grep 'a*phobia myfile would search for all the phobias that began with the letter *a* appearing in the file *myfile,* while grep 'ail*phobia myfile would zero in on all instances of the word *ailurophobia* (if *ailurophobia* is the only phobia that begins with *ail*) in the file *myfile.* The grep command uses a dot instead of the question mark to denote a single character: grep 'Al.x myfile matches *Alx, Alex, Alix,* and any other string with a character or no character between initial *Al* and final x in the file *myfile.*

*praught: We are indebted to Fr. Augustine Whitfield for this putative past participle.

asterism and asterisk come from Greek astēr: as does the now rarely used *asteriscus* (※), which Isidore of Seville (p. 48) says "is put in place of something that has been omitted so as to call attention to the omission." Two signs used in logic that are at least reminiscent of the asterism are ∴ ("therefore," as in "All government officials are suspect; Sen. Porkbarrel is a government official; ∴ Sen. Porkbarrel is suspect.") and ·· ("because" as in "All government officials are suspect; Sen. Porkbarrel is suspect ·· Sen. Porkbarrel is a government official.")

French language discussion site: www.langue-fr.net/A/arrobe.htm. The word *a(r)robe* is traced by several contributors to an old Spanish measurement unit called the *arroba,* itself supposedly from Arabic *ar-roub,* "four(th)."

'pataphysical website: www.h27pataphysicien.net/histoire.htm. The article on 'pataphysics on the French wikipedia site (http://fr.wikipedia.org/wiki/Pataphysique) says that Jarry expressly tacked on the initial apostrophe because, he said, he wanted "to prevent an easy pun"—probably *Pas ta physique!* (Not your (type of) physics!) But he could have known, and been influenced (if only subconsciously) by, the fact that in Greek, word-initial rho (P, ρ) is always preceded by the rough-breathing sign, as in the adjective ῥαθυμος (*rhathymos,* "lazy") or the name Ῥαδυμανθυς (Rhadymanthus), in both of which the initial r̲-sound is aspirated. 'Pataphysical science turns up in the first verse of the Beatles song "Maxwell's Silver Hammer," from the *Abbey Road* album (1970): His hapless victim Joan was quizzically pursuing a course of home self-instruction in it at the time that he asked her out on her fatal movie date. There is no internal evidence either way to suggest or disprove that Rose and Valerie (ibid., verse 3) studied it as well.

editing out white noise: Nor is such excision restricted to the medium of print: Heinrich Böll's story "Murke's Collected Silences" tells the tale of a recording engineer who, instead of consigning to the cutting-room floor the pauses he excised from tapes prior to broadcast, saved the silences and spliced them together for his later private enjoyment.

AP style manual: The Associated Press Stylebook and Libel Manual (p. 180), which goes on to say, "In general, avoid fragmentary quotes. If a speaker's words are clear and concise, favor the full quote. If cumbersome language can be paraphrased fairly, use an indirect construction."

allegory of the blacklist: Jeff Smith, "Are You Now or Have You Ever Been a Christian? The Strange History of *The Robe* as Political Allegory," on pp. 19–38 of Frank Krutnik et al., eds., *Un-American Hollywood: Politics and Film in the Blacklist Era.*

library of Ohio State University: So reports Sherri Linn Kline, who was a student in the OSU folklore department at that time. The perpetrators were never arrested, and the identity of the library insider, while suspected, was never proved.

black mark next to one's name: Claudius, though emperor, was also holding office as one of the Censors at the time of the incident mentioned in the first paragraph of this chapter.

Where do my jokes go…: Demetri Martin. Person.—the periods are part of the title—was premiered on the Comedy Channel on cable TV on January 14, 2007.

the web page where the publisher has reproduced: "Moreover, we know footnotes like anything else on the Web can go *poof!* and disappear," writes Chuck Zerby at the conclusion of *The Devil's Details: A History of Footnotes.*

not supposed to read the footnotes: Anthony Grafton, *The Footnote *A Curious History.*

run to as many words as the body text: See Erving Goffman, "The Insanity of Place," in his *Relations in Public,* especially p. 368: The two footnotes on that page contain 215 words; the body text from which they are called out adds up to 214.

euphemisms, a robust and open-ended class of utterances: A strong candidate for our all-time favorite take on euphemisms is the bumper sticker that reads *Heck is where people go who don't believe in Gosh.*

tales not told out of school: It is British boarding-school tradition that just as in the ads for Las Vegas, what goes on in school stays in school. The principle carries over naturally into government, where keeping the lid on an unpleasant story can make the difference between a government staying in power and toppling on a vote of no confidence.

CHAPTER 7

signifying boldface: Although the marginal marks have been constant for at least a hundred years, there is some variation in how to mark the reverse of boldface and italics within the body text. Older sources—the *Century Dictionary* (1889/1895) and Webster's *New International Dictionary* (1935)—say to mark italics that should be roman with a single underline, and likewise to mark boldface that should be made lightface by using a wavy one. *Webster's Tenth Collegiate* (1993) concurs. However, lists in the 12th edition of the University of Chicago Press *Manual of Style* (1969), Prentice-Hall's *Words into Type* (1974), and the third edition of the *American Heritage Dictionary* (1992) indicate both lightface and roman, where incorrectly set as boldface and italic, by circling the text and marking the margin with a circled *lf* or *rom.* (The *Associated Press Style Manual* [1987] and the second edition of the *New Oxford American Dictionary* [2005] don't commit themselves either way.) The logic of the earlier method is straightforward: Since each entails a binary choice, the underlining means that however the text was set, it should be changed to the opposite. The circling of text, on the other hand, implies that lightface and roman are the default option, so if something deviates from either and shouldn't, then here's what needs to be fixed. Both methods produce intelligible and unambiguous results, and either will be understood by a competent editor.

notes

caret... upside-down caret: In the United Kingdom, proofreaders attach both types of caret to a forward slash, indicating with greater precision and legibility than a caret alone exactly where the mark is supposed to go. Other British symbols differ slightly from American practice as well, e.g., in rendering *stet* as a dashed line under the text and a circled checkmark in the margin.

point of the arrowhead: The caret thus functions as both a *natural sign* and a *conventional sign*, a distinction central to the debate in Athens around 300 B.C.E. between Epicureans and the Stoics; see Paul Cobley and Litza Jansz's profusely illustrated and refreshingly lucid *Introducing Semiotics.*

or octothorn: Square has been used to refer to the # sign on a touch-tone phone, the focus being not on the lines that constitute the symbol but, rather, on that which the lines enclose. A similar origin for the use of the sign as the proofreader's mark for a space was suggested to us by an editor of our acquaintance.

whence also hatchet: Nor, however, *hatch* in either its sense of "(horizontal) opening" or "(cause to) emerge as from an egg," though these may be related to each other with a common ancestor, Middle English *hæc* ("little door")—no relation to Latin *haec* (feminine 'this').

189

e.g., foo#: *Foo* is generally said to be derived from the World War II acronym FUBAR ("Fucked Up Beyond All Recognition"—compare SNAFU, "Situation Normal: All Fucked Up"). However, credible alternate etymologies have been proposed, including a recurrent line uttered by the protagonist in the Smokey Stover comic strip of the 1940s: "Where there's foo there's fire." (Perhaps deriving from this, the nickname *foo fighters* was given to a class of unidentified flying objects that repeatedly turned up in the sky during the Second World War and gave Allied pilots the willies—see the "foo" entry in *The New Hacker's Dictionary*, Eric Raymond, ed., as well as the "foo fighter" entry in the *Random House Historical Dictionary of American Slang*, vol. 1., J. E. Lightner, ed.)

widely used programming language C: Microsoft takes pains to stress that the language is C sharp (and not C pound sign), though, bowing to the limitations of the standard keyboard (which has only the pound sign), allows that a pound sign is acceptable in place of the more proper sharp sign when referring to the language in print. (The Unicode character set distinguishes between the sharp sign [Unicode 266F (♯)] and the pound sign [Unicode 0023 (#)].)

which embrace the space to be removed: The Unicode names for ‿ and ⁀ are *undertie* and *(character) tie*, respectively. (In musical notation, both symbols are known as *ties* when they signify that two successive notes at the same pitch are to be held as though they were a single note. When used to specify that successive notes are to be played legato, they are called *slurs*.) Originally, the undertie was known as a *hyphen*, which the *Century Dictionary* defines as follows: "[<LL. *hyphen*, n. and adv. < Gr. *hyphén*, a sign (‿) for joining two syllables or words, also used in music, prob. to indicate that two notes were to be blended together; prop. an adv., *hyphén*, or rather a phrase, *hyph' én*, under one, into one, together, as one word...] **1**. In *paleography*, a curve placed below the line so as to unite the parts of a compound word, and to indicate that they are not to be separated or read as distinct words...**2**. In *writing* and *printing*, a short line (-) used to connect two words or elements, namely: (*a*) used to connect two words which are so used as properly to form a compound word; (*b*) to join syllables which are for any purpose arbitrarily separated, as in regular syllabication (as in el-e-men-tal), at the end of a line to connect the syllables of a divided word..." Thus, the hyphen in its second (and more generally known) sense is a sort of have-your-cake-and-eat-it-too sign in that it marks a space between two elements between which the space is arguably not a *real* space.

the delete sign: That is, the delete sign that the proofreader writes in the margin of the line from which something is to be deleted, as in the illustration on page 85 in which the deletion of the extra occurrence of *the* is marked by striking it through, and the deletion of the *u* in *honour* is marked by a slash and close space. The delete sign appears in the margin, once for each deletion, the first requiring no further elaboration, and the second being accompanied by the close space marks. Different proofreaders have their own styles when it comes to the delete sign that goes in the margin, all of them resembling to a greater or lesser extent either a backward ampersand or a lower-case Greek delta (δ) short for *delete* or one of its Romance cognates.

general separatrix: Avoidance of needless repetition has given rise to the use of the as in *s/he*. This sort of elision has its pitfalls: the parallel construction implied has to be a valid one, as in "Harsh sentences for lèse-majesté will assure that the king is respected/feared," but not "This sum should be equal/greater than 1." (This is the same problem with which Greek rhetoricians wrestled when it came to their poetic figure called *zeugma*—literally, "yoking"—in which the same verb took two objects, each of which used the verb in a different sense: "I took his advice and a taxi" or "If you don't drop this lawsuit you'll end up out of money and your mind as well!")

Unregenerate gender-grinches might argue that, strictly speaking, *s/he* must stand for *se or he*, and remind us that whoever appears in court *pro se* is for the nonce a lawyer with a fool for a client; but this is pettifogging: If the construction is not quite parallel, it is close enough for a slow freight train to trundle its way along it without derailing; and as the old Winston cigarette commercial poignantly asked, "What do you want—good grammar, or good taste?" Such a construction, however, is actually the mirror image of the "*cur-rere/-ens* means 'run/ning'" sort (same stem but different endings); here *he* and *she* share a vowel at the end but have different stems.

This problem might be solved by adopting the backward slash—see next note—as the sign indicating the boundary at which two dissimilar etymons share a common ending: Thus, *"I don't know/care what the name of your parent/guardian is, young man; but if you don't run along quick/quietly, I'm going to phone him/her and see to it that when you get home s\he shall give you a damned good scol\hiding." Generally, editors discourage this use of the slash, even if, e.g., *X and/or Y* takes fewer words than the preferred (if somewhat clunky) *either X or Y, or both.*

naming DOS/Windows drives: The UNIX convention is to use forward slashes, e.g., /usr/local/bin, a convention subsequently adopted in the specification of URLs.

guillemets: So called because supposedly invented by a printer named Guillaume, of which *guillemet* is a diminutive. They function as quotation marks only in the narrow use of setting off a quoted phrase or word: «*Moi*», *c'est la première personne, et l'article «la» indique la troisième* (" 'Me' indicates the first person, and 'it' indicates the third." The quote is from René Daumal, *La grande beuverie*, in Jacques Drillon, *Traité de la ponctuation française* (p. 295).

Issa's cow: "Dim the grey cow comes / Mooing, mooing, and mooing / Out of the dawn mist," as Peter Beilenson renders it in his Japanese haiku collection.

wasteful in a manuscript scriptorium: James J. O'Donnell, "Pragmatics of the New: Trithemius, McLuhan, Cassiodorus" (http://ccat.sas.upenn.edu/jod/ smnotes.html#1). This paper was delivered at the "Future of the Book" conference held at Umberto Eco's International Centre for Semiotic and Cognitive Studies in July 1994 in the mountaintop republic of San Marino and has been reprinted with the other conference papers in Geoffrey Nunberg, ed., *The Future of the Book.*

says Joseph Moxon in his Mechanick Exercises of 1683: Cited in Percy Sampson, *Proofreading in the Sixteenth, Seventeenth, and Eighteenth Centuries* (p. 50).

a Catalogue of such ambiguous words and compounds: John Smith, *The Printer's Grammar*, cited in Sampson, *Proofreading* (pp. 53–54).

Protestant-turned-Catholic king Henri IV: Famous for remarking that "Paris is worth a mass" (*Paris vaut bien une messe*), the king of Navarre renounced Protestantism in 1593, removing the last serious impediment to becoming king of France in practice, as in theory he had been since 1589 when Henri III died having designated him his successor. His conversion took the wind out of the sails of the occupation of Paris by a Catholic faction allied with the third protagonist in the "War of the Three Henrys," Henri of Guise. Henri IV promulgated the Edict of Nantes in 1598; it continued in force until revoked by Louis XIV in 1685, prompting an exodus of Huguenots to England—including the Revoir family of silversmiths, whose descendant Paul Revere, thanks to two lanterns, a borrowed horse, and a versifier from Maine named Longfellow, would play a quintessential role in America's dramatic mythos of national origin.

the op- *of* opulent: At least according to Ernout and Meillet, *Dictionnaire étymologique*, who trace it (pp. 463–64) to an archaic form *cops, 'abundantly furnished.' Personified, Ops was an agricultural goddess married to the Italic god Saturnus (identified with the Greek Titan Kronos, father of the Olympians); she was honored every year with a festival called the Opalia, celebrated on the 19th of December (the third day of the Saturnalia).

frame a reply to their critics: Thomas Kuhn availed himself of this opportunity by tacking on his 37-page "Postscript," clarifying the difference between a paradigm and an exemplar, seven years after the original publication of his epistemological tour de force, *The Structure of Scientific Revolutions*, when the University of Chicago Press reprinted the book in 1970.

require more than an oral agreement: See Michael Anesko's *Friction with the Market* for how James's shrewd negotiations with multiple publishers got him unprecedentedly favorable contracts at a time when most arrangements between author and publisher remained, by today's standards, astonishingly loose.

dots... to connect in a puzzle: A website now exists that enables the user to create a connect-the-dots puzzle from any picture (www.picturedots.com).

CHAPTER 8

Martin Mull's record album: The *Normal* LP was released on the Warner Capricorn label in 1974. Its dust-jacket note "This album contains no cheap shots at the Carpeters or Carl E. Simon" looks like a version of Epimenides' Paradox, but isn't.

Napoléon... coup of November 9–10: Also known as the coup of 18 Brumaire, its starting date in the French revolutionary in effect until the old Gregorian calendar was restored in 1806. Fabre D'Églantine gave its twelve 30-day months a rational set of nonmythological names evocative of the seasons, such as *Thermidor* ("heat-giver") and *Pluvôse* ("rainy"). Like the Babylonian calendar of antiquity, the French revolutionary year thus consisted of 360 days plus a year-end festival of five days (six in leap year) after which the regular twelve-month cycle would start all over again, the first day of the new year being the Autumnal Equinox.

dollar is divisible: On the stock market, however, the dollar is still divided into eighths ("XYZ traded at 54¾, up 5/8"), thanks to a convention left over from the colonial American circulation of Spanish dollars, i.e., pieces of eight (*reales*, called "bits" in English)—which is also why we still call the quarter coin "two bits."

mercury thermometer: The origin of Fahrenheit's zero point is debated by historians. Some say he determined empirically what the coldest temperature was at which water could be kept liquid by the addition of rock salt (with or without ammonia salts, depending on the source) before it froze, others that his zero point represented the coldest it ever got around Gdansk, where he came from, to avoid the need for negative numbers on his scale.

by mouth: rectal temperatures run about half a degree higher, something forensic pathologists are reminded to take into account when trying to make determinations of time of death from body temperature (C. J. Polson, *The Essentials of Forensic Medicine,* p. 5).

thermometric unit: As such, the Celsius degree helps to define the calorie, which is how much heat it takes to raise the temperature of a cubic centimeter of water 1° Celsius at a moderate temperature (e.g., 20°, or 68° Fahrenheit). A thousand small-c calories make up a grand calorie, properly spelled with initial uppercase C—the ones we're reckoning in when trying to diet our way back into last year's trousers.

degrees Kelvin: Named for William Thompson, Lord Kelvin (1824–1907), who first proposed a scale starting at absolute zero.

and boils at 313.15° K: Temperature, on whatever scale, is reckoned in degrees, the sign for which is a tiny superscript circle: "273.15° Kelvin = 32° Fahrenheit = 0° Celsius." The origin of this sign is surprisingly obscure. C. G. Liungman's *Dictionary of Symbols* says that "[a]n empty circle...smaller than most of the other signs in a given ideographic system" suggests "the idea of something *small* or *weak....* Thus it is used to represent *degrees* when measuring temperature and dividing a circle" [italics in original]. Robert Kaplan, on the other hand, suggests that it may be all that's left of the abbreviation $\mu°$ (short for <u>*moira*</u>, "division, part") current in Archimedes' day (Kaplan, *The Nothing That Is,* p. 18). To complicate matters, the circle, with or without a dot in the middle, is a very old sign for the sun; the heretic monotheist pharaoh Akhenaten had it depicted in sculpture and painting as the lifegiving Aten sun-disk, often emitting rays that terminated in tiny hands signifying the sun's limitless bounty. As a hobo sign, an inconspicuous circle chalked on a house means "you won't get anything here," its simple eloquence conveying an unequivocal sense of emptiness (nothing in the bowl, nothing in the belly).

Hunger can kill; so can hypothermia. "Below 75° death can be presumed," writes forensic pathologist C. J. Polson in his textbook discussion of body temperature and morbidity. A naked body, he says, loses a little more than 2° an hour during the first nine to twelve hours after death, then about 1° per hour thereafter until it reaches the ambient atmospheric temperature, though Polson cautions that there are other factors that may slow this process, such as death by asphyxia, e.g., from strychnine poisoning. "Despite these factors," he concludes, "the body temperature remains a valuable aid" (p. 5).

one-, two-, and three-liter bottles: This innovation is recent enough that people who discard non-returnable plastic pop bottles by the side of the road have yet to be stigmatized with the term "liter-bug," but it's probably only a matter of time.

ounce weighs 28.35 grams: An avoirdupois ounce, that is. In Troy weight, still used by jewelers, the ounce weighs just over 31.10 grams. The Troy ounce is divided into 20 pennyweights, dwt. for short—the same d. (from Latin *denarius*) as was used in the designations £/s/d for the pounds, shillings, and pence of pre-decimal English money. One and a half grams to the pennyweight is not too sloppy an approximation (it's only off by a thirtieth part: The actual ratio is 1 dwt. = 1.555 grams).

light years: There is a still larger unit, the parsec; short for "parallax second," it is the distance (about three and a half light years) to a star whose apparent displacement against the "fixed" ones in the distant background is one second of arc between observations six months apart. The distance from our sun to its nearest stellar neighbor, Alpha Centauri, is roughly one and a third parsecs.

Florian Cajori: His two-volume *History of Mathematical Notations* was published in La Salle, Illinois, by the Open Court Publishing Company in 1928 and 1929; it is presently available in one volume as a Dover reprint, the source for much of the notational information here. Pat Ballew (www.pballew.net/ arithme9.html#decpoint), however, notes Clavius's earlier use of the decimal point than Napier's, as well as the decimal advocacy that had led up to it, especially Dutch mathematician Simon Stevin. Stevin's treatise *De Thiende* ("The Tenth"), written in Flemish, became highly influential after he translated it into French (as *Le Disme*) and published it in 1585. (*Disme*, incidentally, was the name originally given to the tenth-of-a-dollar coin in the monetary system of the fledgling United States.) Stevin's decimal places were indicated by little numbers (1, 2, 3...) in circles over each digit; 946 with a circled 1 over the 4 and a circled 2 over the 6 would be equal to our 9.46.

Clavis Mathematicae: This is the book in which Oughtred also proposed the ∟ sign for his units-tenths delimiter. Unicode, perhaps not surprisingly, distinguishes between x (the multiplication sign), X (the uppercase letter in its various uses), and lowercase x, a distinction easily lost in a handwritten algebra assignment.

Elsewhere in Europe, people use a comma as the decimal delimiter: This is something of an oversimplification. Consider the representation of an American's Lottery savings account balance: $12,000.25 in which the comma separates the thousands from the hundreds, and the dot separates the dollars from the cents (i.e., the decimal from the fractional part). In countries that have adopted the SI standard (the European countries among them), a comma separates the decimal from the fractional part, and a space separates blocks of three numbers when a quantity comprises more than five numbers, as in the French-Canadian representation: 12 000,25 $ (in which a space is also used to separate the amount from the dollar sign).

million millions: David Taylor thoughtfully examines these and other standardization problems in "Elements of Internationalization" www.intuitive.com/globalsoftware/gs-chap4.html.

Agnus Dei: Settings of this text and others designated as suitable for fraction anthems are numbered S-151 through S-172 in the "Service Music" section of *The Hymnal 1982*, now in use throughout the Episcopal Church in America.

monumental two-volume book: Schwaller de Lubicz, by scrupulous measurements and rigorous calculations, attempted to prove that the Temple of Apet of the South at Luxor was a map of the human body, a projection of the Cosmic Man. For his analysis of the Rhind Papyrus, see *The Temple of Man* (pp. 149–87. His deconstruction of the *wedjat* eye into its fractional components is on p. 110).

creation epic: The *Enuma Elish*, which told how the world came into being out of formless chaos, and how Babylon's city god, Marduk, slew the chaos-dragon Tiamat and established order in the universe. Another feature of the festival was that the king got slapped in the face and chased out of the city gates as the people's scapegoat, to return and get swatted again at the festival's conclusion. See N. K. Sandars, *Poems of Heaven and Hell from Ancient Mesopotamia*, especially her thorough essay on the Babylonian epic and worldview (pp. 11–70).

full-moon table: In Cajori, p. 7. Kaplan (*The Nothing That Is*, p. 12) says that a tablet from Kish has been found with a three-hook version of this null placeholder, possibly from as early as 700 B.C.E.

variously translated as "Book of the Abacus" and "Book of Calculation": In the introduction to his translation, *Fibonacci's Liber Abaci* (p. 4), L. Sigler writes, "One should here again make the point, that while derived from the word abacus the word *abaci* refers in the thirteenth century paradoxically to calculation without the abacus. Thus *Liber abaci* should not be translated as The Book of the Abacus. A *maestro d'abbaco* was a person who calculated directly with Hindu numerals without using the abacus, and *abaco* is the discipline of doing this."

ten major branches: For an easily accessible list of Dewey categories to three figures, with some subcategories, go to http://library.bendigo.latrobe.edu.au/irs/WEBCAT/*xxx*.htm, where *xxx* is the Dewey number you want to look at. This will give you access to the library's online cataloguing for that category: Type in 200 and you'll see all the religion categories, or 700 for all the arts. You can then do a finer search by reading the numbers off the subcategories whose links are shown in the list; shamanism, for example, is 201.44; silversmithing self-instruction books are 739.23.

the order in which humanity acquired them: According to Tim Kassinger, a librarian at the Mayfield branch of the Cuyahoga County (Ohio) Public Library.

Cutter-Sanborn author tables: The three tables (Cutter Two-Figure, Cutter Three-Figure, and Cutter-Sanborn Three-Figure) are published by Hargrave House, in Littleton, Colorado (www.cuttertables.com/cutter1.html).

Different cataloguer, different mind-set: Tim Kassinger points out that thanks to the Internet and online catalogues, a library that can't decide on how to classify a newly acquired book can simply search it on the Internet, find a workable classification in some *other* institution's data base (such as the Library of Congress), and use whatever Dewey number the other guys came up with.

Christian Jacob: The quotations are from "From Alexandria to Alexandria: Scholarly Interfaces of a Universal Library," a paper presented at the University of Santa Barbara in March 2002 at a conference entitled *Interfacing Knowledge: New Paradigms for Computing in the Humanities, Arts and Social Sciences* and published on the Internet at "From Alexandria to Alexandria: Scholarly interfaces of a universal library," online at http://dc-mrg.english.ucsb.edu/conference/2002/documents/christian_jacob.html.

the last of its books were burned: The ignition temperature of papyrus, according to papyrologist Mario Capasso, is between 310° and 350° Celsius (e-mail of October 16, 2007, from Dr. Capasso to Timothy Renner, to both of whom we are much obliged for passing this information on). This works out to between about 430° and 480° Fahrenheit. (Ray Bradbury's "Fahrenheit 451" figure, from which he drew the title of his novel about modern book-burning, falls in about the middle of this range.) It is of small consolation that the destruction of the library created a great deal of papyrus ash, which was used as a caustic by physicians in antiquity: Dioscurides mentions in his *De Materia Medica* (78 C.E.) that if applied to ulcers in the mouth, the residue from burnt papyrus would keep them from spreading. (See Elaine Evans's paper "Papyrus: A Blessing upon Pharaoh," at http://mcclungmuseum.utk.edu/research/reoccpap/reoccpr_pyrs.htm.)

notes

how perpendicular the walls seem nowadays: For a more colorful (not to say alarming) appreciation of their omnipresence, first think of pigeons on a railroad platform (Penn Station in Newark, perhaps). Now in your mind's eye replace them with a fast-moving menagerie of galumphing brontosaurian mainframes, skittery desktops darting in and out between their feet like velociraptors, pterodactylesque laptops flapping to and fro amidst swarms of Palm Pilots flitting and scampering en masse to avoid being devoured.

This extravagant fantasy is not so far from reality; the only major omissions are that in the real world some of these entities are disguised as trees or ponds, and not a few have contrived to render themselves as invisible as Cheshire cats. The overwhelming majority of the computers with which we have surrounded ourselves escape notice just so long as they do not malfunction.

the price of memory falls: In 1968, a computer with 16 kilobytes of core memory rented for $1,200 a month; its peripheral devices includes a card-reader for 80-column punch cards, a heavy-duty high-speed printer, and four enormous tape drives, with a ton of air-conditioning running at full blast to keep it all cool. By 1984 for the same amount of money one could own one's own desktop computer with three times as much core memory and peripheral disk drives that held the same amount, with a dot-matrix printer thrown in free. For the same price, in 1990, you could get a 170 megabyte hard drive with built-in 1.4 megabyte disk reader plus full-color printer; in 2000, an 8-gigabyte desktop reading 700-megabyte CDs, in 2004 a laptop weighing under eight pounds with a 36-gigabyte hard drive—and that's not to mention the pocket-size models or those telephones that double as digital cameras, nor the concomitant development of faster and faster processor chips.

even more radical machine, the "Analytical Engine": Babbage's collaborator and fellow mathematician Augusta Ada Lovelace (daughter of the poet George Gordon, Lord Byron) developed the program that would run the Analytical Engine, drawing on the exiting technology for punch-card input to Jacquard looms. Babbage had intended the device to run on steam. (For more of this story, see www.maxmon.com/1830ad.htm.)

cards that are still known by his name: Hollerith cards, also known as IBM cards. Hollerith's company merged with two others in 1911 to become the Computer-Tabulating Recording Company, which was renamed International Business Machines in 1924 (www-03.ibm.com/ibm/history/exhibits/builders/builders_hollerith.html).

development of the vacuum tube: The first triode vacuum tube in commercial production was the Pliotron, developed by Irving Langmuir at the General Electric plant in Schenectady, New York; it went on the market in 1915. The Colossus Mark I had 2000 vacuum tubes, and ENIAC close to 18,000.

197

Ballistic Research Laboratory: This lab would develop a number of computers of its own subsequent to ENIAC, including the Ballistics Research Laboratory Electronic Scientific Computer, BRLESC (an acronym all of a piece with the picaresque army humor of the day; compare SNAFU—"Situation Normal, All F****d Up—and the mnemonic for resistance corresponding to the color spectrum of sheathing for wiring: "Bad Boys Rape Our Young Girls Behind Victory Garden Walls"—variant: " . . . But Violet Gives Willingly"—for the sequence black, brown, red, orange, yellow, green, blue, violet, gray, and white). Instead of the alpha codes ABCDEF, now universally used for 11 through 16 in hexadecimal alphanumeric coding, the Ballistics Lab used KSNJFL, supposed to stand for "King Size Numbers, Just For Laughs."

UNIVAC I: The name was short for UNIVersal Automatic Computer; the ten-ton 5000-vacuum-tube device could perform over a thousand calculations per second. (Other competitors had faster processing, but slower input and output.) The first commercial purchaser was General Electric Appliance Division, for its payroll operations, in 1954 (wwwcsif.cs.ucdavis.edu/~csclub/museum/items/univac.html).

turn up the juice and they become very compliant conductors: This is probably as great an oversimplification as saying that all you need to make a star is to fuse a lot of atoms of hydrogen into helium—both may be true enough as far as they go, but for brevity's sake we leap over several semesters of electrical engineering (or astrophysics) at a single bound. Don't try this at home.

whatsup.doc: A friend of ours who worked at a financial ratings agency routinely assign this filename to the weekly update memo she would send her boss.

this limitation wasn't really a hardship: The evolution of the printer as computer output device is a story in itself. Reduced to its barest bones, the story of transferring information from a computer processor to paper in legible form (typically by inking a page) consists of three basic intertwining themes:

- Whether printing involves a hard object striking the paper—*impact printing* vs. *nonimpact printing* (as exemplified by daisy-wheel and dot-matrix printers vs. laser printers).

- Whether printing proceeds a character at a time in sequence (as with *serial printers*, which print a character at a time along the page and then start a new line, sometimes going the other way back—a method of writing named by the ancient Greeks *boustrophedon*, as it replicated the way an ox [*bous*] would make a turn [*strophē*] at the end of plowing a furrow), a line at a time (as with *line printers*, which may either print a line of dots at a time, constructing the eventual line of characters a line of dots at a time, or print a line of characters at a time), or a whole page at a time. Available memory and the sophistication of the printer driver software that lets the processor talk to the printer are both involved here.

- Whether the basic unit of printing is a whole character or a dot (or a character made up of dots)—typewriter-based printers (e.g., daisy-wheel) print a whole character at a time, while dot-matrix printers, as the name implies, deal in dots. (Nowadays, the pixel has largely replaced its dot ancestor, but the idea is basically the same.) The *matrix* part of dot-matrix refers to the rectangular grid from which a dot is plucked to take its proper place in the formation of a character (or graphic) on the page. The word *matrix* is derived from Latin *matrix*, originally 'a female animal kept for breeding,' and, by subsequent extension, 'womb, place where something originates.' Ultimately, matrix is derived from Latin *mater* 'mother.'

all the way up to the root directory: There is also a command `cd` . whose meaning is "'change' to the current directory." This command doesn't really do anything in DOS but is a relic of UNIX in which it is commonly used (with a preceding slash) to execute a series of commands (in a file called a *script*) from the current directory. Thus, for example, `cd` ./`myscript` will execute the script `myscript.sh` from the current directory.

limit the number of people you can list in the header of a single message: In the case of Juno (now part of its former competitor Netzero), this was 50, which meant that in order to send a message to students in two sections of a course with 40 in each section, it was necessary to maintain separate class lists for e-mailing and send every message twice. Still, this seemed a relatively small price to pay given the volume of spam out there—by some estimates, a third of the entire traffic on the Internet. For an excellent discussion of spam and how to thwart it, see the "Anti-Spamming Techniques" chapter of David Wood's *Programming Internet Email.*

named by Mike Mauss at Berkeley in 1983: Mauss himself says that the name came from sonar, and given the aptness of the analogy one can see why. He adds, however, that later on David L. Mills provided the backronym "Packet Inter-Net Grouper" and it stuck (http://ftp.arl.mil/~mike/ping.html). The term has carried over into gamer slang: Greg Costikyan cites the terms LPB and HPB (short for "low-" and "high-ping bastard") in an article entitled "Talk Like a Gamer" (*VERBATIM* 27:3) the "low" and "high" referring respectively to fast and slow Internet connections (and therefore game response time). An HPB has "such a bad connection that the player is often frozen, offering no help as a teammate and not much challenge as an opponent" (p. 1).

a quick look here.: See Ken Abernathy and Tom Allen, "Converting Decimal Fractions to Binary" (http://cs.furman.edu/digitaldomain/more/ch6/dec_frac_to_bin.htm) for a succinct explanation of how to perform this operation by hand. Typically, you don't have to worry about what goes on under the hood when you enter decimal fractions into a computer program that will then do something with them in binary form.

widely adopted: For a discussion of the historical pull and tug between the proponents of fixed-point and floating-point representations, see pp. 63*ff.* of the second edition of Paul E. Ceruzzi's excellent *A History of Modern Computing.*

called the mantissa: The etymology of the word *mantissa* is foggy: The Latin grammarian Festus said it was Etruscan and meant "makeweight," but it got used in Latin to mean a sauce, a fuss, or a profit. J. Wallis introduced it to England in his 1693 *Opera Mathematica* as a term for the digits after the decimal point in a decimal number, glossing it as "appendage" in his *Algebra* of 1695 (*Oxford English Dictionary* online: dictionary.oed.com/cgi/entry_main/00301499?/query_type=word&queryword=mantissa).

significant digits of a number: That is, the number of places to which a number is presumed to be accurate. Suppose we have a function we wish to test—say, that salaries in Manhattan are on average 1.725 times what they are for the same sort of work in Salt Lake City. We ask our friend who works for the *Deseret Daily* how much they pay him to be night city editor, and he says, "Around thirty thousand." We then multiply $30,000 by 1.725 and are pained when we then ask the city editor of the New York *Stentor-Patroon* if he gets paid something like $52,500, and he tells us, "Yeah...Give or take a few thou, maybe." Where has our precision gone? The answer was that it was never there in the first place: "Around thirty thousand" yields at best one significant digit, the 3 of 30,000.

So the fact that we have a constant in our formula that is of four-digit precision gets smoothed out considerably (three digits' worth) to the one significant digit with which one of the multiplicands began.

In practice this imprecision may not matter at all: We may know that we have exactly 401 hamsters in the lab and that their total granola consumption last month averaged 202.05 grams per hamster per day. But if we're buying by the kilogram, rounding that calculation to 202 times 401 won't make an important difference (just 20 grams out of 82 kilos a day), and uses a lot less pencil and paper.

Moreover, as Joseph Maguire points out (e-mail to AH, October 16, 2007), "to express the distance from here to the moon in four significant digits, I could say:

243.2 thousand miles

15.40 billion inches

1.283 billion feet

427.7 million yards

1.306 light-seconds

It is important to recognize that each of these measurements to the moon is about equally accurate. There is just as much slop in four significant digits of inches as in four significant digits of parsecs."

gives the exponent: However, often a number added to avoid negative exponents, in what is called *excess-n* notation. So, for example, if *n* is 128, 10^{-4} will actually be notated as 10^{124}. There is a convention that the mantissa is always represented with the decimal at the far left before the first number.

(also fixed): So why is it called "floating-point?" Presumably because the radix point "floats" as a reflection of the value of the exponent: A larger exponent puts the radix point farther to the left or right than a smaller exponent.

FLOPS for short: This discussion owes a great deal to the third edition of Valerie Illingsworth, Edward I. Glaser, and I. C. Ayles, eds., *Dictionary of Computing,* particularly those on floating-point notation and FLOPS on pp. 180–81. See also Ken Abernathy and Tom Allen's *Exploring the Digital Domain,* online at http://cs.furman.edu/digitaldomain/home.html.

CHAPTER 10

upper-class Romans: Particularly the friends of Publius Cornelius Scipio Africanus, who come to know and love all things Greek in the course of subduing Greek city-states allied with Carthage during the Second Punic War. After his defeat of Hannibal, Scipio popularized Greek language and culture among his friends at Rome, the so-called Scipionic Circle. Not everyone in Roman high society approved, to be sure; the stern Marcus Porcius Cato, the Censor, wouldn't give anything having to do with Greece the time of day. But the Hellenists eventually won out, and by the time of the early empire, at least a nodding acquaintance with Greek was considered an indispensable part of a Roman gentleman's education. Whence one of the favorite expressions of the emperor of Augustus, whenever he thought someone was trying to hoodwink him: "A radish may know no Greek, but I do!"

down to the present day: The middle dot is still used by lexicographers to show syllable boundaries, as in this entry from *The American Heritage Dictionary* (4th ed.): **syl·lab·i·fy** (sĭ-lăb'ĭ-fī) or **syl·lab·i·cate** (-kāt'). Compare *The Random House Dictionary of the English Language: The Unabridged Edition* (1971): **syl·lab·i·fy** (si lab' ə fī).

Institutio Oratoria: Besides its thoughtful analyses of the science and art of rhetoric, Quintilian's book offers such practical advice as telling a joke to wake up a judge who appears to be nodding off (or, one might suppose, is in danger of concentrating too carefully on the weakness of one's case).

Quintilian (full name, Marcus Fabius Quintilianus) was one of several provincial writers who came to Rome and flourished in Rome's literary "Silver Age" under the Flavian emperors at the end of the first century of the Common Era, as did his fellow Spaniards, the satiric poets Juvenal and Martial. In addition to tutoring several members of the imperial family, Quintilian also was a teacher of Pliny the Younger, whose letters to the emperor Trajan (and expected to be for more public consumption—"*et publice at privatim*," as Pliny tells Trajan in one of them) would rightly come to be held up to students as models of their rhetorical form.

middle dot: The character codes for the interpunct are ASCII 0183 or Unicode U+00B7. This gives a dot darker than today's period, but change the font from 12 to 10 point and it lightens up while staying at the same height, so the series goes like this . · For the uppermost dot, use Unicode U+02D9 "dot above" (·), or you can cheat and type the ASCII code for the middle dot as above and put it in superscript font, as in the three-dot sample concluding the previous sentence.

the complete sentence is called a **periodus:** A *periodus* is literally 'a way around something, a circuit.' Thus *periodos* also referred to the athletes' circuit of games, which included not only the original Olympic games (at Olympia in the Peloponnese) but also other games held at Nemea, Isthmia (near Corinth), and at Delphi (below Mt. Parnassus); many athletes would enter all of them. The games at Athens were not on the formal *periodos* but athletes would often compete there as well. Prizes included ornamental crowns (*stephanoi*) of laurels and other sacred plants; but there were substantial cash awards too: Solon, the legendary *archon* of Athens, in 594 B.C.E. instituted prizes of 500 *drachmai* for Athenian victors at the Olympian games, 100 *drachmai* going to those who won events at the Isthmian games; and a later Athenian law (430 B.C.E., just as the Peloponnesian War was ratcheting up) further awarded winning athletes *sitesis*—the right to chow down at public expense in the *prytaneion* (the Athenian civic dining-hall). Prizewinners at the Panathenian games were paid in jars of olive oil whose exteriors depicted the event they had won and whose contents were a useful and valuable commodity that the athletes often resold: Fragments of such vessels have turned up from as far away as the steppes of Scythia (present-day Ukraine). See Jenifer Neils's lavishly illustrated catalogue raisonné of a touring museum exhibit on the Panatheneia, *Goddess and Polis*.

the **cola** *and the* **commata:** "That is, *membra* and *caesa*" adds Fidel Sebastián Mediavilla by way of clarification on p. 14 of his doctoral dissertation, *La Puntuación en el Siglo de Oro* (Barcelona, Universidad Autònoma de Barcelona, 2002; available on line at www.tesisenxarxa.net/TESIS_UAB/AVAILABLE/TDX-0720101-093447//fsm1de2.pdf). The original Donatus quotation can be found in *Ars Grammaticae*, Vol. IV, p. 372, of Heinrich Keil, ed., *Grammatici Latini*, the Diomedes passage is in ibid, Vol. I, pp. 437–39. He explains that "[i]t is good to pay attention in reading to the '*positurae*' or '*distinctiones*'…, which, while you're reading, measure out the occasions for you to take a breath, without clipping the sense."

in one or another of its forms: For a lively, erudite, and carefully illustrated exposition of early Western punctuation in all its variety see M. B. Parkes, *Pause and Effect: An Introduction to the History of Punctuation in the West*

The English Grammar: Originally published in 1640, it was edited by Alice Vinton Waite and republished in New York by Sturgis and Walton Co. in 1909. The extracts quoted here are from pp. 144 and 145 of that edition. Jonson himself used to sign his name Ben:Jonson; as Sara van den Berg of the University of Washington writes (in her essay "Marking His Place: Ben Jonson's Punctuation"), "It was common practice among bishops, archbishops, and college masters at Oxford and Cambridge to use a colon to abbreviate their first names when they Latinized their signatures. By adopting this usage, Jonson may have sought to identify himself with men in authority, or with learned men who shared his interest in books."

perfect sentences: *Perfect* here comes from Latin *perfectus*, 'complete, thoroughly made' (a compound made from *facere*, 'to make' and the prefix *per-*, 'through [and through]'); this is the sense meant in the King James Bible's translation of Matt. 5:48 as "Be ye therefore perfect, even as your father which is in Heaven is perfect," and surviving in the grammatical term *perfect tense*, i.e., the tense of actions in the past that are complete ('she said') as opposed to ongoing (the *imperfect:* 'she was saying')

important announcement…lump of coal: Both examples conform to the practice of putting an initial capital on the first word after a colon as a visual cue that what follows could stand as a complete sentence, while a colon followed by a word that is initial-lower-case serves to introduce a clause or phrase that cannot. The Associated Press has observed this rule in its stylebook since at least the middle of the 1980s; in the book trades it has been slower to catch on but is often left up to the preference of the author.

corollaries in spoken discourse: Geoffrey Nunberg, in his *The Linguistics of Punctuation* (p. 14), goes even farther: He finds "grounds for doubting whether punctuation can be said to function as a device for 'indicating' or 'signifying' intonational features," though he does concede that "experienced broadcasters [who] often use a combination of pause and ironic tone to indicate the direct quotation in their reading of…*support groups for 'recovering Catholics.'*" In any case it is clear that punctuation can be used profitably to disambiguate when a given utterance, whose tone and accompanying gestures would have an unmistakable import *viva voce*, is reduced to mere words on

203

paper. (One cannot help being reminded here of what is arguably the most famous presidential declaration of the 1990s: "That depends what 'is' is.")

chant:*song*::mer:*sea*: Because French-English *chant*-song is homophonous (more or less) with *chanson*, as *mer*-sea is with *merci*. This slick example of Gallic wit appears in a poem entitled "Chant Song" by the 20th-century French poet, Jacques Prévert.

***question mark* (?)** *to mark the first result:* The question mark also turns up as part of the tags that mark the beginning and end of a Personal Home Page (PHP) script—<?php...?>. The double colon, by the way, also has a specialized use in Computerese: the *paamayim nekudotayim* (Hebrew for 'double colon,' literally, the dual form of *nekuda* 'dot' and the dual form of *pa'am* 'once') in PHP scripting language, where it functions as a scope resolution operator.

War of Thonder-ten-Tronck: A fictional conflict in the writings of François Rabelais, undoubtedly intended to recall to French readers the perennial military expeditions to unpronounceable Lowlands municipalities on their eastern front.

the pioneering printer Aldus Manutius (Aldo Manuzio) the Elder: Sebastián Mediavilla (*La Puntuación*, pp. 26, 53.) has this to say about the birth and promulgation of the semicolon:

> The semicolon [;], which today we call [in Spanish] 'dot and comma' comes on the scene, with fanfare, at the end of the fifteenth century, in the circle of Humanists who gathered around Aldo Manuzio the Elder: in his Venetian press, he printed it for the first time in 1494, in the *De Aetna* of Pietro Bembo. This new symbol had from its very beginnings the appearance of a compromise, a deliberate invention destined to satisfy a need that Aldo Manuzio the Younger explained in great detail in his *Interpungendi ratio*, a manual of orthography for the use of printers, which his Venetian house published in 1561....
>
> Aldo Manuzio the Younger's *Epitome orthographiae* (1561) contains a separate section entitled "Interpungendi ratio" in which he recognizes punctuation as a part of orthography and proposes the following system of signs:...The semicolon: '*punctum semicirculo junctum.*' Intermediate between the comma and the colon. It should be used in those places where "*si semicirculum apponas parum sit; si gemina puncta nimium*" (p. 189). He assigns it two functions: the first would consist of separating opposing nouns or adjectives, where the comma would be insufficient [because, we take it, the semicolon goes in a succession of commas], and a colon would be too much, as in '*Publica, private; sacra, profana; tua, aliena*': while it's not easy to extract the lesson from this, it forms the basis for the first of the functions that the latest edition of the

Ortographía of the Real Academia assigns the semicolon: "To separate the elements of a list when it deals with complete expressions that include commas." [*Ortografía de la lengua españa,* Espase, Madrid, 1999, 5.4.1.] The second application that Aldus assigns the semicolon is to separate not just words but composite phrases when, by the same token, a comma would be too little and a colon too much for the pause that one wants to signal. He opportunely offers an excuse for himself and the many others who will write henceforth, by recognizing that this sign is '*omnium difficilimam,*' the hardest to use of all the *notae* or marks of punctuation.

the excrement falls down: This synopsizes the final couplet of a 16-line poem by Sir John Harington in his *New Discourse on a Stale Subject, Called the Metamorphwsis of A Jax* (London: Richard Field, 1596; reprinted in a heavily annotated Columbia University Press edition by Elizabeth Story Donno in 1961 as *Harington's Metamorphosis of Ajax*), concerning a pious fellow reproached by the Devil for praying while seated in a privy, who concluded his reply with "Pure pray'r ascends to Him who high doth sit: / Down falls the Filth, for Fiends of Hell more fit." (Note his use of the colon where we would nowadays use a semicolon.)

within a single weekend: All these cities and towns lie along U.S. Route 202, a reasonably direct country highway from Bangor, Maine, to Wilmington, Delaware, and a perennial favorite of truckers because it is almost toll-free for its entire length.

you have the horn: This teaser is attributed by Diogenes Laertius (fl. 3d century C.E.) to Eubulides of Miletus, a successor of the Megaric philosopher Euclides—not to be confused with the famous geometer—and teacher of the orator Demosthenes (whose skill was thus not *solely* due to all those hours practicing with pebbles in his mouth at the seashore). According to Diogenes, Eubilides "handed down a great many arguments in dialectics; such as the Lying one;...the Horned one; the Bald one" (quoted from C. D. Yonge's translation of Diogenes' *Lives and Opinions of Eminent Philosophers* [London: Henry G. Bohn, 1853], at www.classicpersuasion.org/pw/diogenes/dleuclides.htm).

The Liar's (or Epimenides') paradox is usually framed as "Said Epimenides of Crete, 'All Cretans are liars.'" The Bald Man is a type of Sorites paradox (*sōros* is Greek for 'heap'), to the effect that you can pluck out one hair from a man's head but he still has hair and is not bald; yet if you keep plucking out hairs, at a certain point an observer would say, "This is a bald man." So at what point is he more bald than not? (While recognized by rhetoricians for many centuries as a fallacy rather than a strict paradox, the Sorites problem has still been a perennial favorite in such discourses as American policy toward indigenous liberation struggles in exotic countries—the Slippery Slope/Domino theory—and cannabis criminalization—the Gateway Drug argument. For a delightfully devastating critique of the latter, and of the War on Drugs of which it is an integral tenet, see the recent collection of parables by California epidemiologist John Newmeyer, *Mother of All Gateway Drugs*.) Quintilian cites a number of these paradoxes in his *Institutio Oratoria*.

separate variables from parameters... associated with that index: Both examples are from http://en.wikipedia.org/wiki/Semicolon (accessed September 13, 2007).

Perl: Said variously to stand for "Practical Extraction and Report Language" and "Pathologically Eclectic Rubbish Lister." The example given here is from the second edition of Randal L. Schwartz and Tom Christianson, *Learning Perl*.

Iacopo Alpoleio da Urbisaglia: Claimed in his *Ars Punctandi* to have invented it: "In truth, observing that exclamatory or admiring sentences are usually expressed differently from declarative or interrogative ones, I marked the ends of such sentences with a simple dot with a tail over it." (Cited in Fidel Sebastián Mediavilla, *La Puntuación en el Siglo de Oro*, p. 26.)

Io Saturnalia!: *Io!* is probably best translated as "Hooray!" or "Huzzah!"

treated the same way: Both quotations are from Fidel Sebastián Mediavilla, *La Puntuación en el Siglo de Oro* (p. 30).

expressions not meant to be taken at face value: See the French oddball punctuation site http://rdereel.free.fr/volPQ1.html. Brahm's original *point d'ironie* looks like this: ⸮ Unaware of Brahm's having beat them to the punch, others have met the perceived typographical need for a mark betokening sarcastic skepticism: Josh Greenman put forth the sarcasm point (a subscript inverted exclamation point [¡] in a 2004 article in *Slate Magazine* ("A Giant Step Forward for Punctuation¡"), and in the early 1980s the current authors proposed the *facetio*—an icon consisting of an eye, nose, and grinning mouth in profile—in our *A B C Et Cetera: The Life and Times of the Roman Alphabet*.

Bazin's contributions are on page 207.

Typographic marks beyond the standard set to help a reader navigate a text with the proper degree of skepticism are nothing new: See, for example, pp. 180–86 for an early medieval take on punctuation marks and *notae sententiarum* ("notations for sentences") from the *Etymologiarum*, the seventh-century treatise on punctuation by the bishop (and saint) Isidore of Seville. Though not strictly speaking punctuation marks themselves, the *notae* were cues to read the passage they marked in a particular light, such as the *obelus* (ancestor of today's *obelisk* or dagger, both single † and double‡), which warned of a spurious passage, and the *phrontis* (Greek for "care"), a phi with a rho's head, indicated text that was archaic or obscure enough to require reading (as Isidore put it) "with solicitude."

ζ

POINT D'IRONIE
(Alcanter de Brahm)

$\dagger$

POINT DE CERTITUDE

$\mathit{!/}$

POINT D'ACCLAMATION

$\varsigma?$

POINT D'AMOUR

$\uparrow$

POINT D'AUTORITÉ

i

POINT D'INDIGNATION

$?$

POINT DE DOUBT

question mark in Arabic (؟)—Unicode U+061F: A similar mark has been proposed for Unicode that would be identical to the *punctus percontativus* found in some medieval Western manuscripts whose purpose was to indicate a merely rhetorical question rather than one requiring or at least expecting an answer: "What was the use of sending you to school?" (Michael Everson et al., "Proposal to add Medievalist and Iranianist punctuation characters to the UCS" (p. 2).

he wondered: Bazin is careful to set his proposals in Chicoutimi, Québec (where *w* would be pronounced [w]), rather than in, say, Paris, France (where *w* would be pronounced [v]).

that form a sort of heart: Bazin, *Plumons l'oiseau,* p. 142. Comic book fans will see this sign as analagous to the funnies' convention of hearts or rays emanating from someone exuding love, e.g., the child Pasquale in Pat Brady's syndicated strip *Rose Is Rose.*

banquet years: An invaluable and highly readable study of the arts in Paris in the 30 years prior to the outbreak of World War I is Roger Shattuck's *The Banquet Years.* For the surrealist "artist's book" in particular, see Marjorie Perloff's *The Futurist Moment.*

point de poésie: Julien Blaine, *Reprenons la ponctuation à zéro.* The reader is never told how to use this mark; but then that's poetry for you, isn't it?

spanked bottom: The first and fourth of these emoticons can be found on the website www.netnude.com/main/emoticon.html; with the exception of the last (one of several "botties" volunteered to us by an informant in the New England BDSM scene who prefers anonymity), the rest are from www. netlingo.com/smiley.cfm. A robust list of Spanish emoticons can be found at www.lenguaje.com/diccionarios/emoticones.php; not to be outdone, Antoine Devillard's site http://adevillard.free.fr/smiley.html offers a mini-anthology of French smilies, funny animals (including <°)))><, "little fish," and <:3)~~ "mouse"), busties (e.g., (—)(—), "bosom flattened against the inside of the shower door") and botties, as well as some smilies from Japan for good measure, such as (-.-)Zzzzzz, "I'm asleep."

V: Derek Wills writes (personal communication): "I have the following note, but I'm not sure if it refers to the above [bat]":

It's about time somebody gave credit to the creator of that terminal art bat that's been kicking around the net for the last couple of years, and shows up in the last Desperado. It's the work of the talented longtime bat freak Bill Wivell, of ESDP/MR. Bill also draws a mean BA123 enclosure backplane removal and replacement procedure, as well as PostScript Batman logos and a Batman skull.

I don't know what the hell myotis lucifigus means, but I think it has to do with bats (though mushrooms or sharks are other possibilities), but that has been his personal name for years.

Wills adds parenthetically that "(the above is many years old now—'last couple of years' was written at least 18 yrs ago)."

CHAPTER 11

sharper focus: This is particularly true if the first words of sentences are not capitalized (as in antiquity they weren't). Here's how the middle of the first paragraph would look with the commas taken out for good measure:

... inconspicuous in itself but decisive in the way it marks the end of declarative sentences and tells us when we're reading them to other people when to let our voices drop and take in some air making written thoughts more intelligible to readers and their listeners is something all punctuation marks do as we have seen in the previous chapter but this is especially true for the period remove the first five periods from this chapter and this paragraph becomes a syntactic thicket in whose tangles we can no longer easily guess where one sentence ends and another begins with the periods in place the meaning snaps into much sharper focus and the text on the page now cues us...

This is quite a word salad and nowadays something only a cryptographer could be expected to read without turning a hair (see "Dit Dah" in this volume). Manuscripts such as Ursicinus's annotated copy (dating from 517 C.E.) of a passage from the historian Sulpicius distinguished the end of sentences with a space and the beginning of the next one with a larger letter; see Parkes, *Pause and Effect*. (pp. 166–67).

to be spoken out loud: Aural transmission is most accurate, of course, at close quarters face-to-face. News reporters learn to dictate copy to editors over the phone sounding out all the punctuation, as well as spelling any unfamiliar words: "Mrs. Metterklume, that's M-E-double-T-E-R-K-L-U-M-E, comma, who taught piano at the Berlin Conservatory before her retirement, comma, played Chopin's, that's C-H-O-P-I-N-apostrophe-S, quote 'Military Polonaise,' that's P-O-L-O-N-A-I-S-E, comma, unquote, to vigorous applause, period." This minimizes the risk of error, but by no means completely eliminates it. (In this connection see, or rather hear, Victor Borge's modest proposal for what he called "Phonetic Punctuation," a favorite with audiences throughout his long onstage career.

scripta continua... *Quintilian:* Quintilian writes that reading a speech aloud from a manuscript requires that "the [orator's] attention must be divided between his eyes [on the page] and his voice (*dividenda intentio animi ut aliud voce aliud aculis agatur*).

"gathered in exile": The phrase is in Vergil's *Aeneid*, Book II, line 798; Donatus's misreading of it is cited in Parkes, *Pause and Effect*. (pp. 11–12).

Cicero's works punctuated (**distincti**) *by Fronto himself:* Parkes (*Pause and Effect*) writes that Cicero himself was "scornful of readers who relied on punctuation" inserted by copyists as an aid to reading aloud; and indeed such texts were rare outside of schools of rhetoric, in which they were used as teaching tools.

its first appearance... 1267: See the *periodus* entry in R. E. Latham, ed., *The Revised Medieval Latin Word-List from British and Irish Sources*.

209

period *is still being used interchangeably with "sentence"*: Sir John Harington's *Metamorphosis of Ajax* (1596) asks

> [W]ould these grave and sober titles [e.g., *A marvelous medicine for the maladies of the minde*] have wonne you to the view of three or four tittles [commas]? Much less three or foure score periodes.

Elizabeth Story Donno (*Harington's Metamorphosis*, p. 181, note 108) shrewdly observes that "in view of the possible pun this may be an early example of its usage as a 'point marking the end of a sentence,'" and if so it antedates the earliest *OED* citation by 13 years. The other sense of period, i.e., as 'sentence,' was still in use at the end of the 19th century: The *Century Dictionary*, whose 10 volumes were published in New York between 1889 and 1896, gives as its sixth definition of *period* "a complete sentence from one full stop to another; a passage terminated by a full pause."

French word for 'sentence' is phrase: In Spanish and Italian, it's *frase*.

the Cepheid variables: The predictability of the magnitude fluctuations in these stars formed the cornerstone of an estimate of the size of the universe advanced by Harlow Shapley, of the Mount Wilson Observatory, in a debate with Allegheny Observatory's Heber D. Curtis held at a meeting of the National Academy of Sciences in 1920, an edited version of which was published the following year by the Academy's Research Council under the title *The Scale of the Universe*. Though Shapley was right about the variable stars, he argued that the globular clusters containing his Cepheids were part of our galaxy and hence that its diameter was about 300,000 light years. Curtis argued for a much smaller galaxy size, maintaining that the clusters were extragalactic, and, like the spiral nebulae, "island universes" in their own right. In the end he was shown to have been correct in this conclusion, though conservative by an order of magnitude in his calculation of the actual size of our own galaxy, the Milky Way.

the versatile verb pungere: Its English derivatives include such words as *punch* (the whack or the tool, not the drink or Judy's husband), *pungent, expunge, puncture, interpunct, contrapuntal, compunction, and punctuation*.

head of a pin: Since angels, like points, were infinitesimally small, the correct answer is "an infinite number." The medieval churchmen were on the whole a bit better at infinitesimals and the notion of a limit than were the Greeks, for whom the idea of something divisible without end caused lots of bother: Zeno of Elea in particular is famous for formulating a number of paradoxes rooted in this problem, the best known being the race between Achilles and a tortoise (itself looking suspiciously like a spinoff of the older Aesopean fable about the race between a tortoise and a hare).

fresco later that day: For a lucid description of pouncing in fresco painting, see Patricia Meilman, *Titian and the Altarpiece in Renaissance Venice.* The noun *pounce* having the sense of 'fine powder' (as in "pouncing bag") comes from *pumex,* 'pumice.' The verb *to pounce* (in the sense "use a fine powder to fill in a design") is derived from the noun. But there are two other verbs *to pounce,* ultimately from *pungo/punctus* probably both via French *ponson* ('piercing tool, puncheon'). One of these means 'to punch little holes (in something),' and the other means 'to seize (as with the talons of a bird of prey),' the sense in Middle English of the noun from which the verb is derived being 'talon,' i.e., a sharp, pointy claw. Subscripts might help to distinguish among these: One *pounces$_1$* the work of art with a pin, then *pounces$_2$* it again with a bag in the hopes that a customer will *pounce$_3$* upon it when it comes up for sale. This is a classic instance of the convergence in sound of two (or possibly three) words of different parentage.

telegraphers abbreviated full stop *to* stop: Texas Country/Western singer-songwriter (and sometime gubernatorial candidate) Kinky Friedman's "Western Union Wire," from his *Sold American* album (Vanguard, 1973) plays on the ambiguity of *stop* as punctuation and as imperative: *You said you'd always love me/How could you...stop.*

book that made the cut: One that did not was the so-called Apocalypse of Peter, dating from sometime in the second century C.E. and describing an afterlife whose imagery draws heavily on traditional Greek notions of Tartarus. See Wilhelm Schneemelcher, ed., *New Testament Apocrypha* (pp. 620–38).

final battle of Ragnarok: See especially chapters 29–36 of Kevin Crossley-Holland, *The Norse Myths.*

who will truly appreciate it: And not, e.g., to cousin Andy, the aspiring artist, who would simply incorporate it, as an *objet trouvé,* in his next frightful dada sculpture, with rude leftovers of dead sea things cemented to it in suggestive places. The nice thing about a will is that as long as one has procured the requisite number of witnesses' and notary's signatures and included the clauses that are mandatory in one's jurisdiction, the probate court will generally wave it on through, notwithstanding any parts of it that might raise questions as to the testator's soundness of mind (e.g., leaving the ancestral tennis racquet to one's cat.)

too smart for his own good: Sisyphus, whose name is a reduplicative form of Greek *sophos* ('wise') and means something like 'Smartypants,' tried to pull a fast one on Hades by getting a furlough to return to the upper world after he died in order to punish his wife for supposedly not performing his funeral rites properly; once back on the surface, he refused to return down below and had to be forcibly dragged back.

Gehenna: Supposedly named for the Valley of Hinnom outside Jerusalem, which functioned in antiquity as the city dump; as a sort of hell, such a smelly, smoky, rat-infested place might well serve for a model, but the imagery of Gehenna, such as it is, probably is indebted to Greek ideas about Tartarus as well.

make it seem less harsh a fact: In the medical arts, this reticence is not confined to euphemisms for death; see William H. Dougherty's delightful 1999 *VERBATIM* article, which gives one of the most elaborate death expressions we have ever encountered: *carried home in the sweet winged chariot that always at my back I hear hurrying near.* Apart from its erudite hat-tip to Andrew Marvell's coy mistress, this phrase offers a combination of semantic and syntactic embedding whose elegance has few if any peers in modern English prose. (That the original chariot actually belongs to Time rather than Death diminishes neither its velocity nor its wingspan.)

the loved one: The title of a bitingly satirical novel by Evelyn Waugh. *The Loved One* was made into a film by Tony Richardson for MGM in 1965 with a script adapted from Waugh's book (and not to the author's liking) by Terry Southern.

placate the spirits of those gone before: The need to appease the malevolence of ghosts has a source of anxiety reaching back at least as far as the Babylonian Empire; see N. K. Sandars's introduction to her translations of the *Enuma Elish* and *Inanna's Descent to the Underworld* (Sandars, *Poems of Heaven and Hell*). Perhaps the most quaint custom required the Roman *paterfamilias* to lead a procession through his house while scattering beans over his shoulder as an offering to the *lemures*, the spirits of the dead who visited their former dwellings during the two nights of the year celebrated as the Lemuria. According to Sir James George Frazer (of *Golden Bough* fame), the beans were a substitute for the souls of the living, whom the dead might otherwise have carried off on account of feeling lonely in the world to come. See F. Guirand and A.-V. Pierre, "Roman Religion," in Graves et al., eds., *New Larousse Encyclopedia of Mythology* (p. 213).

cross the bar: A phrase made particularly popular by Alfred, Lord Tennyson in his poem "Crossing the Bar" (1889) and twigged by Dame Edith Sitwell in her poem "When Sir Beelzebub," the finale to her collaboration with the young composer William Walton, *Façade* (1924).

a litany of clichés: Not to be confused with "The Catechism of Cliché," a recurring feature in the *Cruiskeen Lawn* column Brian O'Nolan wrote for the *Irish Times* under the pen name Myles na gCopaleen. O'Nolan is perhaps better known today under his other pseudonym, Flann O'Brien, as the author of several satiric novels including *At Swim-Two-Birds* and *The Third Policeman*.

bend over backward to be in bad taste: Witness, for example, the possibly apocryphal hospital memo asking all personnel to refrain from referring to the recently deceased "as being 'paws up,' ART (assuming room temperature), CC (Cancel Christmas), CDT (circling the drain), or NLPR (no longer playing records)."

croaked: Possibly an allusion to the "death rattle" of Cheyne-Stokes respiration, the final breathing of those who are not long for this world.

over two hundred euphemisms for death and dying: The site, appropriately entitled "Dead and Buried" (http://phrontistery.50megs.com/longpig/dead.html), was compiled "as part of a course on the sociology of dying and death," Chrisomalis writes. "I know there are tons more out there," he adds, and encourages readers to send them to him for inclusion in the list. The homepage name "Forthright's Phrontistery" pays homage to Socrates' *Phrontisterion* (often glossed as 'Thinkery,' it means something closer to 'Place of Epistemic Due Diligence'—*phrontis* is Greek for 'care') in Aristophanes' *The Clouds*. [*On*] *Death and Dying*, a catchphrase made famous as the title of an influential work by thanatologist Elisabeth Kübler-Ross, is of course a reversal of the normal time sequence of these states, a classic example of the poetic figure called *hysteron proteron* ("later [thing] earlier") .

got 86'd: The origin of "86 the *x*" as slang for 'We're all out of *x*' is obscure, but the expression is common enough throughout the American food-service industry that its metaphoric use as 'kill' appears to be universally understood within the trade as well.

wasted: a favorite of the Vietnam war era, also came to mean 'under the influence of mind-altering substances'—compare *blown away*, which first meant '[explosively] killed,' then 'stoned,' but has since softened in common use to mean merely 'astonished' or 'impressed.'

up the long ladder and down the short rope [*hanging*]: State terrorism, of course, may have its own reasons for wishing to avoid calling death, and particularly death by execution, by its proper name. Thus the Soviet Union referred to the "liquidation" of people, perhaps in keeping with the Marxist view of humanity as *homo oeconimicus* (compare the modern American euphemism *human resources*, commonly shortened to *HR*, for "workers"), while Nazi Germany used *resettled* or *relocated to the east* to mask the deportation of Jews and others to the death camps. (We are indebted to Valentine M. Smith for the last two examples.)

metabolically challenged: The first two examples are from the "Dead and Buried" site (see above); the third is said to have been coined by Ruth Weilgosch.

obituary writer for a northern New England newspaper: David Weinstock; the quotations are from an e-mail he sent us in the spring of 2005.

most frequent editorial task: Our grateful thanks to Erin McKean, editor of the language quarterly *VERBATIM*, whose spring 2005 issue ran an article ("Death's Masks") by one of us (NH) containing much of the material in the preceding section of this chapter.

213

bibliography

Abernathy, Ken, and Tom Allen, "Converting Decimal Fractions to Binary," http://cs.furman.edu/digitaldomain/more/ch6/dec_frac_to_bin.htm.

———, *Exploring the Digital Domain*, http://cs.furman.edu/digitaldomain/home. html.

Adams, Samuel Hopkins, *Grandfather Stories* (New York: Signet/New American Library, 1959).

Alden, John C., et al., *The Central Mass*. (Reading, Mass.: Boston and Maine Railroad Historical Society, 1975).

The American Heritage Dictionary, 4th ed. (Boston: Houghton Mifflin, 2000).

Anesko, Michael, *Friction with the Market* (New York: Oxford University Press, 1986).

Asimov, Isaac, "The Imaginary That Isn't" (*The Magazine of Fantasy and Science Fiction*, March 1961).

Augé, Claude and Paul, eds., *Nouveau Petit Larousse Illustré* (Paris: Librarie Larousse, 1951).

Ballew, Pat, "Decimal Point," in his glossary of mathematical terms online at www.pballew.net/arithme9.html#decpoint.

Barnes, Ken, "Idol Chatter," review of Chris Daughtry's chart progress (May 29, 2007), http://blogs.usatoday.com/idolchatter/idol_airplay/index.html.

Bazin, Hervé, *Plumons l'oiseau* (Paris: Bernard Grasset, 1966).

Beilenson, Peter, *Japanese Haiku* (New York: Peter Pauper Press, 1955).

Benedictines of Solesmes, eds., *The Liber Usualis* (New York: Desclée, 1962).

Bischoff, Hans Peter [untitled lecture], http://www.cs.rit.edu/~hpb/Lectures/20042/AdHoc/all-inOne-19.html.

Blaine, Julien, *Reprenons la ponctuation à zéro* (Ventabren: Collection xeros 2600, Éditions Nèpe, 1980).

Blish, James, "FYI," in Clifton Fadiman, ed., *The Mathematical Magpie* (New York: Simon & Schuster, 1962).

Boehm, Laszlo, *Modern Music Notation* (New York: Macmillan/Schirmer Books, 1961).

Böll, Heinrich, trans. Leila Vennewitz, "Murke's Collected Silences," in *The Stories of Heinrich Böll* (New York: McGraw-Hill, 1986).

Boucqueau, J.-M., et al., "Comment jouer à pile ou face sur l'Internet sans tricher?" Tech. Report CG-1997/1, UCL Crypto Group, http://www.dice.ucl.ac.be/crypto/tech_reports/CG1997_2-1.ps.gz.

Braudy, Leo, *The Frenzy of Renown* (New York: Oxford University Press, 1986).

Brewer's Dictionary of Phrase and Fable, Centenary Edition (New York: Harper and Row, 1981).

Brown, Edward J., *Russian Literature since the Revolution* (Cambridge, Mass.: Harvard University Press, 1982).

Buchanan, Michelle, "Identity and Language in the SM Scene," in Erin McKean, ed., *Verbatim* (San Diego: Harvest/Harcourt, 2001).

Cabana, Paul, "The Rock Heard Round the World" (*Boston Sunday Globe*, December 8, 2002, pp. D2–3).

Cajori, Florian, *A History of Mathematical Notations* (La Salle, Ill.: Open Court, 1928 [Vol. 1] and 1929 [Vol. 2]).

Ceruzzi, Paul E., *A History of Modern Computing*, 2nd ed. (Cambridge, Mass.: MIT Press, 2003).

Chrisomalis, Stephen Andrew, "Dead and Buried," http://phrontistery.50megs.com/longpig/dead.html.

Cobley, Paul, and Litza Jansz, *Introducing Semiotics* (Duxford, UK: Icon Books, 1999).

Code, Murray, *Myths of Reason* (Atlantic Highlands, NJ: Humanities Press International, 1995).

Costikyan, Greg, "Talk Like a Gamer" (*VERBATIM* 27:3 [Summer 2002], pp. 1–6).

Crossley-Holland, Kevin, *The Norse Myths* (New York: Pantheon Books, 2001).

D'Agapayeff, Alexander, *Codes and Ciphers—A History of Cryptography* (London: Oxford University Press, 1949).

Damrosch, David, *The Buried Book* (New York: Henry Holt, 2006).

Domini, John, *Talking Heads: 77* (Los Angeles: Red Hen Press, 2003).

Donahue, Charles, Jr., *Law, Marriage, and Society in the Later Middle Ages* (New York: Cambridge University Press, 2007).

Donno, Elizabeth Story, ed., *Harington's Metamorphosis of Ajax* (New York: Columbia University Press, 1961).

bibliography

Dougherty, William H., "Bromides" (*VERBATIM* 24:1 [Winter 1999], pp. 23–25).

Drillon, Jacques, *Traité de la ponctuation française* (Paris: Éditions Gallimard, 1991).

Erdoes, Richard, and Alfonso Ortiz, *American Indian Trickster Tales* (New York: Penguin, 1998).

Ernout, A., and A. Meillet, *Dictionnaire étymologique de la langue latine* (Paris: Éditions Klicksieck, 1979).

Erzen, Tanya, "Partners in Prayer" (*Boston Globe*, June 11, 2006), online at http://www.boston.com/news/globe/ideas/articles/2006/06/11/partners_in_prayer/?page=4.

——, *Straight to Jesus: Sexual and Christian Conversions in the Ex-Gay Movement* (Berkeley: University of California Press, 2006).

Evans, Elaine, "Papyrus: A Blessing upon Pharaoh," online at http://mcclungmuseum.utk.edu/research/reoccpap/reoccpr_pyrs.htm.

Everson, Michael, et al., "Proposal to Add Medievalist and Iranianist Punctuation Characters to the UCS," online at www.mufi.info/proposals/n3193-punctuation.pdf).

Fadiman, Clifton, ed. *The Mathematical Magpie* (New York: Simon & Schuster, 1962).

"For Whom the Bells Toll" (*Ely Ensign* 182 [January 2005]), online at http://archive.ely.anglican.org/ensign/e2005pdf/e0501.pdf.

French, Christopher W., ed., *The Associated Press Stylebook and Libel Manual*, rev. ed. (Reading, Mass.: Addison-Wesley, 1987).

Fuller, David, "Dotted Rhythms," in Stanley Sadie, ed., *The New Grove Dictionary of Music and Musicians* (New York: Macmillan, 1980), Vol. 5, p. 582.

George, Andrew, trans., *The Epic of Gilgamesh* (New York: Penguin, 2000).

Gilbert, W. S. *The Plays and Poems of W.S. Gilbert* (New York: Random House, 1932).

Glass, Andrew, "The War on Terrorism Goes Online," online at http://www.ksg.harvard.edu/presspol/research_publications/papers/working_papers/2002_3.pdf.

Goffman, Erving, "The Insanity of Place," in his *Relations in Public* (New York: Harper and Row, 1972).

Gopnik, Adam, "Angels and Ages" (*The New Yorker*, May 28, 2007).

Grafton, Anthony, *The Footnote *A Curious History* (Cambridge, Mass.: Harvard University Press, 1997).

Greenman, Josh, "A Giant Step Forward for Punctuation!" (*Slate Magazine*, December 21, 2004), online at www.slate.com/id/2111172/fr/ifr.

Grevisse, Maurice, *Le Bon Usage*, 7th ed. (Gembloux: Éditions J. Duculot, 1961).

Guirand, F., and A.-V. Pierre, "Roman Mythology," in Robert Graves et al., *New Larousse Encyclopedia of Mythology* (New York: Crescent Books, 1987).

Harris, Joseph, "Seeking Mona Lisa" (*Smithsonian* 30:2 [May 1999], pp. 54–66).

Herodotus, trans. Aubrey de Sélincourt, *Herodotus: The Histories* (New York: Penguin, 1972).

Hoban, Russell, *Riddley Walker* (New York: Washington Square Press: 1980).

Huizinga, Jan, *The Waning of the Middle Ages* (New York: Doubleday Anchor, 1954).

Humez, Alexander and Nicholas, *A B C Et Cetera: The Life and Times of the Roman Alphabet* (Boston: Godine, 1985).

Humez, Nick, "Death's Masks" (*VERBATIM* 30:1 [Spring 2005], pp. 21–24).

Illingsworth, Valerie, Edward I. Glaser, and I. C. Ayles, eds., *Dictionary of Computing*, 3rd ed. (New York: Oxford University Press, 1991).

Isidori Hispalensis Episcopi [Isidore of Seville], *Etymologiarum sive Originum* (Oxford: Oxford University Press, 1911).

Jacob, Christian, "From Alexandria to Alexandria: Scholarly Interfaces of a Universal Library," online at http://dc-mrg.english.ucsb.edu/conference/2002/documents/christian_jacob.html.

Jacobs, Arthur, *New Dictionary of Music* (Harmondsworth, UK: Penguin, 1961).

Jonson, Ben, *The English Grammar*, Alice Vinton Waite, ed. (New York: Sturgis and Walton, 1909).

Kaplan, Robert, *The Nothing That Is: A Natural History of Zero* (New York: Oxford University Press, 2000).

Keil, Heinrich, ed., *Grammatici Latini* (Leipzig: Teubner, 1857).

Kessler, Suzanne J., *Lessons from the Intersexed* (New Brunswick, N.J.: Rutgers University Press, 1998).

Kimbrough, Paula, "How Braille Began," http://www.brailler.com/braillehx.htm.

Krutnik, Frank, Steve Neale, Brian Neve, and Peter Stanfield, eds., *"Un-American" Hollywood: Politics and Film in the Blacklist Era* (New Brunswick, N.J.: Rutgers University Press, 2008).

Kuhn, Thomas, *The Structure of Scientific Revolutions* (Chicago: University of Chicago Press, 1970).

Landes, David S., *Revolution in Time: Clocks and the Making of the Modern World* (Cambridge, Mass.: Harvard University Press/Belknap, 1983).

LaRoche, Nancy, ed., *Picturesque Expressions: A Thematic Dictionary* (Detroit, Mich.: Gale Research, 1980).

Latham, R. E., ed., *The Revised Medieval Latin Word-List from British and Irish Sources* (London: Oxford University Press, 1965).

Lightner, J. E., ed., *Random House Historical Dictionary of American Slang* (New York: Random House, 1994).

Liungman, C. G., *Dictionary of Symbols* (New York: Norton, 1994).

Lowe, Lisa, *Critical Terrains* (Ithaca, N.Y.: Cornell University Press, 1991).

Lundmark, Torbjörn, *Quirky Qwerty* (Sidney: University of New South Wales Press, 2002).

A Manual of Style, 15th ed. (Chicago: University of Chicago Press, 2003).

Martin, Judith, *Miss Manners' Guide to Excruciatingly Correct Behavior* (New York: Warner Books, 1979).

Mauss, Mike, on origin of "ping," online at http://ftp.arl.mil/~mike/ping.html.

Mayani, Zacharie, *The Etruscans Begin to Speak* (London: Souvenir Press, 1962).

McCann, Sean, "Dark Passages," in Frank Krutnik et al., eds., *"Un-American" Hollywood: Politics and Film in the Blacklist Era* (New Brunswick, N.J.: Rutgers University Press, 2008).

Mediavilla, Fidel Sebastián, *La Puntuación en el Siglo de Oro*, online at www.tesisenxarxa.net/TESIS_UAB/AVAILABLE/TDX-0720101-093447// fsm1de2.pdf.

Meilman, Patricia, *Titian and the Altarpiece in Renaissance Venice* (New York: Cambridge University Press, 2000).

Mitchison, Naomi, *Memoirs of a Spacewoman* (London: Women's Press, 1985).

Morris, Desmond, Peter Collett, Peter March, and Marie O'Shaughnessy, *Gestures* (New York: Stein and Day, 1979).

Neils, Jenifer, *Goddess and Polis* (Hanover, N.H.: Hood Museum of Art, 1992).

Newmeyer, John, *Mother of All Gateway Drugs* (San Francisco: Haight Ashbury Publications, 2007).

Nunberg, Geoffrey, ed., *The Future of the Book* (Berkeley: University of California Press, 1996).

————, *The Linguistics of Punctuation* (CSLI lecture notes: no. 18, Center for the Study of Language and Information, Stanford Calif., 1990).

O'Donnell, James J., "Pragmatics of the New: Trithemius, McLuhan, Cassiodorus," online at http://ccat.sas.upenn.edu/jod/smnotes.html#1.

Onions, C. T., general ed., *The Oxford Dictionary of English Etymology* (Oxford: Oxford University Press, 1966).

Parkes, M. B. *Pause and Effect: An Introduction to the History of Punctuation in the West* (Berkeley: University of California Press, 1993).

Past Worlds: The Harper Collins Atlas of Archaeology (London: Harper Collins, 1988).

Perec, Georges, trans. Gilbert Adair, *A Void* (Boston: Godine, 2005).

Perloff, Marjorie *The Futurist Moment* (Chicago: University of Chicago Press, 1986).

Petit Larousse grand format (Paris: Larousse/VEUF, 2001).

Petronius Arbiter, Titus, and Lucius Anneaus Seneca, trans. J. P. Sullivan, *The Satyricon and the Apocolocyntosis of the Divine Claudius* (New York: Viking Penguin, 1986).

219

Podolak, Janet, "A Place Where Kid Is King" (*Lake Chatter* [Lake County, Ohio], June 25, 2007, p. 2).

Pohl, Frederik, ed., *Star Science Fiction Stories #2* (New York: Ballantine, 1953).

Polson, C. J., *The Essentials of Forensic Medicine* (Oxford, UK: Pergamon Press, 1962).

Purcell, Jay, Ricky, and Rosamond, *Dice: Deception, Fate, and Rotten Luck* (New York: Norton/Quantuck Lane Press, 2002).

Quantz, Johann Joachim, trans. Edward R. Reilly, *On Playing the Flute* (New York: Macmillan/Schirmer Books, 1966).

Raymond, Eric, ed., *The New Hacker's Dictionary* (Cambridge, Mass.: MIT Press, 1991).

Romer, John, *Ancient Lives* (New York: Holt, Rinehart and Winston, 1984).

Room, Adrian, ed., *Brewer's Dictionary of Modern Phrase and Fable* (London: Cassell, 2002).

Said, Edward, *Orientalism* (New York: Random House, 1979).

Sampson, Percy, *Proofreading in the Sixteenth, Seventeenth, and Eighteenth Centuries* (London: Oxford University Press, 1935).

Sandars, N. K., *Poems of Heaven and Hell from Ancient Mesopotamia* (New York: Viking Penguin, 1971).

Saulny, Susan, "On Hit Lists, Anger Finds an Outlet" (*New York Times*, Thursday, March 22, 2007, pp. E1–2).

Schmandt-Besserat, Denise, "The Earliest Precursor of Writing" (*Scientific American* 238:6 [June 1978], pp. 50–58).

———, "The Envelopes That Bear the First Writing" (*Technology and Culture*. 21:3 [July 1980], pp. 357–85).

Schneemelcher, Wilhelm, ed., *New Testament Apocrypha*, trans. R. McL. Wilson (Louisville, Ky.: John Knox Press, 1992).

Schwaller de Lubicz, R. A., *The Temple of Man* (Rochester, Vt.: Inner Traditions, 1998).

Schwartz, Randal L., and Tom Christianson, *Learning Perl*, 2nd ed. (Sebastapol, Calif.: O'Reilly and Associates, 1997).

Sélincourt, Aubrey de (trans.), *Herodotus: The Histories* (New York: Penguin, 1972).

Seneca, Lucius Annaeus, "The Pumpkinification of Claudius," in Robert Graves, *Claudius the God* (New York: Vintage, 1962), pp. 566–83.

Shapley, Harlow, and Heber D. Curtis, *The Scale of the Universe*, National Academy of Sciences Research Council Bulletin No. 11 (Vol. 2, Part 3: May 1921).

Shattuck, Roger, *The Banquet Years* (New York: Random House, 1979).

Shiel, Mark, "Hollywood, the New Left, and *FTA*," in Frank Krutnik et al., eds., *"Un-American" Hollywood: Politics and Film in the Blacklist Era* (New Brunswick, N.J.: Rutgers University Press, 2008).

Sigler, L., *Fibonacci's Liber Abaci* (New York: Springer-Verlag, 2002).

Smith, Jeff, "Are You Now or Have You Ever Been a Christian? The Strange History of *The Robe* as Political Allegory," in Frank Krutnik et al., eds., "*Un-American*" *Hollywood: Politics and Film in the Blacklist Era* (New Brunswick, N.J.: Rutgers University Press, 2008).

Sobel, Dava, *Longitude* (New York: Walker, 1995).

Speer, Laurel, "Our Photos," in *Sin* (Tunnel, N.Y.: Geryon Press, 1990).

Squiers, Susan, *Babies in Bottles* (New Brunswick, N.J.: Rutgers University Press, 1994), p. 181.

Suetonius Tranquillus, Gaius, trans. Robert Graves, *The Twelve Caesars.* (Harmondsworth, UK: Penguin, 1979).

Sullivan, J. P. (trans.), *The Satyricon and the Apocolocyntosis of the Divine Claudius* (New York: Viking Penguin, 1986).

Tarachow, Sidney, *An Introduction to Psychotherapy* (New York: International Universities Press, 1963).

Taylor, David, "Elements of Internationalization," online at www.intuitive.com/globalsoftware/gs-chap4.html.

Travers, T. H. E., "Gallipoli: The Allied Failure," online at http://www.worldwar1.com/neareast/gallfail.htm.

Tunis, Edwin, *Weapons: A Pictorial History* (New York: World Publishing, 1972).

United States Government Printing Office, *Style Manual* (Washington, D.C.: USGPO, 1984).

Unterberger, Richie, review of *Spaghetti Westerns Vol. I,* online at http://music.msn.com/album/?album=41639439&menu=review.

Uzzi, Jeannine Diddle, *Children in the Visual Arts of Imperial Rome* (New York: Cambridge University Press, 2005).

Van den Berg, Sara, "Marking His Place: Ben Jonson's Punctuation" (*Early Modern Literary Studies* 1:3 [1995], pp. 21–25), online at http://purl.oclc.org/emls/01-3/bergjons.html.

Wallechinsky, David, and Amy Wallace, *The New Book of Lists* (New York: Canongate, 2005).

Waugh, Evelyn, *The Loved One* (Boston: Little, Brown, 1947).

Wells, H. G., Julian Huxley, and G. P. Wells, *The Science of Life* (London: Cassell, 1931).

Wood, David, *Programming Internet Email* (Sebastopol, Calif: O'Reilly and Associates, 1999).

Wosk, Julie, *Breaking Frame: Technology and the Visual Arts in the Nineteenth Century* (New Brunswick, N.J.: Rutgers University Press, 1992).

Zerby, Chuck, *The Devil's Details: A History of Footnotes* (Montpelier, Vt.: Invisible Cities Press, 2002).

SOUND RECORDINGS

The Beatles, *Abbey Road* (Apple: 1970).

The Big Gundown: *Reggae Inspired by Spaghetti Westerns* (Trojan Records TJCCD062, and Earmark Records EM303DLP: n.d.)

Catches and Glees of the English Restoration (Allegro Records ALG 107[mono]/3008 [stereo]: n.d.).

Cosby, Bill, *Why Is There Air?* (Warner Brothers W-1606: 1967).

Friedman, Kinky, *Sold American* (Vanguard: 1973).

The Fugs, *Virgin Fugs* album (ESP-Disk ESP1038:1965).

The Mothers of Invention, *The Mothers Live at the Fillmore East* (Bizarre Records: 1971).

Mull, Martin, *Normal* (Capricorn CP 0126: 1974).

Spaghetti Westerns Vol. I (Koch Entertainment:1995).

Waits, Tom, *The Black Rider* (Island Records: 1993).

ANONYMOUS WEBSITES

http://adevillard.free.fr/smiley.html (French emoticons).

http://dentongenealogy.org/Jeremiah%20Andrew%20Denton.htm (Denton's captivity).

http://en.citizendum.org/wiki/SOS (distress call origin and bibliography).

http://en.wikipedia.org/wiki/Alfred_Vail, accessed August 7, 2007 (Morse's telegraphy business partner).

http://en.wikipedia.org/wiki/FOB, accessed August 22, 2007 (F.O.B.).

http://en.wikipedia.org/wiki/Semicolon, accessed, September 13, 2007 (semicolon).

http://fesrouge.free.fr/neologismes_fessologiques.htm (French spanking neologisms).

http://fr.wikipedia.org/wiki/'Pataphysique, accessed August 9, 2007 ('pataphysics).

http://homepages.cwi.nl/english/codes/morse.html (Morse codes in many lands).

http://info.astrian.net/jargon/terms/Alice_and_Bob.htm (cryptographers' jargon).

http://ir.westernunion.com/press/news.cfm (Western Union Mexican expansion).

http://lcweb2.loc.gov/ammem/today/may24.html (S. F. B. Morse as painter).

http://library.bendigo.latrobe.edu.au/irs/WEBCAT/*xxx*.htm (Dewey Decimal classifications).

http://pc-facile.com (glossary of cybernetic terms).

http://rdereel.free.fr/volPQ1.html (French punctuation innovations).

www.britannica.com/eb/article-9002217 ("Data Encryption").

www.bigbandsandbignames.com/shay.html (Dorothy Shay).

www.blackballcorp.com/catalog/fuzzy_dice_281204_products.htm (fuzzy dice manufacturers).

www.citi.umich.edu/techreports/reports/citi-tr-01-11.pdf (cryptologosts examine suspect .jpg files).

bibliography

www.cuttertables.com/cutter1.html (Cutter-Sanborn author tables).

www.dice.ucl.ac.be/crypto/introductory/pileouface/pof.html (French heads-or-tails).

www.drinkingsongs.net/mp3s/1600s/1600s--1950s-catches-and-glees-of-the-english-restoration-(LP)/index.htm (mp3 files of English Restoration catches).

www.h27pataphysicien.net/histoire.htm ('pataphysics).

www.kloth.net/radio/qcodes.php (Q code list).

www.kryptonitelock.com/OurStory/History.aspx (Kryptonite bike locks).

www.langue-fr.net/A/arrobe.htm (French language discussion group: "@" sign).

www.lenguaje.com/diccionarios/emoticones.php (Spanish emoticons).

www.maxmon.com/1830ad.htm (Babbage's protocomputers).

www.netlingo.com/smiley.cfm (emoticons).

www.netnude.com/main/emoticon.html (more emoticons).

www.picturedots.com (do-it-yourself connect-the-dots pictures).

www.redhen.org/files/pdf/1888996463.pdf (first chaper of John Domini's novel *Talking Heads: 77*).

www.spammimic.com (steganographic encoder).

www.tackyliving.com/crafts/fuzzyDice.html (instructions for making fuzzy dice).

www.urbandictionary.com (online Urban Dictionary).

www.whatsis.com (etymologies).

www-03.ibm.com/ibm/history/exhibits/builders/builders_hollerith.html (Hollerith and IBM).

wwwcsif.cs.ucdavis.edu/~csclub/museum/items/univac.html (UNIVAC).

223

index

227

228

229

Chopin, Fréderic, 177n
Chrisomalis, Stephen Andrew, 158–59, 213n
Christianity, encoding in, 23
Christopher, saint, 10–11
Cicero, Marcus Tullius, 209n
CINDEX (indexing software), 88
cipher(s), 16
  alphabetic, 170n
  vs. codes, 20
  Kerckhoffs' Law, 171–72n
  trellis, 17
circumflectere, 85
circumflex accent, 85
class (Java), 129
claudere, 151
Claudius, emperor of Rome, 69, 166n, 167n, 187n
Claudius the God (Graves), 166n
clause, 151
clausula, 151
Clavis Mathematicae (Oughtred), 103, 194n
Clavius, Christopher, 194n
Cleese, John, 158
Cleopatra, 11
climbed the Golden Stair, 158
Clinton, Bill, 181n, 204n
clocks, seagoing, 165n
close one's eyes forever, 159
The Clouds (Aristophanes), 213n
#Cludge starts here, 87
COBOL, 58
Code, Murray, 178n
codes and ciphers, 13–27
Codex Expurgatorius, 77
coin (Fr.), 6
coinage, 166n
  ancient, 5–6
  design conventions of, 6–7, 134
  pre-decimal, British, 98–99
  as propaganda, 11–12
  See also money

coin-flipping, 7, 8
  See also heads or tails
Coleridge, Samuel Taylor, 80
collectam exilio/ex Ilio, 150
colon, 133, 135–37, 203n, 204n, 205n
Colossus Mark I, 112–13, 114, 197n
comestible, 92
Comintern, 56
comma, 137–38, 205n
  in Ben Jonson's grammar, 136
  as decimal delimiter, 102, 125, 195n
comma (Lat.), 133–34, 135
comment character, 141
commercial a, 72
  See also at-sign
commercial number codes, 21
compunction, 210n
computers
  CPU, 125
  filing systems, 115–18
  hierarchical notation, 127–30
  history of, 111–14
  languages, 114–15
  omnipresence of, 197n
  operating systems, 115
  printers, 198–99n
  punched-tape/film input, 126
  ubiquity of, 111
condition non-conducive to life, 159
congiaria, 12
connect-the-dots puzzles, 95, 192n
"Contract on Love" (song), 94
"Contract with America," Republican, 94
contrapuntal, 210n
conventional signs, *vs.* natural signs, 189n
conversion at the point of the sword, 153
Cooke, Francis Judd, 174n
cooking for the Kennedys, 159
Coolidge, Calvin, 67
Copernicus, Nicholas, 77

231

232

233

237

239

241

242

243

247

248

249

index

251

252

253

255